General Editor: David Daiches

Women and Marriage in Victorian Fiction

WOMEN AND MARRIAGE
IN VICTORIAN
FICTION

Jenni Calder

New York

OXFORD UNIVERSITY PRESS

1976

© 1976 THAMES AND HUDSON LTD, LONDON

Printed in Great Britain

Library of Congress Catalogue Card Number: 75-42965

ISBN Number: 0-19-519856-5

For my mother and father

*I am grateful to the staff of
the National Library of Scotland
who help to make the Library one of the
most congenial environments for
working that I know.*

CONTENTS

GENERAL EDITOR'S INTRODUCTION

DURING THE last forty years or so we have been taught by some of the most sophisticated and influential critics of the English-speaking world, especially by academic critics in America, to consider works of literary art as timeless structures to be read and valued for the skill, imagination and subtlety with which they have been welded into a complex unity. We have learned about the relation between structure and texture, about kinds of tension, of irony, and of rhetoric that can fruitfully exist within a work, about the way in which imagery is related to plot, about different ways in which symbolism can operate, about the importance of point of view, about 'aesthetic distance', and about many other matters which, if we bear them in mind as we peruse the text, can help us to read works of literature with keener and more precise awareness of the kind of unity they possess. This has been a permanent gain to our reading habits. Accepting this, we can now turn back with renewed confidence, and perhaps with greater skill in reading, to consider themes which earlier critics thought obvious and which the so-called New Critics (no longer new) tended to neglect in their anxiety to distinguish literature from life and literary criticism from history. These themes can be summed up quite simply as the human (and more particularly the social) base out of which literature arose in the first place, the kinds of human situation that literature reflects, and the ways in which it reflects them.

The Victorian novel is a particularly suitable subject for an investigation of this kind, for the Victorian novelists reflected in a peculiarly vivid and urgent way the social anxieties of their time, and their concern with the moral and psychological adequacy of the institutions through which social and economic life was organized emerges in their work in a fascinating variety of ways. They were both critical of those institutions and, in varying ways and degrees, trapped in them. Of those institutions marriage and the family were the ones that most directly engaged the novelists' imagination, for the Victorian novel was concerned with domestic relationships above all others. The ambivalence of feeling resulting from this combination of rebel and victim, from being conditioned by the very institutions of which they were most critical, even from accepting the necessity of many of the social norms they most criticized, led many of these novelists to build into their work enough paradoxes and complexities to satisfy the subtlest of modern analytic critics, while their joint role of critic of Victorian society and public entertainer – their dependence on the very society their novels probed and exposed – tended to compound the ambivalence of their attitudes.

If then we approach Victorian novels from the social side, as it were, asking ourselves not only what were the actual social institutions and norms of behaviour that provoked their imagination, but also how that provocation worked in their novels, we can get a fascinating new perspective on the nature of their achievement. While the great novelists are not diminished, both their achievements and their limitations can be seen in a new light. We see more clearly where Dickens' imagination failed, where George Eliot stopped short of the implications of her own insights, where Mrs Gaskell achieved what some greater novelists were unable to, and how Meredith emerges as a subtler and more honest novelist than many critics have believed him to be. It is not that the purely 'literary critical' evaluations have been reversed; but they are often modified, qualified, extended or illuminated. The writer of this study is not naïve enough to believe that social history is a substitute for literary criticism, but by using social history in an *explicatory* way in a full literary reading of the novels she is able to throw light on the human anxieties and breadth (or narrowness) of vision that set the novelists' imagination working in the way it did.

We live in a time when the role of women in society is the subject of impassioned debate, and the question of marriage, the family, sexual behaviour, the relation between freedom and constraint in society, recur in moral, sociological, political and literary discussion. A study of marriage and the family in Victorian fiction is therefore of particular interest to our generation, which is far from being the first to be concerned with such matters. Such a study is bound to concentrate on the role of women, and again and again in the chapters that follow it will be found that a novelist can be, if not finally, at least interestingly and illuminatingly judged by the way he presents that role. From this point of view, Meredith emerges as the writer of strongest contemporary interest. And if we say that this is not a literary judgment, it can be replied that, as Mrs Calder presents it, it *is* a literary judgment, for it is based on a sensitive reading of the texts as well as on a knowledge of the social background. This is not to say that it is the final literary judgment, if indeed any such thing is possible, but it points to something real and significant in the novelist's achievement. This study is full of such pointers, which lead us not only to Victorian life and Victorian fiction, but also to ourselves and our own problems and anxieties.

David Daiches

FOREWORD: FAMILY HAPPINESS

OF ALL THOSE writers who immersed themselves in the problems of marriage and the family during the period with which this book is concerned, the greatest was Tolstoy. His drab, depressing story, *Family Happiness*, published in 1859, is an emblem of nineteenth-century married life. In spite of its Russian character and location it is strikingly relevant to the Victorian novel, for it knits together, with deliberate and sober lack of drama, many of the major themes preoccupying English writers.

Masha is seventeen. Her mother dies just when she is about to be launched into Petersburg society, so that she now must spend her time in the country, cut off from the social world. Her father has long been dead and her only companions are her sister and her governess. Masha becomes very depressed. 'I was told that I was growing thin and losing my looks; but even that failed to interest me. What did it matter? For whom? I felt that my whole life was bound to go on in the same solitude and helpless dreariness, from which I had myself no strength and even wish to escape.' She feels she is being denied the arena in which she could have been expected to find a husband, and there is no alternative occupation for her.

After a dismal winter her guardian, Sergey Mikhaylych, a man of early middle age, arrives to take up his responsibilities. He considers himself too old to marry, but through his intimacy with Masha's family, their friendliness, and the warm influences of spring and summer in the country, he falls in love with Masha. Her vision of him is not as a lover but as an energetic influence bound to make everything different. 'I had ceased to ask that terrible question – what is the good of it all? Now it seemed quite plain and simple: the proper object of life was happiness, and I promised myself much happiness ahead. It seemed as if our gloomy old house had suddenly become full of light and life.'

The warm intimacy between Masha and Sergey develops over the summer. He tries to preserve his role of father figure, but finally betrays himself. Masha declares her love, overjoyed, and they marry. Their courtship has been conducted in an atmosphere of music and moonlight, of sunshine and cherry-picking. Masha appears a natural country girl; Sergey's professional interests are all in his estate. But the chill descends at the moment of their wedding. 'I attended to the words of the prayers and repeated them, but they found no echo in my heart. Unable to pray, I looked listlessly at the icons, the candles, the embroidered cross on the priest's cope, the screen, the window, and took nothing in. I only felt that something strange was being done to me . . . I was only frightened and disappointed: all was over, but nothing extraordinary, nothing worthy of the sacrament I had just received, had taken place in myself.'

Masha had anticipated marriage as a release into happiness. It would give her existence a purpose, working for others, helping her husband. What she gets is at first a secluded, selfish happiness, all too soon followed by dissatisfied boredom, while Sergey is absorbed in running the estate. Masha's happiness disintegrates, the differences between herself and her husband become formidable, loneliness takes over. The solution appears to be a trip to Petersburg. Sergey agrees, reluctantly, but society life only worsens their situation. He is committed to life in the country and sees the habits and values of Petersburg society as destructive. She is enlivened by the company and the occasions but, in the eyes of her husband, she is corrupted.

By the time Masha and Sergey arrive in Petersburg three-quarters of the story is over. Their marriage is already blighted. The birth of two children does not alleviate their mutual resentment. 'Fashionable life, which had dazzled me at first by its glitter and flattery of my self-love, now took entire command of my nature, became a habit, laid its fetters upon me, and monopolized my capacity for feeling.' The crisis comes when Masha almost succumbs to the importunities of a frivolous young officer who looks uncannily like her husband. Shocked, Masha rushes to her husband, but he is disillusioned and cannot allow himself to respond to her in the way he once did.

Back in the country there is a kind of reconciliation. But each still accuses the other, and each has to admit that the quality of their early love has disappeared. But it is quite clear that Tolstoy considers the fault to be Masha's, and her reproaches of Sergey reveal that she herself accepts this: 'Why did you never tell me that you wished me to live as you really wished me to? Why did you give me a freedom for which I was unfit? Why did you stop teaching me? If you had wished it, if you had guided me differently, none of all this would have happened.' Finally it is Masha's children who help her accept 'a quite different happiness', that is not the selfish, exaggerated happiness of youth, but the sober satisfactions of a responsible woman. As a mother she experiences 'a new feeling of love', for her children and for her children's father. At the end of the story Masha's happiness, family happiness, rests entirely in her acceptance of a quiet, domestic, country life, undisturbed by the corruptions of the city, fulfilling her responsibilities as wife and mother.

The story is throughout in a low key. It is a very basic moral that Tolstoy is setting before us, independent of personalities and dramatic situations. Romantic love is an illusion, life in society, beyond the influence of the family, is artificial and corrupt, and true moral happiness lies in the quiet performance of domestic duty. The moral is distinctly pointed in the direction of women. Sergey perhaps fails in a fully responsible enactment of the paternalistic role, but it is Masha who is exposed to corruption and temptations, Masha who is weak and nearly falls. There is no sentimentalization of 'family happiness', no recourse to insubstantial images to veil reality; it is much more a question of duty than of bliss. But it is significant that Tolstoy himself was unable to retain this view of family life. The frenzied *Kreutzer Sonata*, written thirty years later, is witness to that, and his own stormy but tenacious married life belies the viability of the family as an enclosed, inward-looking, duty-bound unit.

Of course no Victorian English writer exactly matches Tolstoy's approach and interpretation – the Russian-ness does make a difference – but *Family Happiness* contains the germ of so much that is essentially Victorian, and so much that appears consistently throughout the writing of the period. Tolstoy does not fall for the images of domestic bliss that tantalized many English novelists, but his picture of domestic happiness as essentially an island cut off from the social world is typical. The Victorian view of the home was precisely of a haven isolated from the trials and temptations of the 'real' world outside. Women presided over this haven, partly because that was pre-eminently where they ought to be, but also – and this emerges in a great deal of Tolstoy's writing – because they could not be trusted in the outside world.

There are anomalies in this. While Victorian society regarded women as its moral guardians, moral strength was clearly not sufficient protection in itself from society's pitfalls and dangers. Women were simultaneously the supporting pillars and the helpless parasites of society. Tolstoy is less inclined to see the moral virtues of women: he is too much aware of their exploitability. His women, whatever their class, tend to have in their nature a susceptibility that needs to be guarded and controlled by the strength of men. As soon as women go beyond the world of home and children they are liable to become weak, dangerous, corrupted and corrupting. Yet Tolstoy's intuition warred against his intellect; one of his greatest creations, Anna Karenina, does precisely that.

Just as it lies in the nature of women to be morally weak, it lies in the nature of fashionable society to be dishonest, artificial and destructive. Almost all the threats to marriage come from this area; at the same time, in the normal course of things, almost all upper-class marriages are made there. The fact that the marriage of Sergey and Masha was not is implicitly the reason for their initial happiness. In avoiding a commercial or a social marriage they get a romantic marriage but, Tolstoy says, the latter is no more real or right than the others. In the end only duty is a suitable antidote to weakness.

Tolstoy was never able to come to terms with his highly equivocal attitudes towards women which clearly influenced his approach to ideas and realities of the family. While English Victorians had a tendency to rationalize attitudes to women Tolstoy worried at this fundamental problem throughout his life. He was vastly more honest than the average Victorian novelist, but also more damaging in his view of women and their potential.

Certainly most Victorians, both men and women, would have shared Tolstoy's view of the husband as guide and mentor. Sergey's fault lies not in his attitudes but in his failure to apply them strongly enough. The paternalistic husband is ubiquitous in Victorian literature, yet some of the most interesting writing of the century questions or attacks the concept of male mastery. In Victorian eyes criticism of paternalism challenged not only the structure of the family but the structure of society also. It was a profoundly radical criticism, although it was never fully realized or explored as such until Samuel Butler wrote *The Way of All Flesh* in the last years of the century. But the germ was there in the writing of the Brontës, in the analyses of George Eliot, in the cutting exposures of Meredith, and in the less proficient but honestly felt forays on the part of lesser novelists.

The questioning of the family as the essential moral centre of society was brought very clearly into focus by the questioning of the obligations of women to produce children. This remained largely an underground discussion, but by the 1880s it was being openly suggested that motherhood need not be the only or even the most desirable route to female fulfilment. Motherhood is a very important theme in Victorian literature, although it is a theme that tends to be assumed rather than discussed. Childbirth is of course one of the most recurrent dramatic episodes in literary family life. But by the end of the century men and women were writing novels that were deliberate attempts to take women away from the marriage and family theme. Throughout the century there had been attacks on those who married for the wrong reasons. Now there were attacks on marriage itself.

But marriage and courtship held their own as major themes in British fiction, and continued to hold their own through periods, the 1920s for instance, where we tend to consider that marriage and the family became increasingly irrelevant in fiction. In fact, the more marriage itself was questioned as an institution, the more it changed, the more it was challenged, the more novelists were likely to be preoccupied with it. That certainly remains the case with many contemporary novelists.

In Victorian fiction almost the whole of human life could in a sense be contained in the family, for that part of life which lay beyond the confines of the family was usually considered to be incompatible with a moral view of human relations. 'Goodness' required a home, a wife, children, and servants. It needed a door to shut against temptation, corruption and threat. The Victorian novel may be said to be about men and women, but particularly women, seeking protection and fulfilment, and that ideally both are found in the same sources. The sources are financial security, property, a spouse, and children. These provide us with an image of the middle-class family in the nineteenth century. Hard work becomes a moral achievement because it contributes to the sources of fulfilment and protection. It is rarely seen as a source of fulfilment in its own right.

The situation of women is what makes marriage not only of central importance in Victorian fiction but also of vital interest. Denied for the most part opportunities for an identity other than that of wife and mother, women's attempts to find their own level in the fiction of Victorian life provide endless fascination. Quiescent, ambitious, immoral, peculiar, like dolls or like dragons, women are seen to be multifariously engaged in a contest with an overwhelmingly paternalistic society. It is no accident that Masha tells the story of family happiness in her own words. It is *her* life that marriage and the family are primarily about. That is the crux of the story. And it is women and their contest with society that provide the crux of this book.

THE ONLY SOLUTION

1

THE ASSUMPTION in many eighteenth-century and early nineteenth-century novels is that men are predators. All but the worthiest of them are liable to take advantage of women at the slightest opportunity. Women must be continually on their guard, and this is what most of their education is about. Etiquette, accomplishments, due regard for parents and property, obedience to those in religious and moral authority, all these are means of protection against the male predatory instinct.

Very often in the fiction of this period high drama is provided by abduction and elopement. The helpless female borne off by the villainous male or, worse, the susceptible female compliant to the false promises of the unscrupulous male, were staples of popular and serious fiction. In the widely read Gothic romances published at this time, the main threat to the young girl usually at the centre of the tale is invariably from a man. The unnamed horrors that lurk in dark passageways take second place.

Fanny Burney wrote continually of females hedged with dangers. As soon as they set foot outside the parental home, and sometimes within its walls, they are exposed to the calculations of men. In *Camilla* (1796) a young heiress is abducted and terrorized into marriage. Her abductor, Bellamy, threatens to kill himself if he is refused, and she, like any truly feminine woman, is so tender-hearted that she submits. Once she and her money are his he drops his mask of desperate love and her sufferings really begin.

The vicious Bellamy goes to immense lengths to acquire possession of Eugenia. Is it worth it? The answer is yes, although in his case he comes to a suitably bad end before he can enjoy the fruits of his efforts. Until almost three-quarters of the way through the nineteenth century a wife had no right of ownership. She and everything she possessed, money or property, belonged to her husband. A man who married a rich woman was indeed marrying money, and so the economic realities of marriage were bound to be of the greatest significance. A woman could easily be no more than a pawn in the hands of the economic aspirations of men.

Because of women's lack of economic rights the dowry, usually involved in society marriages, was a literal payment from father to husband. Thus the frequent appearance in fiction of the worried father of many daughters who fears he may not be able to finance their marriages. In return for this the husband would usually negotiate with the father the terms of a marriage settlement, which might include specific financial provision for the wife. It was a lax parent who failed to ensure that the terms were as good as the dowry deserved. In other words, a girl's personal financial prospects after marriage tended to be directly related to the wealth and status of her father. A great deal depended on the generosity of her husband, of course, and many a tale is woven around that all-important quality.

The vulnerability of women, therefore, stems not just from feminine weakness, but from their lack of economic status. Eugenia is a victim of this. A happier fate is reserved for Camilla herself, who manages to win through innumerable dangers and difficulties unscathed. In the turmoil of her sister's abduction, her brother's affair with a married woman, and her cousin's elopement, she preserves her wits and her virginity. At the heart of all this activity lies money: on the one hand, the ambitions of impecunious bachelors to ally themselves to rich wives; on the other, the desirability of the daughters of respectable but modest families marrying financial security. Camilla's story is brought to an appropriate finish when she marries a young neighbour of property and serious intentions. On the final page we read:

Thus ended the long conflicts, doubts, suspenses and sufferings of Edgar and Camilla; who, without one inevitable calamity, one unavoidable distress, so nearly fell the sacrifice to the two extremes of Imprudence and Suspicion, to the natural heedlessness of youth unguided, or to the acquired distrust of experience that had been wounded. Edgar, by generous confidence, became the repository of her every thought; and her friends read her exquisite lot in a gaiety no longer to be feared. . . . (Volume v, Chapter 14)

Camilla's gaiety is no longer to be feared because, being married, she is able to indulge her natural temperament without being thought a flirt inviting attention. Her marriage to a generous husband brings her not only financial security, but a harbour amidst the storms and risks of society. In the novels of Fanny Burney, as also in those of Jane Austen and most contemporaneous novelists, marriage is not only the proper ambition of well-bred young ladies, it is their only safe refuge. Between the parental home and possession by a husband there is no viable alternative.

Camilla only exists to be married, and in spite of the fact that she is a lively and almost over-spontaneous girl she is characterized negatively. Her talents can take her only towards marriage. She is typical of pre-Victorian fiction. It is a great relief to find in Jane Austen that, although her heroines are indeed to be married off, they are characterized so much more positively and individually than we find elsewhere. Susan Ferrier, for instance, in *Marriage* (1819) writes, however briskly and amusingly, about women who simply hang about waiting for husbands. They have no reality except in terms of the marriages they are to make, or fail to make, or make and then ruin. Perhaps the highest praise we can award Jane Austen's heroines is that in almost every case we can believe that they might not have married, like Jane Austen herself, and yet lived, within the narrow limits of their confining society, purposeful and interesting lives.

Even in the Gothic novel, where the heroines appear to be more involved in action beyond the limits of polite society, the main resolution of the plot generally entails marriage to a young man who could have stepped out of the pages of Fanny Burney. These young men are sometimes poor and foot-loose, but they usually manage to inherit something to make the marriage suitable. The heroine of Mrs Radcliffe's *The Mysteries of Udolpho* (1794) follows a route to marriage that is very similar to that of Camilla. The details are different but the dangers are much the same. Morally, it hardly matters if a forced marriage takes place in a ghost-filled castle or at Gretna Green. In the Gothic novel we are not led beyond the influences of polite society, for it is consistently by its standards that events are judged. The extremities of murder, poison and frustrated love are seen through the eyes of, usually, a well-bred young lady who is a victim of these curious events, though not to the extent of death or a fate worse than death.

In *Udolpho* we experience everything through the well-tutored sensibility of Emily. Amidst extremes, she does not respond with extremity. She is appreciative of the proper standards, whether in landscape or in behaviour, but avoids passion. Those who come to a bad end are those who love and hate too passionately, which leads them to commit radical moral mistakes although they may not be evil in themselves. They are unable to judge true worth in their life and their surroundings; Emily has been carefully taught to maintain her equilibrium, and an appropriate marriage is a part of her reward.

When Jane Austen taught that sensibility without moral sense was dangerous, she was taking up a theme that was at the heart of a number of novelists. As later novelists would emphasize duty, writers of this earlier period were very much concerned with balance, a rational moderation that avoided extremes of action or feeling. Emily, by her response to natural beauty, phrased as it is in conventional eighteenth-century terms which brought it within the realm of culture, is able to preserve her balance in extreme situations. This balance, controlled response to danger, love or beauty, was crucial in the moral view of marriage that most of the pre-Victorian novelists portrayed.

The usefulness of Gothic was that it allowed for extremes in a situation where it was conventionally accepted that there should be no extremes. In Jane Austen's world, although Lydia Bennet does elope, and Jane Fairfax's betrothal to Frank Churchill is almost improper, and Maria Bertram goes off with Henry Crawford, these are presented in terms of social *faux pas* rather than human cruelty. There is no torture, physical, mental or emotional. People do get upset, but suffering is relative. Mr Knightley loves Emma, and Fanny Price loves Edmund, but there is no passion here that might lead to poisoning or rape, or even to hysterics and smelling-salts. Fanny Burney's heroines have a tendency to faint and suffer on couches, but Jane Austen's are too sensible, too positive.

Polite society provides a convention, not a norm. We learn more about Regency society from Thackeray, looking back, than from Jane Austen focusing on her surroundings. Yet the standards of Jane Austen's little world are of great significance. They impose some order and control on a situation that in fact gave scope for great suffering and disastrous marriages, a situation in which a woman had no status except as a daughter or a wife, and where, if she were deprived of her belief that marriage was both a worthy ambition and her salvation, she would be deprived of life. The fact that marriage was not necessarily the comfortable and moderate institution that Jane Austen's ideal suggests did not interfere with this belief.

We think of the Victorian family as being of surpassing size. But women of a previous era bore just as many children – the attenuations of childbirth were that much greater. Both mother and child were less likely to survive. The glitter of Georgian society tends to disguise this aspect of marriage, just as it deflects attention from the subjection of women. Many contemporary moralists regarded Regency marriage as being in a bad way. In fashionable society it was considered *à la mode* for husband and wife to lead separate lives, extra-marital affairs were accepted, and it was not regarded as necessary to invite a married couple together to the same social function. Married women were the legitimate prey of unattached young men, who thus tested their sexual prowess, and we can find hints of this in Fanny Burney. In Susan Ferrier's *Marriage* the elopement of a recently married young woman with a dashing young man is described without much excitement. The family is not particularly shocked and the consequences are not disastrous. In later novels it is rare for a woman to get away with such a misdemeanour without severe punishment.

But the outstanding fact in the marriage situation of this period is the insecurity of women. No writer of the period allows us to forget this insecurity, although it is such a built-in assumption that it sometimes emerges in spite of the writer. Fanny Burney tells us repeatedly that a girl must be careful, must be protected and guided, must never say a rash word or commit a rash action, must guard her spontaneity and liveliness. And all this is necessary because there is so much at stake. A young man may sow his wild oats, is sometimes positively encouraged to do so, but a girl can only watch and wait. She is allowed to cultivate certain restricted, acceptable accomplishments, and because this is all she is allowed to do these become of immense importance. Yet she must not take them too seriously, she must not play the piano or draw too well, for that suggests professionalism, and even Jane Austen had to write her novels secretly and hide the manuscripts when someone came into the room.

Manuals advising on the behaviour of young ladies began to grow numerous as the century progressed. Similar manuals had existed for more than a century, but the concentration on the female sex had previously been less distinct. They can be seen as a response to a confused and contradictory situation. On the one hand young girls were brought up under severe restriction. On the other they were encouraged to look towards marriage as liberation, where they would achieve the acknowledgment of adulthood and as much freedom to control their own lives as was consonant with their sex. In fact, the freedom was largely illusory, for most young women exchanged the control of a father for the control of a husband. Restriction was an ill education for liberty, and most of them passed straight from childhood to the responsibilities of matronhood without any chance of testing their strength as young women, except in the marriage market.

The sheer futility of much of female existence is exposed in this passage from John Gregory's *A Father's Legacy to His Daughters* (1774):

The intention of your being taught needle-work, knitting and such like is not on account of the intrinsic value of all you can do with your hands, which is trifling, but . . . to enable you to fill up, in a tolerably agreeable way, some of the many solitary hours you must necessarily pass at home. (page 51)

At least there is no attempt here to burnish the faded image of female usefulness. Yet there also existed a strong belief in the good influence of women, which was absorbed and reiterated by the Victorians as part of their rationalization of the servitude of women. And it is just this that Thackeray shatters in his portrayal of Becky Sharp. He knew that, given motive and opportunity, women were not like this, and that many women did not want to be like this.

There were others who refused to soften the hard facts surrounding marriage. Just before Victoria came to the throne Bulwer Lytton wrote, in *England and the English* (1836):

A notorious characteristic of English society is the universal marketing of our unmarried women; – a marketing peculiar to ourselves in Europe, and only rivalled by the slave merchants of the East. We are a matchmaking nation. . . . We boast that in our country, young people not being affianced to each other by their parents, there are more marriages in which the heart is engaged than there are abroad. Very possibly; but, in good society, the heart is remarkably prudent, and seldom falls violently in love without a sufficient settlement: where the heart is, *there* will the treasure be also! Our young men possessing rather passion than sentiment form those *liaisons*, which are the substitute of love: they may say with Quin to the fair glovemaker, 'Madam, I never make love, I always buy it *ready-made*.' (page 57)

Lytton adds to this a condemnation of the female side of the contract. 'The ambition of women absorbed in these petty intrigues, and debased to this paltry level, possesses but little sympathy with the great objects of a masculine and noble intellect. They have, in general, a frigid conception of public virtue: they affect not to understand politics, and measure a man's genius by his success in getting on' (p. 58). If we ignore Lytton's revealing arrogance, his remarks are indicative of both the confines and the inutility of the lives of upper- and middle-class women. His picture of women ruled by pettiness, bought and sold, is sad and futile. It is worth bearing it in mind in view of the countless Victorian novels that describe just what Lytton is writing about here, but without censure.

What Lytton says here had been said already, with greater astringency and with a more intimate involvement. Mary Wollstonecraft, inspired by her exposure to the French Revolution, wrote *A Vindication of the Rights of Women* (1792) partly as a reply to Rousseau, who insisted that women should be educated only to please men. She wrote:

Women ought to endeavour to purify their heart; but can they do so when their uncultivated understandings make them entirely dependent on their senses for employment and amusement; when no noble pursuits set them above the little vanities of the day, or enable them to curb the wild emotions that agitate a reed, over which every passing breeze has power? To gain the affections of a virtuous man, is affectation necessary? (Chapter 2)

No, Jane Austen would say, with emphasis. She demonstrates that affectation is a positive barrier to gaining the affections of a virtuous man. But would Emma ever have employed her talents in match-making if she had had better things to do? Mr Knightly loves her precisely because he can see through the veneer of her affectation and recognizes that she herself will learn to become aware of it. It is artificiality that Mary Wollstonecraft condemns. Women are *trained* to be artificial, she argues, and as long as they are so trained there will never be equality.

From reading Fanny Burney and the great majority of later novelists it would be assumed that a degree of artificiality was an essential part of a woman's *moral* training. Let us look, for instance, at a piece of literature that figures frequently in the nineteenth-century novel as approved reading for young ladies, Fordyce's *Sermons*:

I am astonished at the folly of many women, who are still reproaching their husbands for leaving them alone, for preferring this or that company to theirs, for treating them with this and the other mark of disregard or indifference; when, to speak the truth, they have themselves in a great measure to blame. Not that I would justify the men in anything wrong on their part. But had you behaved to them with more *respectful observance*, and a more *equal tenderness; studying their humours, overlooking their mistakes, submitting to their opinions* in matters indifferent, passing by little instances of unevenness, caprice or passion, giving *soft* answers to hasty words, complaining as seldom as possible, and making it your daily care to relieve their anxieties and prevent their wishes, to enliven the hour of dullness, and call up the ideas of felicity: had you pursued this conduct, I doubt but not you would have maintained and even increased their esteem, so far as to have secured every degree of influence that could conduce to their virtue, and your mutual satisfaction; and your house might at this day have been the abode of domestic bliss. (Quoted in *A Vindication of the Rights of Women*, Chapter 5)

Mary Wollstonecraft quotes this as an example of the dominant attitude towards women. What Fordyce is recommending here is straightforward dissembling – for what else is a woman's denial of her own personality and existence in order to beguile her husband? Domestic contentment is a woman's responsibility, and any disruption of it necessarily her fault. If she cannot keep her husband at home, she has failed.

Jane Austen rewards her heroes and heroines by bringing them together in balanced and complementary unions. Fanny Burney tells us about a young girl who longs to marry to gain freedom from parental control, only to find that the husband she gets oversees her life with even greater authority. There is some suggestion of this process in Jane Austen. On the simplest level, so many of the husbands are considerably older than their wives. It was customary at the time for girls to marry very young, men only when they were settled in life. Mr Knightley, Mr Darcy, even Edmund, are paternal figures, and certainly in the first two cases the balance is between a spirited but good-hearted girl and an experienced older man. The nasty young men – and they are usually young – in

Jane Austen's novels are those who are in rebellion, if not against actual fathers, then against symbolic paternalism. The moral distinction between father figure and son is quite clear, and it could be argued that there is even a psychological necessity in it. There are, it is suggested, two kinds of men, fathers and sons, the sons indicative of the perils of society while the fathers hold moral law together. Within such a pattern it is obviously of some importance that Jane Austen's heroines marry fathers rather than sons.

One of the reasons that a balanced moderation is so important in her unions is that her marriages operate in static situations; they are likely for the duration to be subject to the same kinds of influences and pressures. The details of daily domestic life are unlikely to change, even the arrival of children does not make a very considerable difference. Families were less likely to move house, to change their physical surroundings, or their occupations. Under these circumstances adultery, financial distress, or the loss of property could be absolutely disastrous. (As a correction to the decorous impression of her novels it is enjoyable to look at Jane Austen's letters, where she comments with gay sarcasm on the habits of her acquaintances. She prides herself on her ability to pick out an adulteress in a crowded room.)

A marriage that is financially dubious can cause much greater opprobrium than an elopement, for an elopement can lead eventually to a suitable establishment and the resumption of the accustomed way of life. Lack of money could alter life radically. It was accepted that it was a parent's duty to provide for his children, to launch his sons into adult life suitably endowed, and his daughters similarly into marriage. A recurring theme in nineteenth-century fiction involves the worry of parents that they might be unable to give their children a good financial send-off. The head of the family was the economic prop of everyone else, and of course this increased both his power and his responsibility. It was not considered right that children should be economically independent, though questions of inheritance interfered here, as the eldest son's right to inherit usually meant that younger sons had to fend for themselves even when there might have been plenty to go round. Daughters, for whom independence was considered a disaster, were where possible provided for by the eldest son until husbands could be found. In lieu of husband or father, the first-born son took on the paternal role.

Deprived of dependence a woman would find herself in the unfortunate position of having to earn her own living. In the early part of the Victorian period it was virtually impossible for a well-bred woman to do this except as a governess, and there were not even that many opportunities for a respectable young man. The young heroes of early and mid-Victorian fiction tend to be very limited in their occupations. Many have private means. Law is a favoured profession, if a profession is necessary, for the heroes of fiction. Writers are also acceptable. Thackeray's Pendennis and Dickens' David Copperfield both become writers after starting out in the law. Clergymen are always proper, and later captains of industry feature prominently in novels located in the north. But it is interesting to reflect on the growing number of interesting and exciting professions that do not feature widely in Victorian fiction, medicine for instance, or science. Elizabeth Gaskell in *Wives and Daughters* (1867) features a country doctor, and her hero is a natural scientist, but few of her characters are typical of the fiction of the period.

Jane Austen's heroes, the men her heroines marry, that is, are clergymen, officers, or country landowners. All these occupations are seen as ways of life rather than ways of work. We do not see *Mansfield Park*'s (1814) Edmund in action in his profession as clergyman, nor Captain Wentworth, in *Persuasion* (1818) aboard ship. There are a few hints of Mr Knightley's occupation as a landowner, but we see very much more of his social life than of his working life. Again this emphasizes how important Jane Austen's well-balanced marriages are, for the men as well as the women have very little in the way of a distinctive occupation. It is vital that they should behave decently and politely to each other, that they preserve certain formalities, keep strictly to certain routines, such as the hour for dinner, the hour for visiting, and so on. These things provide necessary anchors for married life. It is an offence to be late for dinner, or to visit too early, because such things have a major place in life. They anchor marriages and social life too, and through that sometimes an entire community.

Alongside the vulnerability of women goes the vulnerability of ownership. Throughout the century the economic theme marches hand in hand with the marriage theme. They are inseparable, and further into the century the economic theme becomes increasingly dominant as money and the objects it can buy become increasingly in evidence. We can see it at a peak in Dickens' *Our Mutual Friend* (1865), and later pursued vigorously by Gissing. Jane Austen could write about money and property as if there was no reason why, once possessed, it should ever be lost. This is part of the static quality of her novels, part of her apparent unawareness of outside forces. Even property under entail can be guarded by judicious marriage – that was to be the object of Elizabeth Bennet's marrying the rejected Mr Collins – and if at the worst daughters were deprived of property the chances were that it would go to a male cousin, and thus at least stay in the family.

Most of Jane Austen's contemporaries had cause to worry about ownership. Even without the disturbing events across the Channel which conjured up visions of wild mobs attacking decent establishments, the threat of adversity was always present. Sudden changes of fortune, through foolishness, or bad luck, or gambling, or a squandering son, or a rash investment, form a common ingredient of nineteenth-century fiction. Often the sudden loss of money is used to make a moral point about the desirability of a modest life. It certainly can be the focus of great drama. Later in the period not only do such reversals occur, people worry constantly that they might occur, and if they have money and security they want more money and security. The preoccupation with money is present, not always with Dickens' ruthlessness, throughout Victorian fiction. Money is a major factor in Thackeray, in Elizabeth Gaskell, in George Eliot, and in a host of minor novelists nibbling away at the problems of a middle class that became more confident, yet more worried, as it grew.

Thackeray tackles the theme directly. Money and marriage cannot be separated. And he tackles it in a more intimate and robust way than Jane Austen. Money is not just a question of status and life-style now, but a grittier problem of hard cash and gambling debts, ambition and independence. He writes of the Regency period, but in a way that prepares us for Dickens' passionate analyses of Victorian greed. At his best Thackeray's amiable irony does not disguise the sharpness of his vision, and his novels are very much about men and women whose activities and moral outlook are tempered by their degree of access to cash.

A Becky Sharp in a Jane Austen provincial household is an outlandish idea, and it is true that Becky needs to feed on London society, or London society transplanted, which Jane Austen largely avoids. Yet she prepares the ground for the likes of Becky, indeed demonstrates before us well-bred young ladies of equal calculation, if less courage. Above all she shows us how important status and security are, and how men and women, but especially women, will go to the greatest lengths to win them. Jane Austen helps us to believe in Becky Sharp, and to understand her.

While Jane Austen's irony, whatever its depths in the exposure of human frailty and deceit and silliness, never suggests that this quest of status and security is other than basic and ultimately acceptable in human life, Thackeray attacks the system itself, in a friendly way very often, wryly, as one who had fought and won the battle for security himself, but always with a sharpness, and at times with a savage bite. He wrote of a period when women were seen to have no existence except in terms of their relationship to men; a period of moral contradictions, where 'official' morality had little to do with the behaviour of the majority, before middle-class respectability triumphed. He wrote of a time when people were still in a state of excitement and fear in response to the ideas generated by the French Revolution and the more concrete threat of Napoleon.

He was the first novelist to reject marriage as a happy ending. Except in the case of Pendennis and the, fortunately, inimitable Laura – Laura Bell, who shares the name of one of the most notorious prostitutes of the Victorian era – his intimations of marital happiness are rare. Many of his novels are very much concerned with exposing flawed marriages – *Barry Lyndon* (1844), *Vanity Fair* (1847), *The Newcomes* (1855) – and even where, as in *The Newcomes*, he throws a sop to his sentimentally inclined public, it has little weight in the total impression of the novel. He too, along with most of the more sensitive and aware novelists of the Victorian period, wrote about the grim workings of marriage capitalism.

THACKERAY, writing in the 1840s and '50s, genuinely believed in love, in marriage as a happy and workable union, in the contentment of home and children. These things were not for him a remote ideal but a perfectly feasible reality, given common as well as moral sense. Yet he found difficulty in conveying this belief convincingly in his novels. He never really succeeded. It is the cruelties and failures that are the most striking.

One of the most pleasing features of his work is its modest idealism. But this is also responsible for some of his worst writing, for he rather enjoyed an amiable sentimentality, the kind of thing of which there is rather too much in *Pendennis* (1849). On the whole, though, his belief in human good is restrained and sharpened by irony. We rarely find in a single character an exemplum of a right and moral way of life, and when we do, in *Pendennis*'s Laura, it is impossible not to regard her critically. Laura is only able to be 'good' because she is deprived of everything that might make her interesting, and we cannot accept her as a moral measurement. Other women in the novel, Fanny or Blanche Amory, provide more serious tests for the book's hero.

Laura is Pendennis's reward for learning the right lessons in time. But there is a suggestion in the novel's denouement that union with Laura is a step beyond criticism, and this goes contrary to the whole tendency of Thackeray's writing. His fiction is a continuous process of judgment. Characters may be redeemed, but their mistakes cannot be forgotten. Thackeray does not cast his men and women in specific and predictable roles, but gives them considerable freedom, and thus gives his readers a free range of assessment. This is partly a result of the way he draws us in such a relaxed way, yet with pointed reminders of what he is up to, into the narrative. For all that, he never lets us forget that his novels are artefacts – he is pulling the strings of puppets, presenting fables – but makes it quite clear that he does not deal in black and white judgments. Poor Laura is a puppet with only a couple of strings; her movements are severely limited and her existence as a positive moral force has little credibility. Yet, at the time Thackeray was writing, many of his readers would have believed that two strings were enough for a female puppet, and Thackeray himself, in *Pendennis* of all his novels, was oversensitive about public taste. If he thought he was providing an ideal of womanhood, the best reward a man could have, it is fairly clear that Laura bears little relation to the way Thackeray saw and understood the women in his own life.

Thackeray himself was a man who made mistakes and acknowledged them. He squandered his patrimony as a young man and was familiar with the gaming tables that feature so significantly in his novels. He found a great deal of pleasure in the moderate luxury which he attained, yet did not grow unaware of his own motives. He had to cope with considerable personal tragedy, yet avoided bitterness and pessimism.

In 1836 Thackeray married Isabella Shawe, a young, immature girl with no money. At this time he was having to work hard as a journalist, and soon after became entirely dependent on freelance work for supporting himself and his wife. Their first child was born in 1837. It was an extremely difficult birth, and the survival of both mother and child was threatened. A second child was born a year later, but died at the age of three months. Two years later there was a third child, and although there were no problems with this confinement the effect on Isabella of her second daughter's death and the suffering of her first experience of childbirth was profound.

There seems no doubt that the Thackeray marriage was a reasonably happy one, yet it was not without problems. There was little money. Isabella had married, as so many very young girls were bound to do, with no experience at all of adult responsibilities. She was a hopeless housekeeper, which in a household lacking funds was a serious matter. Although Thackeray appreciated her warm, simple personality she took no interest in the world of ideas, or of politics, in which Thackeray was increasingly involved. Nor did he encourage such interest. He was not neglectful, but there was clearly a sharp division between his working life and his home life, a great deal that his wife could not share.

Isabella, depressed before the birth of her third daughter, never recovered her spirits. She was in fact well on the road to madness. She took no interest in her children, attempted suicide, needed constant attention, and it was all an almost unendurable strain on Thackeray. Isabella never fully regained her sanity, and she spent the greater part of her remaining life in an asylum. We can see the reflections of these experiences in much of Thackeray's writing. The circumstances of his three daughters' birth were not unusual, but Isabella had neither the physical, nor the emotional nor the mental strength to sustain them. It is hardly surprising, for she had had no opportunity to prepare herself for such events. In proportion to their unpreparedness women had the more to endure physically and emotionally from marriage, and we can see Isabella as a case history of this. It was an experience from which Thackeray learnt a great deal. He is in his fiction unable to see anything desirable in helpless innocence in women. In his most impressive novels such women are invariably either destroyed or destructive. They are not allowed to be simply negative, as they are in so much lesser Victorian fiction.

Thackeray's own experience showed that a happy, unpretentious marriage was a possibility, but that dangers and threats lurked in the most ordinary events. He does not as a rule deal in happy marriages, yet the whole basis of his criticism of the arranged marriage, the marriage of convenience, the marriage of consent not love, is not only that it is damaging to individuals and to society, but also that there are alternative ways of uniting men and women. He is not against marriage; he is against a certain kind of marriage contract.

In 1842 Thackeray met Jane Brookfield, the wife of an old college friend, William Brookfield. A friendship developed which could only have enhanced his astringent views of marriage, for a major factor in this friendship, which was profound but Platonic, was William Brookfield's treatment of his wife. He was away a great deal, and it never occurred to him to apply the same standards of freedom to his wife as he applied to himself. This is how Gordon Ray, Thackeray's biographer, describes their marriage:

Although after his fashion he loved Jane profoundly, he regarded it as his duty to insist on the essential inferiority of the wife to the husband. . . . He thought it Jane's chief duty to be an efficient housewife and censured severely any sign of domestic incompetence. He did not allow the demands of home to interfere in any way with his social pleasures, attending bachelor feasts as the opportunity offered, and often not returning until early morning. Characteristically he did not hesitate to report to Jane an ambiguous compliment that Kinglake paid him, 'that I had been very happy in my marriage . . . that you appeared to have a perfect temper, and "to fall in with my bachelor ways" '. (*The Age of Wisdom*, 1958, page 125)

But Jane was not quiescent. She described herself as 'a neglected young wife eating my heart out with rage and bitterness' (Ray, p. 49). It was not surprising that she responded to the sympathetic interest of Thackeray, and that Thackeray found in her an understanding confidante. The friendship flourished until 1851, when Brookfield forbade its continuance.

Thackeray rarely presents us with comfortable little domestic scenes to suggest an ideal of domestic harmony, although we do get hints of such scenes in his own life through his letters. His briefly enjoyed marriage and his relationship with his much-loved daughters was relaxed and full of the pleasure to be found in relatively modest comforts. But this is not apparent in his novels. Often the tension is contained precisely in those moments of ordinary familiarity, in meals taken together, in family gatherings, or at times of celebration, where it might be expected he would allow his protagonists some ease. Unlike Dickens, Thackeray never lets the shared enjoyment of a steak pudding contain a flavour of moral ease and human well-being. Thackeray was always alert to human weakness: men and women were often at their worst when eating and drinking.

Although we never cease to be aware of Thackeray's benign personality, the general tendency of his novels is pessimistic. People, he suggests, are destructive creatures, and the closer their alliance with each other the more damage they are likely to do. At best uneasy compromises can be reached, helped by a degree of self-awareness and moral sensitivity. But these qualities will not themselves guarantee happiness, and certainly the conventionally approved qualities (in women at least) of placidity, mildness of temper and dependence can be disastrous. In men good humour and good manners will not necessarily bring any reward. Thackeray is contra-Victorian because his belief in people does not come easily, and a belief in God is for him scarcely relevant. When he admits sentiment it is not with the commitment of Dickens, but with a theatrical gesture that is thoroughly alienating. His public did not like his lack of serious acknowledgment of their escape routes.

Thackeray often claimed to be soft-hearted and sentimental, but this emerges not so much as a lack of realism as an affirmation of his open, and in some ways unconventional, enjoyment of the important relationships and activities in his life. In an age when hypocrisy seems to us now to have been a characteristic feature, Thackeray was not a hypocrite. Hypocrisy, above all, was what he attacked.

Marriage is the key relationship in Thackeray's social critique, marriage and the family relationships that are a part of it. In his novels marriage is generally a union of families, often financially strategic, a union with all kinds of social implications, bringing in its wake elevations and descents, gains and losses, property and mothers-in-law. His scene is much wider than that of Jane Austen, and the implications of marriage cannot be so self-contained. He does not at any time indicate what he might have considered an ideal of marital harmony – the marriage of Pen and Laura is too sketchily presented to operate like this, even if it were more credible – but we can be fairly sure that he had little faith in a simplistic view of honest, humble love. But that precisely is the characteristic version in the Victorian novel, and it is worth looking at it in some detail.

In Anne Brontë's first novel, *Agnes Grey* (1847) the heroine has to take the governess route to a modest marriage. Anne, like her sister Charlotte, was herself a governess, and for both the experience was significant. Agnes shoulders the responsibilities of breadwinner after the death of her father, and after some trying times gets a decent husband. But it is the marriage of her parents that has created for her a moral example and taught her the importance of honest love. Here her parents' marriage is described:

Finding arguments of no avail, her father, at length, told the lovers they might marry if they pleased; but in so doing, his daughter would forfeit every fraction of her fortune. He expected this would cool the ardour of both; but he was mistaken. My father knew too well my mother's superior worth not to be sensible that she was a valuable fortune in herself: and if she would but consent to embellish his humble hearth, he should be happy to take her on any terms; while she, on her part, would rather labour with her own hands than be divided from the man she loved, whose happiness it would be her joy to make, and who was already one with her in heart and soul. So her fortune went to swell the purse of a wiser sister, who had married a rich nabob; and she, to the wonder and compassionate regret of all who knew her, went to bury herself in a homely village parsonage among the hills of ——. And yet, in spite of all this, and in spite of my mother's high spirits and my father's whims, I believe you might search all England thoroughly and fail to find a happier couple. (Chapter 1)

Agnes' parents defy convention and marry for love without money. This is presented as an act of moral courage, but it is of interest to pause for a moment at the language used here. First, Agnes' mother as a 'valuable fortune in herself': her mother, we are to understand, has great moral qualities, but these are presented in terms of monetary value. Virtue becomes a saleable commodity. Then, 'embellish': it is a word that suggests beautiful objects, decorative things, lifeless ornaments. Vitality is contradicted. Then, 'he should be happy to take her on any terms': the condescension, the further suggestion of a financial transaction – he pays for her by foregoing her dowry, the payment to *him* for taking her. Finally, 'would rather labour with her own hands': behind this the assumption, which we take very much for granted in the Victorian novel, that in the normal course of things no well-bred young woman would do such a thing. While he condescends to take her without cash, she is ready for the ultimate sacrifice to make him happy. I should add that the Grey household is thoroughly paternalistic.

In the Victorian novel it is virtually impossible to get away from the concept of marriage as a financial transaction. The idea of money is there even when the cash is absent. Thackeray attacks this, not by presenting a sentimental, or morally self-conscious, or deliberately humble alternative, but by showing how these basic assumptions about the union of man and wife actually work.

Even if we accept this humble version of marriage as morally superior, it is as hard to believe in it as it is to approve of the mercenary marriage. In theory, of course, Victorian sensibility did not approve of mercenary marriages. But it is hard to reconcile this with the strong belief in duty, both of children to parents and of parents to children, and practical common sense. To the most unambitious middle-class girl marriage meant 'setting up an establishment', and without money that wasn't possible. There are many moral tales about innocent young things who are sure they can manage on very little, and then discover just what the absence of money cannot buy. And a man had very little to gain except a licit sex life, probably soon to be disrupted by pregnancies and babies, by marrying without a modest competency. Financial difficulties would make it less likely that he would acquire either an efficient housekeeper or a pleasing companion.

Thackeray is concerned with the way the system operates. In *Pendennis* and *The Newcomes* he demonstrates its operation through the activities and difficulties of two young, personable heroes, just the sort of young men, he explicitly says, who *ought* to be the heroes of novels. They are the victims of the system, Clive Newcome much more so than Pen, who is let off lightly. They are victims of social assumptions about what young men ought to want, and victims in particular of hopeful parents, scheming women, and their own inability to carve an independent way through a mass of pressures. This inability is bred of the society in which they move or, to be more accurate, to which they have aspirations.

Women were taught to dissemble, and men were taught to encourage and accept this dissembling. Pendennis, in his progress from gullible youngster to rakish undergraduate to young man of the world, becomes a self-conscious cynic because he thinks he's got to the bottom of this operation. Of course he hasn't; his friend Warrington who has, of necessity, opted out of the game altogether, usefully continues to expose the extent of Pen's illusions. Behind this are the expectations of others concerning the heroes of the two novels: that they should of course marry, and set up suitable establishments, and take up their positions in the social world. No one has any doubts about the desirability of marriage. Even Pendennis at his most cynical never questions the institution, although he thinks he has a realistic view of what it will be like. Parents worry about the activities of unattached young men. Colonel Newcome in particular is troubled by the temptations that surround his son; marriage would save Clive from loose women.

There is little to suggest a positive attitude to marriage, or even a personal attitude. Motives other than money, property and the acceptance of convention are barely relevant. Marriage is a part of one's progress in the world, and the idea of marriage permeates the thinking of young women and young men long before any particular choice is considered. When Pendennis marries Laura we cannot help suspecting that he does so because, in the circumstances, it is the easiest way of providing himself with the appendage that the world deems necessary for establishment.

Novelists were writing romances, yet love, even sexual attraction, had little to do with marriage, not only in Thackeray's novels, which are concerned to expose this, but also in general attitudes. Young women were told that they would 'grow to love' their husbands after marriage, and conventions of court-ship were such that there was very little opportunity to know one's future spouse well before marriage. As we have seen, men chose their wives for their value, whether it was economic, moral or decorative or, if very lucky, all three. In Mrs Craik's *Agatha's Husband* (1853) (and Mrs Craik was a prolific writer of much-read books) there is a solemn chronicle of a girl, aged nineteen, who accepts an offer of marriage out of loneliness and a desire for change, and 'learns to love' her priggish husband after many trials and desperate emotional suffer-ing. It is a curious book, ambiguous in its sympathies, for although it clearly indicates that it is Agatha's obligation to make the running in the learning process, her husband is so unsympathetic and unhelpful that we do not feel he deserves it. Thackeray's husbands and wives tend to learn to hate their spouses as the disguises donned in order to effect capture are left off. At best mutual tolerance is achieved.

Women, and men too, occasionally, were instructed in various methods of preserving these disguises, indeed of perfecting them. This is *The Family Friend* (1849) providing some 'Hints for Wives':

Don't imagine when you have obtained a husband, that your attention to personal neatness and deportment may be relaxed. Now, in reality, is the time for you to exhibit superior taste and excellence in the cultivation of your address, and the becoming elegance of your appearance. If it required some little care to foster the admiration of a lover – how much more requisite to keep yourself lovely in the eyes of him to whom there is now no privacy or disguise – your hourly com-panion.

It did not seem to strike the mid-century mind that pretence was a dubious activity – hence the common hypocrisy and the ambiguity of novels like *Agatha's Husband*. Agatha does not disguise the way she feels; her resentment and discontent are plain, and these are in themselves unacceptable emotions. She must learn to tame them, even if she has good cause to feel them. Her husband is superior, condescending and less than honest, and Agatha herself is sympathetically portrayed. But Mrs Craik clearly feels that it is a woman's great strength to overcome petty and selfish feeling, and to go more than half way to recognize and support superior worth. Agatha has to be shocked into discovering that her husband really is a fine man, and that she really does love him. Underneath this Mrs Craik appears to be saying, yes, it is often hard for young wives, but they mustn't give up the struggle.

Mrs Craik would certainly have approved of the following typical piece of advice to the young wife, and it relates directly to a certain type of Thackeray heroine, to Helen and Laura in *Pendennis*, Rosey in *The Newcomes* and Amelia in *Vanity Fair*:

Domestic comfort is the chief source of her influence, and the greatest debt society owes her; for happiness is almost an element of virtue, and nothing conduces more to improve the character of men than domestic peace. A woman may make a man's home delightful, and may thus increase his motives for virtuous exertion. She may refine and tranquillise his mind, – may turn away his anger or allay his grief. Her smile may be the happy influence to gladden his heart, and disperse the clouds that gather on his brow. And she will be loved in proportion as she makes those around her happy, – as she studies their tastes, and sympathises in their feelings. In social relations adaptation is therefore the true secret of her influence. (Mrs John Sandford, *Woman in Her Social and Domestic Character*, 1831, Chapter 1)

To make any sense of this we have to assume a good income; this is a picture of a woman with nothing much to do. Her purpose is to 'improve the character of men' and thus of society, and this version of woman as the moral uplifter of society is emphasized throughout the period, and even becomes entwined in late-century feminism. And again the question of value is present: 'she will be loved in proportion as she makes those around her happy'. Just as in *Agnes Grey* we saw the unconscious suggestion of virtue as a saleable commodity, here love, good works, self-effacement emerge as goods to be bartered. Behind this is a more prosaic intimation: if you make a man's home comfortable enough, he won't go out in the evenings and find his pleasure at the club, the opera or the brothel. It is Fordyce's *Sermons* again.

The suggestion that all human qualities are marketable permeates Thackeray's fiction. Although he does not write of money in human relations so drastically as Dickens, he exposes the layers of culpability. His characters trade on the elements of their 'value', which may be cash, or rank, or beauty, or devotion, self-sacrifice, usefulness. Those who do not find purchasers are those who fail, and in general the unwed are to be found amongst them.

It was an age that found it easy to clothe the morally dubious in decent and demure garments. By the emphasis on submissive devotion in women, wives were taught to bear with appalling treatment, and only slowly as the century progressed did the law begin to cope with the results of such a situation. Thackeray writes basically about two types of women, those who submit (Amelia, Rosey, Helen, Lady Lyndon in *Barry Lyndon*, Rachel Castlewood in *Henry Esmond*) and those who rebel (Mrs Mackenzie, Becky Sharp and, less damagingly, Beatrix Castlewood and Ethel Newcome). Both types of women are destructive, Becky scarcely more obviously so than Amelia, the one openly deceitful and aggressive, the other self-deluded, sentimental and suffocating.

In *Pendennis* it is Helen, Pen's mother, who is cast in the latter role. On one level she is presented as the perfect lady, gentle, self-sacrificing, devoted to her son, uncritical, living her whole life through her hopes for Pen. But gradually single words and phrases appear that indicate Thackeray's irony at work undermining the ideal that he appears to be setting up, an ideal that he knows is thoroughly acceptable. Helen is a 'foolish woman', a 'good, tender, *matchmaking* woman'; we are enabled to interpret her hopes as schemes, her devotion as destructive, her possessiveness as damaging. 'Ponto licked his hand and shoe, as they all did in that house, and Mr Pen received their homage as other folks do the flattery which they get' (Chapter 27). Between them Helen and Laura promote the self-conceit that creates Pen's difficulties. Having been tutored by these women to consider himself at the centre, he has to enact this role, and is resentfully cynical when he perceives the havoc he causes. His opinion of women and their lives is, not surprisingly, negative. 'In the country a woman has her household and her poor, her long calm days and long calm evenings,' he says. It does not occur to him, as he moves in sophisticated town circles, that the country life of Helen and Laura is anything but appropriate. In fact, he needs to have them there, as quiet unsophisticated influences to remember from time to time when city life gets difficult.

Pen, in his cynical phase, says, 'We don't marry for passion, but for prudence and for establishment' (Volume II, Chapter 7). If he is complacent about the life of women in the country, he is scathing about the life of the fashionable lady. He takes a tough view of the facts of society, but it does not occur to him that he might be an instrument of change. It is revealing of the lack of bite in the novel as a whole that Pen, although at the end redeemed – if that is the right word – by Laura, is still complacent. In *The Newcomes* some of the characters do try to change things, which is one of the reasons why it is a much more interesting book.

Pen fails to see that he himself is implicated in the acceptance of the values he sees operating around him, and I think Thackeray himself fails to focus on this to the extent that the novel demands. Pendennis is let off too lightly. We could say the same of Colonel Newcome in the later novel, but there his not very convincing adoption of Christian humility comes so near the end of his life that it carries much less weight in the moral balance of the book. At every point Pen is saved from committing himself so deeply that his fight back has to be radical. He is weak rather than wicked, selfish rather than savage. He doesn't actually seduce little Fanny, he doesn't actually ruin his mother and Laura. Of course we are intended to see Pendennis throughout as, *au fond*, a decent fellow, but the point is, or should be, that a decent fellow who is taken in so readily by the surfaces of things is likely to be a moral failure.

In the Fanny episode we see Pen's view of himself as the superior and condescending young gentleman completely exposed. 'I may call you Fanny, because you are a young girl and I am an old gentleman. But you mustn't call me anything but sir, or Mr. Pendennis, if you like; for we live in very different stations, Fanny . . .' (Volume II, Chapter 8). The way in which Pen treats Fanny illuminates the way he treats other women. He would like to condescend towards them all. He can't manage it with Blanche, but he does with Helen and Laura, and there is a distinct flavour of condescension in his ultimate marriage. He can congratulate himself on taking Laura, and on doing what his now dead mother had spent her life wishing for.

His lack of moral conversion is underlined by his rejection of Blanche Amory. Blanche is false, but she has more reality than Laura and certainly operates more actively in the world she lives in. Pen outgrows his imagined love for her, but then sees her suitability, represented by money, as a wife. When he discovers that her father is an escaped convict, he realizes that marriage would be impossible. He is reinforced by Warrington: 'Arthur Pendennis can't marry a convict's daughter, and sit in Parliament as Member for the hulks' (Volume II, Chapter 31). Until this moment Pen has been perfectly prepared to acquiesce in the scheme his uncle initiated to marry him into cash and politics. When the spectre of the convict comes into view he is suddenly able to see the intrigue in its true light. Thus illuminated he rejects Blanche for the wrong reasons, not because he doesn't like or respect her but because he cannot stomach the nastiness and the extent of the intrigue in which he is involved. His ability to reject the *situation* is laudable; his rejection of Blanche – and the moral rejection remains even though, at Laura's insistence, he goes to her prepared to have her if she wants it – is not. Thackeray further undermines even the most generous interpretation of Pen's motives by revealing that Blanche was intending to cast *him* off in favour of his rich friend Foker. He is even deprived of making a meaningful self-sacrificing gesture.

Pendennis was never intended to be an astringent moral tale. Yet I think Thackeray's irony makes it quite clear that we are to criticize Pendennis, and that the best we can say for him is that, for a fallible human being, he hasn't performed too badly. The conclusion is low-keyed, as it is in most of Thackeray's novels. Let us, he says, 'give a hand of charity to Arthur Pendennis, with all his faults and short-comings, who does not claim to be a hero, but only a man and a brother' (Volume II, Chapter 37). In other words, let us recognize that it is a tough, imperfect world, and be as tolerant as sympathetic judgment will allow. This conclusion emphasizes the 'soft' Thackeray, the Thackeray with a tendency to level humanity, to expose us gently but not savagely, and leans right away from the attacking Thackeray, the critic who stabs mercilessly at the fabric of society's values.

To some extent we are to believe that Pendennis is redeemed by his wife. She, perhaps, represents the standard towards which we should all strive. Yet Laura does not work. In a book characterized by its lack of taut commitment we cannot accept Laura as a constructive moral ideal, partly because the whole flavour of the book suggests that such an ideal cannot operate. Added to this, Laura shares too much of Helen's 'parasite' role, and has too little of the independent vigour that makes Ethel in *The Newcomes* so much more attractive. We need something more positive than Laura to counteract the image of marriage that Thackeray himself strikingly provides:

Damon has taxes, sermon, parade, tailors' bills, parliamentary duties, and the deuce knows what to think of; Delia has to think about Damon – Damon is the oak (or the post), and stands up, and Delia is the ivy or the honeysuckle whose arms twine about him. Is it not so, Delia? Is it not in your nature to creep about his feet and kiss them, to twine round his trunk and hang there; and Damon's to stand like a British man with his hands in his breeches pocket, while the pretty fond parasite clings round him? (Volume II, Chapter 18)

The image is damaging to man and woman. The mention of tailors' bills in the list of male duties clearly indicates that Thackeray has no very high regard for the activities of husbands, and the hands in the breeches pocket certainly suggest inertia rather than activity. But the 'pretty fond parasite' comes out rather worse than the British man. The theme of the parasitic woman is not at its strongest in *Pendennis*, partly because it is undermined by the complacent tone of the novel. It is much more present in *The Newcomes* and dominates the end of *Vanity Fair*.

However, the close association between woman as parasite and the influence of parents is apparent in *Pendennis*. The parasitic woman is almost always an over-protected daughter or wife, tutored to lean on husband or father. In Helen there is a dual role, for although she attempts to wield parental authority it is almost as if she sees in her son a substitute husband. She is much more dependent on him than he is on her. And of course her wish that he should marry Laura, an extension of herself, reinforces this. To bring him up and then let him go is an eventuality she cannot tolerate.

In Thackeray's fiction, wherever there is a parent who cares a great deal about his children there is damage done. One of the reasons that Ethel is able to operate with some independence is because her parents have little to do with her. As they haven't tried to make something of her, she can make something of herself. In *Vanity Fair* Mr Osborne cannot tolerate his son's acting independently, and the Sedleys stifle the inadequate Amelia. They arrange a marriage for her and encourage her to fall in love with a vain, empty-headed young man and she can be nothing but compliant. She has no tastes or opinions of her own because she has never been allowed the space for them to grow. When her parents and herself get into trouble they are all inadequate to each other because none of them has any independent resources.

Before pursuing the parent-child theme, which is central in Thackeray's novels, it is worth enquiring *why* it is that marriage is the fulcrum of action. Nineteenth-century fiction is full of snobs, full of an awareness of snobbery, full of an aloof condemnation of both the outward signs and the inward strivings of snobbery. It is permeated with a love-hate relationship with aristocracy and conspicuous wealth. The space that is used in describing the details of status, the appurtenances of living, servants, carriages, clothes, crests, estates, town houses, dinners, wine, is immense. One reason for this is that this was an age when conspicuous wealth was able to challenge aristocracy, and readers and writers alike were fascinated by that territory where the upper reaches of the *nouveaux riches* (most of the untitled *riches* in Victorian fiction are *nouveaux*) shade into aristocracy. It is just this territory that Thackeray occupies, just this territory where the strivings towards status and rank and cash mean most, where the little upstart Becky Sharp wages her war, and where marriage can be pivotal.

The family is the crucial unit in all this. It is over points like the inheritance of titles and fortunes that the haggling takes place. 'Life is a transaction,' says Pen, excusing his own part in transactions. Life is a market-place – Vanity Fair. Parents sell their daughters, trade titles for riches, buy commissions in the Army or seats in Parliament for their sons. A family can stand or fall by the marriages the children make. Again, it is something we take for granted in the Victorian novel, but Thackeray does not take it for granted. He exhibits this area of society in terms of families. The whole system is presented as a kind of tribal warfare, with the families themselves weakened by internal feuds. What emerges from this is the sheer cruelty of spouses to each other and parents to children. As long as families are obedient to society the cruelty is inevitable.

In *The Newcomes* the Colonel himself, that admirable, kind, decent old man, is guilty. Gradually the nature of his marriage emerges. He married for the wrong reasons, out of pity. He had no love for his wife, who was a silly, empty, unhappy woman whom he felt it his duty to marry in order to protect. She made life very difficult for him, and his marriage was a dismal affair. In spite of this his attitude to women is above all protective, and his attitude to marriage is highly romantic. He sees Clive as a young prince 'in a gold coach with a Princess beside him' (Volume II, Chapter 13). The princess he selects for Clive is the helpless Rosey. The Colonel imposes on his son a marriage as disastrous as his own had been.

Clive's marriage is flanked by the amorous adventures of his cousin Ethel, whom he himself loves, and the marriage of his cousin Barnes the banker to Lady Clara, another weak, submissive female. It is overshadowed by the presence of his father and Rosey's mother. The latter is a savagely portrayed woman who in the vulgarity of her cruelty far outdoes Becky. But the well-meaning Colonel is as guilty as Mrs Mackenzie of the ruin of Clive's happiness, and of course Clive is guilty too. Like his father, Clive marries for the wrong reasons, but he can only see this in terms of his own submission, not as a wrong done to Rosey, the most extreme example of Thackeray's parasitic women. 'So everybody, somehow, great or small, seems to protect her; and the humble, simple, gentle little thing wins a certain degree of goodwill from the world, which is touched by her humility and her pretty sweet looks' (Volume I, Chapter 24). The problem is that Rosey operates as a well-groomed, sweetly-dressed limb of her appalling mother, unable to do or say anything without reference to her. Before marriage and the financial disaster brought about by the Colonel's anxiety to set up his son, this is seen by the kindly men who surround her as charming. Flung into the whirlpool of real life, deprived of money and style and comforts, Rosey becomes a ghastly puppet.

Rosey is eaten away by her mother and marriage. 'She sat under Mrs Mackenzie as a bird under a boa-constrictor, doomed – fluttering – fascinated; scared and fawning as a whipt spaniel before a keeper' (Volume II, Chapter 35). Her deterioration is dramatically enacted in terms of constant pregnancies and confinements. As Rosey becomes weaker physically she becomes more negative, less human, and Mrs Mackenzie becomes increasingly overbearing and vicious. We have an impression of Clive being completely excluded from the blood-sucking mother and daughter relationship. 'I am not quite the father of my own child, nor the husband of my own wife' (Volume II, Chapter 31), he says. In spite of which Rosey has no time to recover from one still-birth before she is in expectations of another, and she dies in childbirth. The cruelty in this situation implicates them all, father and son, mother and daughter, husband and wife.

Rosey is the absolute victim, the victim of greed and ambition in others, the victim of parents and men. She shares this role with another woman in the novel, Lady Clara, the wife of Barnes Newcome. Barnes, an antithesis to the handsome, pleasing Clive, has power, money and rapacity, and his treatment of his wife is savage. Clara is seen as an animal, repeatedly referred to as a well-broken horse that will respond to spur and bit. But Barnes is overactive with the whip and spurs, and Clara bolts, though scarcely to a happier life. Thackeray's handling of Barnes and Clara needs to be ruthless, for not only must we be told the worst about mercenary marriages, but Thackeray needs to shock Ethel Newcome into avoiding such a marriage herself.

Ethel, Barnes' sister, is enmeshed in aspirations that dictate that she too must marry into the aristocracy. This branch of the Newcome clan has made its money through banking, and needs to give its wealth respectability with a title. Ethel, cynically accepting these pressures, becomes engaged to Lord Farintosh, who has very little to recommend him except the largeness of his estates. She is a dashing, attractive, independent-minded young woman, and although she becomes thoroughly implicated in the worst aspects of the marriage market, Thackeray has to make it clear that she is redeemable. He tries hard to get the moral perspective right, to relate Ethel and her independence to the pressures operating in society and the family, and her relationship with her cousin Clive that is an important part of this. Here Thackeray attempts to clarify how we should judge Ethel:

The least unworthy part of her conduct, some critics will say, was that desire to see Clive and be well with him: as she felt the greatest regard for him, the showing it was not blameable; and every flutter which she made to escape out of the meshes which the world had cast about her, was but the natural effort at liberty. It was her prudence which was wrong; and her submission, wherein she was most culpable. In the early church story, do we not read how young martyrs constantly had to disobey worldly papas and mammas, who would have had them silent, and not utter their dangerous opinions? how their parents locked them up, kept them on bread and water, whipped and tortured them, in order to enforce obedience? – nevertheless they would declare the truth: they would defy the gods by law established, and deliver themselves up to the lions or the tormentors? Are there not Heathen Idols enshrined among us still? Does not the world worship them, and persecute those who refuse to kneel? Do not many souls sacrifice to them; and other bolder spirits rebel, and, with rage in their hearts, bend down their stubborn knees at their altars? (Volume II, Chapter 15)

Thackeray obliquely reproves Ethel for being too prudent and submissive, and thus makes us reflect on the bold, unorthodox Ethel with whom we have become acquainted. The passage puts Ethel very precisely in her place; the whips and the tortures and imprisonment have more than allegorical relevance. We already know that her brother Barnes has physically beaten Clara and soon we will see him locking her up. Ethel does rebel in time, although we might complain that it is too quiet and modest a rebellion. Thackeray could be accused of taming Ethel rather than allowing her to rebel with a force proportionate to her spirit. In spite of this, the significance of Ethel as the only character through whom Thackeray activates a morally acceptable and *successful* rebellion should be emphasized. Whether we accept his ironically suggested, take-it-or-leave-it happy ending does not matter. What matters is that Ethel did rise up against the 'Heathen Idols' and stood against society and her family. In this case it is Clive who is the sacrifice, Clive whom she rejected against her better judgment, who is thrown to the lions in the painful process of Ethel's learning independence.

Inevitably we return to the parent-child theme. At an early stage in the novel the Colonel worries that he does not understand his son. Clive is attractive, bright and easygoing. His father is proud of him and wants the best of everything for him. Colonel Newcome is innocent and old-fashioned. He represents values that appear to be out-of-date. But although we are intended to respect these values, they are clearly not adequate. Once again, innocence fails to cope, and in doing so becomes destructive.

Money is an important part of what he does for his son, but he doesn't understand money, although he does understand, or thinks he does, what constitutes a gentleman, and an important part of gentility is the avoidance of earning a living. It is this, a profoundly bred, well-intentioned snobbism, that comes between him and his understanding of his son who wants to be an artist, an activity which at that time was considered to be not so much a profession as a trade. The most positive and creative part of Clive's existence baffles him. The tragedy is that there is not so very great a difference between the Colonel's attempt to destine his son for a life of gentlemanly leisure, and Mrs Mackenzie's fiendish dedication to marrying her daughter well, or Lady Kew's malevolent interferences in the marriages and fortunes of her grandchildren.

Clive loves his father too much to rebel. Ethel is less inhibited by affection for her elders. And when children bow to their parents they not only worship false idols, they help to sustain what is ultimately the political *status quo*. They acquiesce in the existing social *mores*, the existing hierarchy, the existing operation of money and rank as major influences. Thackeray does not leave us to guess at the political link, for he demonstrates trading in parliamentary seats and political power as part of marriage transactions. He shows us that political power is impossible without money and, conversely, that money and status mean power. Barnes enacts this, as does Mr Osborne in *Vanity Fair*, and Colonel Newcome too is implicated. As a rich man he buys himself a seat in Parliament, and tries to buy a wife for his son. But he has to give up his seat when he loses his money, because political power is something he would need to go on paying for, and he cannot buy Ethel for Clive because that branch of the family doesn't need cash; its needs nobility.

I think even more than in *Vanity Fair* marriage in *The Newcomes* is a crux in the power game. But, as in *Vanity Fair*, money is the final test. It is through her generosity with *money* that Ethel redeems herself: she buys redemption. It is through loss of money that the Colonel is punished for his *hubris*. It is through lack of money that Clive is forced to work for a living and thus to make something of himself. At least in *The Newcomes* the loss of money does work in a morally positive way, and thus although it is a more sombre novel than *Vanity Fair* it is more optimistic.

Thackeray is attacking a system in which marriage is essential, and it is in terms of married life that we see the grossest cruelty and the most profound unhappiness. There would be little point in the attack if Thackeray did not intend us to believe that there were other possibilities. But what are they? His ironically happy ending cannot be taken very seriously, nor can the fringe relationship of Laura and Pendennis. In fact, the penultimate images of Ethel and Clive are much more constructive than the romantic evocation of their eventual union. Ethel is preferable as a calm, independent woman who has opted out of what she herself calls the 'haggling' over marriage, who has come to terms with herself and has found a purpose in the care of her brother's children, themselves the victims of a disastrous marriage. There is a slight taint of sentimentality in her modest devotion, but I don't feel it is too damaging. The lasting image of Clive is of a man scarred but surviving, earning a modest living, and caring for his small son with whom he has a lively, intimate relationship. While the Colonel sent his son from India back to England for his training as a gentleman, and did not see him again for many years, Clive and Tommy are companions, sharing interests (Tommy drawing in the corner of Clive's studio) and pleasures. Where wealthier parents consign their children to the care of servants and governesses, Clive cares for his own son – as Ethel, it is clear, is closely involved with her niece and nephew.

The moral creativity of these relationships is reinforced by the way in which the parent-child theme has been established. The errors and the culpability have been displayed. We have seen adults judged in terms of their attitudes to children. Clara, for instance, has little interest in hers, and this is shown to be a disquieting sign of human deficiency. Lord Kew gets on well with children: this helps to suggest that he is a decent fellow in spite of his bad habits. Colonel

Newcome loves children, and children love him. He makes mistakes but his heart is right.

The novel is full of children, although the process by which children are tailored for the adult world is much more detailed in *Vanity Fair*, where we see the young Georgy and the young Rawdon growing up. In *The Newcomes* they are a more pervasive presence, and it is appropriate that the most positive note in the finale should be so closely associated with them. It is the theme of parental destruction that is so devastating, and to have a glimpse of children as the companions rather than the victims of their parents is salutary.

3

Vanity Fair was written before *Pendennis* and *The Newcomes*, published in monthly parts, as all Thackeray's novels were, from 1847 to 1848. It discusses the marriage theme with the focus on women and society, and is in many ways less digressive and more consistent in its confrontations than the later two novels. This does not mean that questions of moral choice and moral approval are made any easier: far from it. But an acquaintance with Pendennis and Clive, with Blanche and Rosey and Ethel, helps to focus the ripples of implication in *Vanity Fair*, and also suggests that it is a much more complex, more deeply thought out book, than critics sometimes indicate.

Thackeray sets out his characters in ranks that at first sight seem as irreconcilably opposed as the two armies at Waterloo, which features so strikingly in the novel. But wars are compounded of ambivalences artificially fashioned into opposing sides, and thus we have, while the armies fight it out and George Osborne, 'that selfish humbug, that low-bred cockney dandy, that padded booby' (Chapter 67), as Rebecca calls him, is killed fighting valiantly, the population of Brussels ready to embrace the victorious French with as much alacrity as they made money out of the British. Loyalties in war are as fluctuating as those in societies, families and marriages. Becky, while her husband is on the battlefield, envisages herself settling down profitably under French occupation.

All of Thackeray's characters are, as it were, reflected simultaneously in several different mirrors. One shows the image reflected by the conventions and hypocrisies of society, another the self-centred, internal image, another the image in the consciousness of characters whose moral judgment we think we are being led to approve, another the image the author himself reflects. In order to assess Thackeray's people and his purposes with them we have to compose these various images.

The novel hinges on two women, Amelia Sedley and Rebecca Sharp, who represent alternatives for a successful career in society. Amelia, from a substantial middle-class background is kind, good-natured and pretty, but she is also indiscriminate, inexperienced, self-deluded and unintelligent. She is therefore helpless, at the mercy of her parents and the man her parents have chosen for her. We have already seen in Rosey and Lady Clara that helplessness in women is disastrous, especially deliberately cultivated and unintelligent help-lessness.

Becky's parents are dead, and she is quite free from family pressures. Her dubious Bohemian background contributes to the slight exoticism of her looks and manner. She is insubordinate and unscrupulous, ambitious and deceitful, but she is also clever, an intelligent judge of character, and honest with herself. Without parents, she has to forge her own career. She cannot afford to be helpless, she has to think and plan and act for herself.

According to the conventions of the time, Becky is regarded dubiously be-cause of her uncertain background. During her visit to the Sedley household she is found wanting because she is not sufficiently humble. The servants don't like her because she appears to compete with them. Becky is being criticized, but once again this is a situation where a character is condemned for the wrong reasons; and while we appreciate the wrong reasons, we appreciate also that Becky does deserve criticism, but on quite other grounds. Thackeray thus uses Becky's dubious character as a means of exposing both her and society's motives.

Becky's deceit is precisely what has been encouraged by the guardians of morality. She pretends to be what everyone tells young girls they ought to pretend to be. Amelia's sweetness wins the admiration of gentlemen who have been taught that this is a desirable quality in women, but it is no positive help to her in making her way socially. After reading the early chapters of *Vanity Fair* we might be tempted to say, Amelia will fail where Rebecca succeeds, but she will be all the better for it. As the novel proceeds we discover that Amelia's position is not a simple one of social failure and moral success. We discover not only the flaws nestling in Amelia's weakness but the destructive potential too.

Becky's understanding of society, and her grasp of what she wants out of it, give her flexibility in adapting to its exigencies. Where defeat devastates Amelia, Becky is not bothered. She has many of the characteristics of Ethel Newcome – we can see Ethel perhaps as Thackeray's apology to Becky, a realist and a schemer whom we can forgive – but whereas Ethel is in a position to indulge these characteristics, Becky has to make them work very hard for her. One of the features they share, of course, is the centrality of marriage in their schemes. Marriage is the yardstick of a woman's social success; there is absolutely nothing else. By it Ethel hopes to acquire an aristocratic seal of approval which will guarantee social conquest, and Becky aims for anything society offers that will ensure money and power. The modest Amelia's parents want security and a suitably polished exterior.

Neither Becky nor Amelia has any choice in the roles they play, Becky because of her background, Amelia because of her lack of intelligence and her deference to her parents. She operates only in response to her parents' control, falls in love with the man they choose and later, when circumstances have altered so drastically, gives up her son under pressure from them. In the marriage market Amelia is a prize – 'What a blooming young creature you seem, and what a prize the rogue has got!' (Chapter 5) thinks Dobbin when he meets her, and thus incidentally reveals his own attitude to women – and Becky is an asset. Becky has talents which can help a man get on. As the relationship between Amelia and George Osborne is elaborated, Amelia's vulnerability becomes increasingly apparent. It is just this vulnerability that attracts Dobbin, and makes credible his long attachment to her, and his precipitate return at the end of the book. Once Dobbin has established his feelings of protective responsibility towards her, out of loyalty he cannot give them up. It ceases to be a question of love. Some critics have suggested that Dobbin's long-lasting attachment to Amelia is a sign of his stupidity, especially when he admits himself that she isn't worth it, but I would rather see it as a sign of his awareness that, having through his better nature encouraged her to depend on him, he is unwilling to forego his responsibility. His feeling is a combination of sentiment and loyalty.

Amelia's vulnerability is demonstrated not just in terms of her uncritical attitude to George, but in the context of social intercourse as a whole:

'We are kind to her,' the Misses Osborne said . . . and they treated her with such extreme kindness and condescension, and patronised her so insufferably, that the poor little thing *was* in fact perfectly dumb in their presence, and to all outward appearance as stupid as they thought her. (Chapter 12)

The Osborne sisters are jealous and eager to condemn Amelia: the point is that Amelia appears to conform to the opinion they have of her. George neglects her:

Poor little tender heart! and so it goes on hoping and beating, and longing and trusting. You see it is not much of a life to describe. There is not much of what you call incident in it. Only one feeling all day – when will he come? only one thought to sleep and wake upon. (Chapter 12)

While we do not regard Amelia unsympathetically – it is of some importance that neither Amelia nor Rebecca alienates us entirely – we are aware of the essential negativity of her life. It is hard to respect her. As Rosey only operates as the limb of Mrs Mackenzie, so Amelia only operates as the destined bride of George.

Both she and Becky are surrounded by ominous images, which are a challenge to Becky but a threat to Amelia. One of these images is contained in Thackeray's portrait of the marriage of Sir Pitt Crawley to his second wife. She is the daughter of an ironmonger, deliberately selected by him as a woman who would be modestly grateful for such elevation and, of course, happy. And, having taken her from her own milieu, Sir Pitt neglects her, and pursues his own life:

As the only endowments with which Nature had gifted Lady Crawley were those of pink cheeks and a white skin, and as she had no sort of character, nor talents, nor opinions, nor occupations, nor amusements, nor the vigour of soul and ferocity of temper which often falls to the lot of entirely foolish women, her hold upon Sir Pitt's affections was not very great. Her roses faded out of her cheeks, and the pretty freshness left her figure after the birth of a couple of children, and she became a mere machine in her husband's house, of no more use than the late Lady Crawley's grand piano. (Chapter 9)

This could be Amelia, a useless object, and such a marriage was already on the cards when George's timely death brought it to an end. In awarding Amelia the miseries of poverty and widowhood Thackeray saves her from becoming 'a mere machine in her husband's house'. She has no conception of positive cruelty, no thought about the implications of marriage, and no understanding of the character of her husband.

Amelia continues to love a dead, idealized George for fifteen years, although we know that he was about to embark on an affair with Becky when he died. This is Lady Crawley: 'Her heart was dead long before her body. She had sold it to become Sir Pitt Crawley's wife. Mothers and daughters are making the same bargain every day in Vanity Fair' (Chapter 14). If George had not died we would have seen Amelia's marriage in the same light, as a bargain contracted by the parents, in the case of Amelia to consolidate the relationship between two families already mutually involved in business. It is a bargain convenient to the business and social relationships of the parents, but devastating to the wife: the husband has the means to avoid the devastations of such a marriage. George is Sir Pitt in embryo.

So while Thackeray shows us how necessary marriage is to the hopes and ambitions of young girls, he also demonstrates what marriage is like. We see ambition, deception and cruelty operating to such an extent within marriage – often on a small scale and with limited objectives, but no less pervasive for that – that we are prepared for anything marriage might entail and married people might do to one another. Yet it is a tribute to the highly organized structure of the book that Thackeray can still take us by surprise, and use the unexpected with a superbly creative sense of drama. We know about Becky and Lord Steyne, yet we can still share Rawdon's fury and injury when he discovers them together. We know that Rawdon is not such a bad fellow; we have seen his affection for his son, his regard for his sister-in-law, his decency to Amelia, yet we can still find this injured manifestation of his positive qualities rewarding.

Becky's vulnerability is quite different from Amelia's. It works positively, it creates her independence. We can see just how it operates in this passage, describing Becky as a governess in the Crawley family:

. . . it became naturally Rebecca's duty to make herself, as she said, agreeable to her benefactors, and to gain their confidence to the utmost of her power. Who can but admire this quality of gratitude in an unprotected orphan; and, if there entered some degree of selfishness into her calculations, who can say but that her prudence was perfectly justifiable? 'I am alone in the world,' said the friendless girl. 'I have nothing to look for but what my own labour can bring me; and while that little pink-faced chit Amelia, with not half my sense, has ten thousand pounds and an establishment secure, poor Rebecca (and my figure is far better than hers) has only herself and her own wits to trust to. Well, let us see if my wits cannot provide me with an honourable maintenance, and if some day or the other I cannot show Miss Amelia my real superiority over her. Not that I dislike Amelia: who can dislike such a harmless, good-natured creature? – only it will be a fine day when I can take my place above her in the world, as why, indeed, should I not? Thus it was that our little friend formed visions of the future for herself – nor must we be scandalized that, in all her castles in the air, a husband was the principal inhabitant. Of what else have young ladies to think, but husbands? Of what else do their dear mammas think? (Chapter 10)

Thackeray's irony is clearly working on several levels here, as he writes of Rebecca's duty to make herself agreeable, as he looks at Amelia through her eyes, but he is also showing how Rebecca is responding realistically to her situation, and at the same time is doing what would conventionally be expected of her. It was expected that one in her situation should be grateful and prudent, and pleasant to everyone. But prudence, for instance, can involve both calculation and selfishness, and we are intended to see this applying to more than just Becky. Who is more selfish and calculating than Miss Crawley?

Again, when Thackeray uses the words 'alone' and 'friendless' his intention is to prod us, for although they suggest pathos, in Rebecca they motivate her independence. They are positive, not negative. It is Amelia we feel sorry for, with her 'ten thousand pounds and establishment secure'. Becky knows that she is superior to Amelia in intelligence, and in attractions too; the problem is that she must prove it, and the only way in which she can do so in terms that everyone will understand is by taking a place 'above her in the world'. And the only way that can be done, because a woman is nothing on her own, is by securing the right husband.

This paragraph is vital to the way in which Thackeray intends us to see Becky. She is not only clever and ambitious, operating independently in a world she is determined to conquer, she is also a victim of established pressures. 'Of what else have young ladies to think of but husbands? Of what else do their mammas think?' We have to look at Amelia in order to understand fully what Thackeray is doing with Becky. Both girls have had the same education, both have the same curtailed prospects before them, both have been taught that marriage is not only the yardstick of success but the only means of avoiding failure. Both have been deprived of choice. It is their response to this deprivation that differs so radically, but the response itself has been dictated by the difference in their backgrounds.

Rebecca's superior wits operate to great advantage through her observation of people and manners. Amelia's interest in other people, apart from George, is very limited, and her understanding of them as individuals even less. Becky watches everyone, and puts to good use what she sees. She captures Rawdon Crawley because she understands and anticipates him, and sees what sort of a woman attracts him, and then becomes that sort of a woman. She does the same thing with George Osborne. 'He thought her gay, brisk, arch, distinguée, delightful' (Chapter 25). She deliberately emphasizes qualities that make her as different as possible from little Amelia, while at Queen's Crawley she presented herself as a pleasing but self-effacing amanuensis. Amelia has not a clue about her husband's character, and has not the means to compete with Becky even if she were so inclined.

Thackeray uses animal imagery a great deal to describe and reflect on human behaviour. In *Vanity Fair* the whole of society is characterized by suggestions of wild beasts, savagery and cannibalism. People maul each other and feed on each other. Within this Rebecca operates as a snake or a serpent. The image is not only contained in that memorable paragraph towards the end of the novel where Thackeray himself seems to recoil from the portrait he has painted of a sea-monster feeding on the corpses of the drowned. It is specifically present quite early on. Dobbin remarks, 'She writhes and twists about like a snake' (Chapter 29), which is both morally and physically suggestive – we see her sinuously turning her white shoulders. A little later George leaves the note in Becky's bouquet which proposes that they should run away together – 'there lay a note coiled like a snake among the flowers' (Chapter 29).

But Rebecca shares the snake image with others, and is associated with the idea of poison which involves the Sedleys as well as the Crawleys. Amelia shrieks out when her mother is trying to administer medicine to the infant Georgy, 'I will *not* have baby poisoned' (Chapter 38), and her mother responds with equal vehemence. 'Yes; I've nursed five children, and buried three: and the one I love best of all . . . says I'm a murderess. Ah, Mrs Osborne! may *you* never nourish a viper in your bosom. . . .' The snake and poison imagery draws everyone into the destructiveness of Becky, and applies especially to members of the same family damaging each other. Old Mr Osborne is a part of it too:

He firmly believed that everything he did was right, that he ought on all occasions have his own way – and like the sting of the wasp or the serpent his hatred rushed out armed and poisonous against anything like opposition. (Chapter 35)

Selfishness and self-centredness are poisonous, and there is scarcely a character in the book free from them. The imagery is taken into the Sedley camp and the Osborne camp, Amelia is implicated, the door of Lord Steyne's house has a bronze Medusa's head as its knocker, Rebecca's hands when she is discovered with Steyne by Rawdon are 'covered with serpents and rings' (Chapter 53).

I emphasize the way in which this particular image penetrates almost everywhere, because I think it effects the interpretation of that surmounting emblem of the serpent which has been so often discussed. That writhing sea-monster does not represent the final dismissal of the hideous Rebecca from the moral vantage point of the society she has fed on. It is society itself. When Thackeray protests that he is innocent of flouting the conventions, that he has politely refrained from telling us what really went on, he is exposing those same conventions, and exposing society:

I defy anyone to say that our Becky, who has certainly some vices, has not been presented to the public in a perfectly genteel and inoffensive manner. In describing this siren, singing and smiling, coaxing and cajoling, the author, with modest pride, asks his readers all round, has he once forgotten the laws of politeness, and showed the monster's hideous tail above the water? No! Those who like may peep down under the waves that are pretty transparent, and see it writhing and twirling, diabolically hideous and slimy, falling amongst bones, or curling around corpses: but above the water-line, I ask, has not everything been proper, agreeable and decorous, and has any the most squeamish moralist in Vanity Fair the right to cry fie? When, however, the siren disappears and dives below, down among the dead men, the water of course grows turbid over her, and it is labour lost to look into it ever so curiously. They look pretty enough when they sit upon a rock, twangling their harps and combing their hair, and sing, and beckon to you to come and hold the looking-glass; but when they sink into their native element, depend on it these mermaids are about no good, and we had best not examine the fiendish marine cannibals, revelling and feasting on their wretched pickled victims. (Chapter 64)

Only in a cannibalistic world can Becky the cannibal make use of her talents. Thackeray is simultaneously particularizing and generalizing. The siren is 'she', but also 'it' and 'they'. The 'monster' is hypocrisy and deceit in general, the corpses all those who have failed according to society's artificial standards, and in a cannibalistic world you either are a corpse, or you are feeding on a corpse. And the siren represents all women – Amelia too has sat upon her rock and twangled her harp, and Dobbin in the end comes and holds the looking-glass. But there is another layer to the irony in the entire passage. It is not only an exposure of social activity in Vanity Fair, it is an invitation to acknowledge that, by the standards of society, by their logic, we must indeed accept Becky as genteel and inoffensive. When Thackeray claims that he has offended no one he is not just saying that he has conformed to the laws of politeness, he is showing how the whole of society conspires to hide the serpent's tail, and thus to enable the Becky Sharps to appear perfectly acceptable.

Amelia's place in this is clear. She has fed on a corpse – the dead George – as well as twangled a harp, and others have fed on her. On her marriage to Dobbin, she feeds on him; she has become a parasite. Dobbin, fortunately, is able to sustain her, and in that consists the only positive aspect of their marriage. Thackeray underlines Amelia's involvement in the above characterization of society by depicting, as part of the final episode, Amelia and Becky at Boulogne. Only once in the book has Amelia been so near the sea; at Brighton immediately after her marriage to George. Now she awaits Dobbin on the shore: 'she looked out westward across the dark sea line, and over the swollen billows which came tumbling and frothing to the shore' (Chapter 67). Now Amelia is the siren, already once and firmly rejected by Dobbin, luring Dobbin to her.

The moral of Thackeray's tale is that both Becky and Amelia are cannibals. And whereas Becky's cannibalism is a fairly straightforward process of deceit and consumption, Amelia's involves the complex workings of sacrifice, of parents feeding on children, of the gradual effects of slow-working poisons. And while it is not difficult to expose Becky, Amelia is surrounded and protected by convention, by sentiment, by her own sweetness and tenderness. But it is just these things, Thackeray shows us, that contribute to her cannibalism.

Amelia is complacently self-centred. Only with her own son does she act positively, and that, we can see, sustains her selfishness, and does Georgy no good either. The words most frequently used to describe her are 'tender' and 'clinging'; but her tenderness does not mean warmth, an outgoing response to people, but rather suggests a need to be soothed and cared for. Even Georgy is used for this, and very soon becomes her prop. She worships him, but also depends on him, so that she clings to her child just as she tried to cling to her father and to George, and continues to cling to Dobbin. Yet Amelia's vulnerability is real; everything has conspired to deprive her of self-sufficiency. Here she is, nine days after her wedding, the achievement of her major aim in life:

Was the prize gained – the heaven of life – and the winner still doubtful and unsatisfied? As his hero and heroine pass the matrimonial barrier, the novelist generally drops the curtain, as if the drama were over then: the doubts and struggles of life ended: as if once landed in the marriage country, all were green and pleasant there: and wife and husband had nothing to do but to link each other's arms together, and wander gently downwards towards old age in happy and perfect fruition. But our little Amelia was just on the bank of her new country, and was already looking anxiously back towards the sad friendly figures waving farewell to her across the stream, from the other distant shore. (Chapter 26)

We see how difficult it is for her, since almost everyone is ready to reinforce her self-absorbed image. Dobbin in India nurses a mental picture of a 'gentle little woman', 'happy and loving', but Thackeray comments:

Very likely Amelia was not like the portrait the Major had formed of her: there was a figure in a book of fashions which his sisters had in England, and with which William had made away privately, pasting it into the lid of his desk, and fancying he saw some resemblance to Mrs Osborne in the print, whereas I have seen it, and can vouch that it is but the picture of a high-waisted gown with an impossible doll's face simpering over it – and, perhaps, Mr Dobbin's sentimental Amelia was no more like the real one than this absurd print which she cherished. (Chapter 43)

But perhaps, we have to wonder, Amelia is 'a high-waisted gown with an impossible doll's face', and Dobbin's illusion lies, not in being unable to see the real Amelia, but in seeing the real Amelia in a more favourable light than she deserves. The passage is damaging to both of them. Amelia is reduced to the picture of a doll, Dobbin to a foolish victim. Dobbin is able to recover his focus on reality before the book ends, but Amelia never sheds her doll-like personality.

Dobbin and Rawdon Crawley are the only important characters in the book who do not take advantage of women, and they are both also shown to be socially awkward and dull. The implication is that the socially skilled are most likely to take advantage of the opposite sex – this applies to women as well as to men. Clearly it is to Rebecca's advantage to choose a husband who will not fight her back, and to Amelia's to choose a husband who will support her parasitism without reprisal. Most of the other male characters exploit women, out of habit or deliberate scorn and cruelty, or a combination of both. The elder Sedley and the elder Osborne, George, Sir Pitt, Lord Steyne – whether they are daughters or wives these men treat the women of their households as slaves: only Rebecca escapes this. Only Rebecca is able to turn the tables on the men. 'Who are you to give orders here?' Lord Steyne says to his daughter-in-law. 'You have no money. You have no brains. You were here to have children, and you have not had any' (Chapter 49). The vicious Lord Steyne, the one character whom we can unreservedly abhor, illuminates one of the most significant layers in the novel.

Lord Steyne's attitude to his daughter-in-law is directly related to the attitude of all *Vanity Fair*'s parents to their children, particularly to their daughters. The Iphigenia clock in the Osborne's drawing-room has reference to much more than the Osborne household, ruled as it is by a tyrannous, mean-spirited old man. When Dobbin goes to break the news of George's marriage to Miss Osborne and 'the tick-tock of the Sacrifice of Iphigenia clock on the mantlepiece became quite rudely audible' (Chapter 23), this is an inanimate comment on both the sacrifice of Amelia and the enslavement of Miss Osborne, in other words on the two alternatives open to the well-bred middle-class young woman: to be either a wife or a daughter. Rebecca is ultimately neither, and her vagabond life is the price she has to pay for this escape. We are not asked to applaud Becky's bid for independence, but nor are we asked to admire Amelia, 'the tender little parasite' feeding on Dobbin, 'the rugged old oak' (Chapter 67).

At various periods in the century there were waves of attack on the artificiality of society, on marriages of convenience, on the enslavement to money and status. But there were few writers who exposed, in the way that Thackeray did, the process of internal poisoning that these things produced. He cast more light on the damage caused within *normal* close relationships than Dickens. A crucial part of his exposure is his depiction of the older generation, obsessed with perpetuating their own false values, dominating and damaging the young. And it is not only the obviously malignant who do this, not only the old Osbornes and the Miss Crawleys and the Lady Kews, but often more homely and likeable parents. We see this in *The Virginians* (1857–59), a lax and less gritty book than most of Thackeray's novels, where the genial Lamberts react with horror at the possibility of George Warrington marrying their daughter without his mother's consent. It is a question of authority and of money, the one bolstering the other, and the implications of this are much wider than the effect on the individuals concerned. It was risky to challenge parental power as long as heads of families were able to control so absolutely the property and finances of adult children completely untrained for any kind of profession. Inheritance is a major theme in *The Virginians*. Parental power is what much of Thackeray's fiction is about, and he understood it much better than most Victorian novelists. His understanding of its political significance, its inevitable tendency to reinforce the *status quo* politically and socially, each permeating the other, is at the centre of his approach.

Thackeray does not produce a convincing alternative to the toughly bargained marriage, although he does try. There are Laura and Pendennis, and, very similarly presented in terms of style and tone, George and Theo Warrington in *The Virginians*. In this case courtship and marriage are discussed with a generous helping of sentiment, which is scarcely appetizing after the astringency that Thackeray's best writing accustoms us to. Theo and Laura are very similar: good-natured, well-intentioned girls who will do anything for their husbands except falsify their moral response to other people. The suggestion is that marriage, a happy and fulfilled marriage, is in Thackeray's ideal a kind of benevolent paternalism which leaves the wife free to make her own judgment of individuals and society. The fact that Laura and Theo are both highly critical of artificiality and pretence, and are genuinely loving and prepared for humility, is important. Unlike Laura, Theo seems to be entirely free of an ironic undertone in her characterization. But the whole book is less severe, and most of Thackeray's satire emerges through digressions and interludes rather than directly through characterization.

In *Henry Esmond* (1852) Thackeray attempts to resolve the parent-child dilemma, and in doing so illuminates from a more tangential angle the centrality of this relationship in perpetuating an invalid society. In a sense Henry Esmond marries his mother, reverses the accepted system of authority by marrying a woman whom he has long looked to as a mother figure. He thus echoes Pendennis's marriage. Like Becky, Henry is without parents, ostensibly an orphan, and thus free from the tie that would make it difficult and risky for him not to conform. But in marrying Lady Castlewood and renouncing his claim to the title he puts himself in an anomalous position, and having meddled with the customary processes, ultimately renounces society itself by going to Virginia.

There is in Thackeray's portrayal of marriage considerable ambiguity. Clearly he enjoyed indulging in the marriage of George and Theo, and wanted to allow himself a ration of sentiment. But there is no ambiguity in the way he shows parent-child relationships operating, personally and socially. Parents can destroy children while appearing to sacrifice all for them – we need look no further than Amelia and the young Georgy to see the uninterruptible process of suffocating love and care forcing Georgy along the way to the irresponsible vanity of his father. In *The Newcomes* Thackeray tells us plainly that there are times when children must rebel, and in a softer vein in *The Virginians* George Warrington reflects that there have to be moments when youth flouts the authority of age. He is discussing the American Revolution, and using a parent-child analogy. There are times when rebellion is the only moral action, yet the rebel must be prepared to accept the full consequences of what he does.

Ethel Newcome, we feel, is prepared to do this, which is why the offered happy ending of *The Newcomes* can hardly be taken seriously. George Warrington is rescued from the consequences of his rebellion – poverty – by a timely inheritance. Thackeray's avoidance of the issue here is all the more exposed by his insistence that the newly married Warringtons are all the happier for having no money, and have much nicer friends as a consequence of not moving in society. However, it is from Thackeray's strong novels that we retain a lasting impression, and in *Vanity Fair* there are no rescues.

THE MAINSTREAM of fiction in the 1840s and '50s stuck close to an uncritical presentation of the Amelia type in heroines, and a corresponding interpretation of marriage. There were some remarkable exceptions – the Brontës and Mrs Gaskell in particular – but generally the fiction of the period contains not only a stereotype of femininity and marriage, but a stereotype that is intrinsically less interesting than, for instance, the Fanny Burney heroine hedged by dangers. It is less interesting because the sphere of action narrows considerably. Fanny Burney's heroines needed protection, but they moved freely and widely. As the Victorian age took shape necessities became conventions, and as the walls closed in on the Victorian heroine and the Victorian marriage, two features grew into dominance: stasis and boredom.

Jane Austen's heroines are not bored. They may not always be useful, but they are usually busy. They know how to find pleasure in passing the time in what seem to them useful activities, needlework, sketching, music, visiting. In Jane Austen's novels languor and boredom, such as we find in *Mansfield Park*'s Lady Bertram, are a reflection of character, not of society. Amelia isn't bored, but we suspect she might be if she had more imagination. In Thackeray's novels a judgment of society is always involved in characterization, and we have seen how Amelia's helplessness is the inevitable product of the attitude of society in general, and her parents in particular, to a pretty young girl with money but no talents. Many of Thackeray's heroines avert boredom through nervous indulgences. In *The Virginians* Lady Bernstein plays cards. In *Pendennis* Helen makes life interesting through her obsession with Arthur. In *The Newcomes* Lady Kew machinates and match-makes because she has nothing else to do. For younger women the readiest cure for boredom is love. Married women have their flirtations and perhaps their adulteries to make life interesting. Unmarried women nurse secret passions and sometimes choose marriage from the sole motive of wanting to escape a dull and confined life.

In Mrs Craik's *Agatha's Husband*, Agatha marries because she has literally nothing to do and her empty life is intolerable. We have seen how some of those who concerned themselves with the moral worth of women's lives took pains to suggest that many of the activities that were considered proper were virtually useless. How then was a woman to render her life worthwhile? By marriage, and by devotion to her husband, and her children, if she had any. In herself she was nothing. Only by relating to husband and children could she develop and fulfil her moral personality.

A solid core of fiction was concerned above all with strengthening the ramparts of what we tend to regard as a typically Victorian view of marriage. Not only the domestic novel narrowed its sphere of interest and action. The Gothic, or what remained of it, also became increasingly limited and flatly stereotyped, allowing less and less scope for the conventional heroine to experience unconventional situations. In magazines in particular, the Gothic tale and the historical romance, which in magazine stories were virtually indistinguishable in their ingredients, lingered on without providing any worthwhile contrast with the domestic love story.

The treatment of marriage in popular fiction of this kind, in the stories and serials that appeared in women's magazines, is extraordinarily trite even by the standards of what we now expect from popular romantic fiction. A favourite theme, much present in novels too, is the 'learning to love after marriage' theme, which is used in the most blatant fashion to rationalize the subordination of women in marriage. It is almost always the women who have to learn to love their husbands, and who undergo various crises in the process. Emily Eden's *The Semi-Attached Couple* (1860, but written thirty years earlier) is a perfect example. These crises often involve a near-entanglement with another man, as it does in Emily Eden's book, the point being that if a wife does not make it exaggeratedly obvious that she dotes on her husband she becomes a prey to the misconceptions of other men. Invariably the heroine remains innocent, and is shocked into expressing her devotion to her true mate. In *The Semi-Attached Couple* the crisis also involves the husband's prolonged absence from home because he thinks his wife does not love him. It is up to the wife to prove to him otherwise, so that he will stay at home.

We have seen that young women were given quantities of advice about how to keep their husbands at home, and that it was generally considered their fault if the men turned elsewhere for their pleasures. This attitude is scarcely less explicit in the fiction of the period. The usual view is that marriage rescues women from a life that is at best unsatisfactory, and that therefore it is their duty in return to love their husbands and provide comfortable domestic surroundings. Yet this retains, as we saw so clearly in *Agnes Grey*, the strong suggestion of a bargain, a transaction, and even as conventional opinion was hardening a reaction was taking root.

Two quotations from a very popular novelist of the 1840s and '50s provide an idea of the dominant image of women in love. These are taken from two novels by Geraldine Jewsbury, in her time widely read and much reprinted:

Nothing teaches humility like love. The more conscious she became of her influence over Everhard, the more earnest was the desire to make herself worthy of him; her manners became soft and timid; an indescribable air of womanliness tinged every action, and made her attractions the more irresistibly subduing than ever. (*Zoe*, 1845, volume II, Chapter 11)

Kate needed to be loved, protected, guided. Her intelligent passivity was to Charles an intense attraction; her noble nature seemed to fertilise under his culture. (*Constance Herbert*, 1855, volume I, Chapter 4)

Geraldine Jewsbury provides us with all the words we need to describe this typical portrayal: 'humility', softness and timidity, the need for protection and guidance, 'intelligent passivity', the 'noble nature' needing a man in order to grow. We meet with this type of loving woman repeatedly throughout the century. It is still very much alive as the century closes, although by then it has been significantly attacked. And it is closely linked with the emphasis on the moral influence of women which is found in writers like Ruskin and Kingsley. Both contribute powerfully to the rationalization of women's position, and swell a vein that runs strongly through the whole of Victorian literature.

Geraldine Jewsbury backs up her passive version of women in love and marriage by commenting with great disfavour on women who go into public life, thus reflecting typical mid-century attitudes. Earlier the usual reaction to 'active' women was contempt and laughter, but this became a more earnest concern with pointing out the serious error of women with public aspirations. But there was one aspect of the position of women which did engage concern at about this time, and that was the situation of unmarried women. With so much enhancement of the worth of women in marriage, with so great an economic motive involved in marriage, with marriage traditionally an event to be celebrated ostentatiously, publicly and expensively, and with opportunities of employment for women of gentility being negligible, women who did not marry were a class of unfortunates. The Brontë sisters had direct and personal experience of having to make their own way without the aid of either inherited wealth or husbands, and the first reflections of this appeared with the publication of *Agnes Grey* and *Jane Eyre* in 1847. In the same year Thackeray had given the public his interpretation of these circumstances in the person of Becky Sharp.

As so often, public opinion lagged behind fiction, and it was not really until the end of the 1850s that serious attention was paid to single women who had to find a way of supporting themselves in an acceptable fashion. Later, magazines ran columns on the employment of women, with suggestions as to how to make money in a genteel fashion. In 1857 *Chamber's Journal* ran a series of articles called 'A Woman's Thoughts About Women' which, though characterizing women's role in terms of duty and self-sacrifice, laid great emphasis on the necessity of education and appropriate training for 'self-dependence'. They contained a plea to raise the status of the single woman. This gradually became respectable, but ten years earlier Charlotte Brontë had been bitter on this subject, and even in 1857 the anonymous author of these articles has to hedge her suggestions with a solidly conventional, anti-feminist attitude.

Her approach is an interesting reflection on the uncertain state of the marriage market:

Dependence is in itself an easy and pleasant thing: dependence upon one we love perhaps the very sweetest thing in the world. To resign oneself totally and contentedly into the hand of another; to have no longer any need of asserting one's rights or one's personality, knowing that both are as precious to that other as they were to ourselves; to cease taking thought about oneself at all, and rest safe, at ease, assured that in great things and small we shall be guided and cherished, guarded and helped – in fact thoroughly 'taken care of' – how delicious is all this. So delicious, that it seems granted to very few of us, and to fewer still as a permanent condition of being. (*Chamber's Journal*, May 16, 1857)

This is a wholly explicit and idealized characterization of marriage as the total subordination of wife to husband. It is, as expressed here, an ideal to be longed for but granted to few: throughout the nineteenth century there were many more women than men, so it was not possible to count on marriage as a solution to the problem of superabundant females, and a realistic attitude to the necessity of self-dependence did not need to have anything to do with feminism. It is worth remembering, in connection with the advances in female education in the century, that the more enlightened view of the education of women often had nothing to do with a belief in women's rights.

The general consensus, in fiction as well as in journalism, was that marriage was the core of social life and social aspiration, and that the onus was on the wife to make marriage a success. Wives had a duty to love their husbands, except in extraordinary circumstances, in which case they had a duty to make the best of things. And they had a duty to ensure that their husbands loved them. In fact most of popular middle-class literature was at this time consolidating what amounted to a reaction against the critical ironies of Thackeray. There were of course exceptions, and one of the most striking is Charlotte Brontë.

Charlotte and her sisters were at various periods in their short lives self-dependent women, and this fact is the moving force behind the fiction of

Charlotte and Anne – it is more difficult to generalize usefully about Emily's *Wuthering Heights*. Charlotte's central female characters are not only required, in most cases, to earn their own livings, but are also extraordinarily isolated from family, friends, a known locality, or a corner of society in which they can feel at ease. Jane Eyre and Lucy Snowe not only have to support themselves, they are alone, and the novels in which they figure, *Jane Eyre* (1847) and *Villette* (1853) are steeped in solitariness. In these novels the context of love and marriage is very different from that with which Thackeray has made us familiar, and which the run-of-the-mill mid-century novel habitually employs. The workings of the marriage market, of the standards of upper-class society in selecting mates and making marriages, are seen through the eyes of outsiders for whom there is no possibility, indeed no desire, of becoming involved. The drily critical attitude of Lucy Snowe to the antics of her upper-class pupil, Ginevra Fanshawe, is only possible because of her isolated independence. Much of the passion in the experiences of Jane and Lucy arises from the fact that they want to love and to be loved, but they cannot barter their emotions, not only because of their moral personalities but also because they are excluded from the market-place. Although they despise the auction they both have a keen sense of how unsatisfactory their isolated positions are.

This isolation both exposes and protects. They are protected from the destructive workings of convention, because they are excluded, but they are also vulnerable because of temptations to marry merely to escape, and because they have none of the emotional outlets that friends and society normally provide. Lucy and Jane experience intense emotional crises which have physical effects. It may be argued that, for instance, Jane hearing the voice of Mr Rochester calling her a hundred miles away is completely unrealistic, but in fact Charlotte Brontë does not go psychologically wrong here. Jane is under extreme pressure from St John Rivers to become the kind of woman that society would approve, to live a life where duty is pre-eminent, to submerge her own personality, and that she should react by responding super-sensitively to the man she does love is convincing. Jane rejects St John, seeing in him the dangers of highly spiritual but conventional religious and moral attitudes. It is significant that what she is rejecting is the role of missionary's *wife*, not of missionary itself. (She is clearly tempted by what would have been a logical extension of her well-tried self-dependence.) But more revealing is her acceptance of Rochester, and the brief indication at the end of the novel of the kind of marriage they have.

Jane marries Rochester not in his dominating prime but in his frustrated helplessness. He has been tamed. Their marriage is quietly domestic, with Jane devoting herself to her husband's care. But, interestingly, the novel ends not on this note but with two paragraphs describing the activities of the 'resolute, indefatigable pioneer' St John Rivers. Yet the contrast between the stern, ambitious, energetic St John, unlikeable though he is, and the blind, inactive Rochester is telling, and introduces, or re-introduces, a suggestively ambiguous note as the novel closes.

When Jane's relationship with St John is first developing she is very conscious of what she herself describes as her 'servitude'. She becomes dominated by his standards and expectations. 'By degrees he acquired a certain influence over me that took away my liberty of mind: his praise and notice were more restraining than his indifference.' And then:

As for me, I daily wished more to please him: but to do so, I felt daily more and more that I must disown half my nature, stifle half my faculties, wrest my tastes from their original bent, force myself to the adoption of pursuits for which I had no natural vocation. (Chapter 33)

Throughout her initial relationship with Rochester, a relationship between employer and employee, she insists on her freedom. 'I am a free human being with an independent will,' she says (Chapter 23). Yet Rochester has thoroughly mastered her, not only as her employer but as a man. A few pages earlier she has reacted like this when she sees him in the distance on her return after a month's absence:

... every nerve I have is unstrung: for a moment I am beyond my own mastery. What does it mean? I did not think I should tremble in this way when I saw him, or lose my voice or the power of motion in his presence. (Chapter 22)

Rochester and St John both master Jane, and in both cases she insists on her independent will. Yet she is afraid of St John's power, and afraid of Rochester up to the moment of her near-wedding. (After that disaster Jane loses her fear: 'But I was not afraid: not in the least. I felt an inward power; a sense of influence, which supported me. The crisis was perilous; but not without its charm: such as an Indian, perhaps, feels when he slips over the rapid in his canoe.' When Rochester is struck down – the associated image of a tree struck by lightning occurs twice in the novel – Jane gains the ascendant and also experiences an exhilaration which is an important part of her character.) The theme of mastery weaves around Jane from the moment in the first chapter when the atrocious John Reed insists that Jane call him 'master' to the final paragraph where St John (the similarity in name is interesting) addresses the God he has laboured for as 'my Master'.

Jane is coping with contradictory forces. She wants power, she wants to be active, she wants to experience the world in a positive and constructive fashion.

At the same time, like Shirley Keeldar in *Shirley* (1849), she can only contemplate marrying a man who can be her master. We can see similar contradictions at work in many of the century's most interesting heroines, in novels by George Eliot, Mrs Gaskell and Meredith, and increasingly towards the end of the century. But in *Jane Eyre* I think they are at their most naked. And it is the physical and emotional features that are conventionally the least acceptable – she is passionate, she lacks humility, she is small and plain – that are at work.

Jane Eyre has become a pattern for a basic type of romanticism which is still easily detectable in fiction today. The passionate woman submitting to the powerful man is a combination of ingredients that has a lasting attraction. Jane is attracted to Rochester because he has been a wanderer, because he has been wronged, because he has had experiences that she will never have – in fact because he is a Byronic type. Is it too much to suggest that she, so thoroughly isolated and ill-equipped for life's difficulties except through her own strength of character, finds in him a surrogate for the life she can never have? Does she choose Rochester because she cannot be free, she cannot go where she wants, do what she likes, enter into love affairs, even friendships (St John won't accept her as a companion; only as a wife would their association be proper) with men as she feels inclined? When she finally marries Rochester it is as if she is choosing to live through his past.

It is important that she does choose. For although Rochester is tamed when she returns to him, she herself is freer. She now has money, which represents a very significant kind of independence. She does not need to work, or to serve, and she does not need to call anyone master. In the course of an argument with St John, he says she will surely want to 'look a little higher than domestic endearments and household joys' as she plans for the future. But, she rejoins, they are 'the best thing the world has!' (Chapter 33). It is hard to believe that the passionate, inquisitive and ambitious Jane will rest content with 'domestic endearments and household joys', yet this, it is suggested, is what marriage brings her. The ambivalence which, throughout the novel, has been nagging and productive is ultimately unconvincingly resolved.

The final image of Rochester, and by association of Jane, bears a surprisingly close resemblance to Thackeray's valedictory portrait of Amelia. Jane says to Rochester:

'You are no ruin, sir – no lightning struck tree: you are green and vigorous. Plants will grow about your roots, whether you ask them or not, because they take delight in your bountiful shadow; and as they grow they will lean towards you, and wind round you, because your strength offers them so safe a prop.' (Chapter 37)

Here is Rochester as the oak tree, and Jane with a suggestion of the parasite about her. The point about Byronic heroes and passionate women is that domestic bliss is not readily conceivable.

If *Jane Eyre* ends on a note of ambivalence which is not wholly satisfactory and *Villette* on a more consistent note of unresolved and unfulfilled possibilities, *Shirley* ends with such easeful reconciliation that it almost amounts to a betrayal of all that is most striking in the novel. At its close their author provides both her restless, dissatisfied, aspiring heroines with restraining mates. It is generally considered an unsatisfactory novel and the need to make it a novel about the acquisition of husbands is a major reason. Yet who in the nineteenth century was to write about women without writing about love and marriage? It took the dogged courage of George Gissing to attempt this.

Shirley's two heroines, the young isolated Caroline Helstone and the more experienced and authoritative Shirley Keeldar, both seek independence, yet they both seek men. Caroline, increasingly aware of herself as an entirely superfluous member of society, wants to go away and earn her own living. Shirley, economically independent and unconventional, wants to be treated as an equal in a man's world. The whole novel is permeated with the awareness of a double standard operating not just in sexual morality but in education, manners and occupation. Caroline is painfully aware of her superfluity, and the uncle who has brought her up is contemptuous both of Caroline's restlessness and of women in general. There is a strong suggestion that he destroyed his own wife by his total repression of her.

The most interesting feature of Caroline's personality is her rejection of the idea that 'service' should be the female role:

... certain sets of human beings are very apt to maintain that other sets should give up their lives to them and their service, and then they requite them by praise: they call them devoted and virtuous. Is this enough? Is this to live? Is there not a terrible hollowness, mockery, want, craving, in that existence which is given away to others, for want of something of your own to bestow it on? I suspect there is. Does virtue lie in abnegation of self? I do not believe it. Undue humility makes tyranny; weak concession creates selfishness. (Chapter 10)

This is surely a direct statement from Charlotte Brontë herself, and it is the most explicit repudiation to be found in the literature of the period of the 'service and humility' syndrome. It is just this kind of thing, along with her assertions of female passion, that provoked accusations of coarseness and impropriety from many of her reviewers, accusations that angered her greatly.

Later Caroline reflects on the implications of the double standard:

Look at the numerous families of girls in the neighbourhood . . . The brothers of these girls are every one in business or in professions: they have something to do: their sisters have no earthly employment, but household work and sewing; no earthly pleasure, but an unprofitable visiting; and no hope, in all their life to come, of anything better. This stagnant state of things makes them decline in health: they are never well; and their minds and views shrink to wondrous narrowness. The great wish – the sole aim of every one of them is to be married, but the majority will never marry: they will die as they now live. They scheme, they plot, they dress to ensnare husbands. The gentlemen turn them into ridicule; they don't want them; they hold them very cheap: they say – I have heard them say it with sneering laughs many a time – the matrimonial market is overstocked. (Chapter 22)

Caroline herself, overwhelmed by the stagnant state of things and disappointed in love, declines into one of those illnesses that so frequently attack Victorian females. Ultimately she gets her man, a vigorous and tough mill manager. Others consider that she will be an excellent wife, quiet, devoted. She allies herself with progressiveness in the shape of her husband, but has she really gained any of those things that she herself was so acutely aware of as being denied her?

Shirley is both more fanciful and more dramatic when she images the situation of women. In a passage that is extraordinarily reminiscent of Thackeray's sea-monster in *Vanity Fair*, all the more extraordinary as she arrives at it by way of Scott's *The Pirate*, she characterizes what she most condemns in women. She is talking to Caroline:

'I show you an image, fair as alabaster, emerging from the dim wave. We both see the long hair, the lifted and foam-white arm, the oval mirror brilliant as a star. It glides nearer: a human face is plainly visible; a face in the style of yours, whose straight, pure (excuse the word, it is appropriate), – whose straight, pure lineaments, paleness does not disfigure. It looks at us, but not with your eyes. I see a preternatural lure in its wily glance: it beckons. Were we men, we should spring at the sign, the cold billow would be dared for the sake of the colder enchantress; being women, we stand safe, though not dreadless. She comprehends our unmoved gaze; she feels herself powerless; anger crosses her front; she cannot charm, but she will appal us: she rises high, and glides all revealed, on the dark wave-ridge. Temptress-terror! monstrous likeness of ourselves! Are you not glad, Caroline, when at last, and with a wild shriek, she dives?' (Chapter 13)

She rejects the monster temptress role of women, and clearly has taken

Thackeray's portrayal very much to heart. But she is not at all sure what is to be substituted for it. Charlotte Brontë presents a vivid picture of Shirley's ability to act on her own, making her own decisions and scorning a conventional sub-servience, but allows her to marry a man, who in spite of her assertion that she could only marry a man who could be her master, is negative in action and unpleasant in thought. He *is* her master in the sense that he has been her tutor and knows more than she does, and this is important to her, but his own attitude to his position as tutor and lover is sententious and self-important:

I wish I could find such a one: pretty enough for me to love, with something of the mind and heart suited to my taste: not uneducated – honest and modest. I care nothing for attainments; but I would fain have the germ of those sweet natural powers which nothing can rival: any temper Fate wills – I can manage the hottest. To such a creature as this, I should like to be first tutor and then husband. I would teach her my language, my habits, and my principles, and then I would reward her with my love. (Chapter 36)

Shirley reacts to this with scorn, which seems fair enough – yet she marries him. In the course of the scene from which this passage is taken Louis Moore wears Shirley down to the point where she exhibits her powerlessness and acknowledges his superiority. It is almost as if Charlotte Brontë was afraid to commit herself wholly to the masculinity of Shirley and her endeavours. As the scene comes to an end more and more phrases conventionally employed to describe feminine behaviour are used: 'the grace, the majesty, the modesty of her girlhood', 'a sweet, open, earnest countenance'. Her lively scorn and readiness for combat diminish.

At the same time the author is trying to communicate a version of marriage as companionship and mutual assistance. But it is wrapped up in Shirley's acceptance of an inferior, a pupil's role – 'teach me and help me to be good', she says. In the case of Jane and Rochester it is Rochester who sees Jane as his good influence, and Jane accepts his attitude to her. Here the roles are more or less reversed, yet with Louis's remarks still ringing in our ears it is hard to accept the reversal. We sense that there is too much interfering with what Charlotte Brontë really wants to say. She cannot quite realize either Caroline or Shirley as fully developed personalities. They are both nipped in the bud by marriage, and there they are left.

They remind us a little of George Eliot's Dorothea Brooke, but if Charlotte Brontë has a greater commitment to making something positive out of her heroines' lives she does not have George Eliot's thoughtful control. They sug-gest, too, a parallel with a very different kind of writer interpreting differing social developments, Turgenev writing of mid-century Russia. Turgenev's characteristic heroines are young girls longing to broaden the scope of their lives, longing for action, longing for commitment. They exist in gentle vacuums of inaction, exasperated with their daily companions and the daily frittering away of time. They want not so much independence – for in fact Russian women were much freer economically and socially than their British counterparts – as an experience of real life. In *On the Eve* (1859) and *Virgin Soil* (1877) the heroines' longings are channelled into love for men whom they see as opening the gates to action and a positive life.

Turgenev was two years younger than Charlotte Brontë, though much of his work was published after her death. Although he was writing about a different society and different movements in society he was subject to very much the same influences as Charlotte Brontë. They both belonged to the generation that was so highly susceptible to the ideas and energies of the period of revolution in Europe that reached an abortive climax in 1848. And when they write about love and marriage from the point of view of women they are handling very much the same syndrome. Both writers see in women untapped potential which should be utilized for their own sake and for the sake of society. Yet there is an essential and significant difference in their approach. In Charlotte Brontë's novels the male characters are generally positive, energetic men, men with professions, men who work, men of experience. But Turgenev is writing mostly about men who have as little to do as the women, and who are highly conscious of the lack of a positive role. She takes an optimistic view of the way men *can* contribute to progress, whereas his men torment themselves about their own inaction, and those who have something positive to do tend to go abroad to do it.

Perhaps what brings Turgenev and Charlotte Brontë closest together is the way they allow their female characters to control their destinies and to make their own choices. The heroines of *On the Eve* and *Virgin Soil* put themselves in positions similar to those forced by necessity on Jane Eyre and Lucy Snowe. And although in Charlotte Brontë's novels the economic aspect tends inevitably to be to the fore, fundamentally she and Turgenev are concerned with the same things, with women who are seeking a way of making a positive contribution to life and to society, beyond the limits imposed by tradition. It is rich territory and, handled with spirit and imagination, as rewarding a subject as any the Victorian novel can offer.

Turgenev is a novelist of acute political awareness and so his concern is closely linked with his political themes, which help to give his restless women intensity and direction. It is political commitment that his heroines discover, and through that discovery that they can indeed act on their own once the initial break has been made. What Charlotte Brontë's heroines crave is recognition, recognition of their existence as individuals and of their rights with or without marriage, or perhaps more than anything else, in spite of the ambiguities in her work, acknowledgment of the irrelevance of marriage as a standard by which to judge the success or failure of women.

Turgenev can be set beside Meredith as a man who found women interesting and vital in their own right, and in fact his influence on Meredith and other writers towards the end of the century is apparent. In the meantime it is Dickens who dominates the scene, and with him family life takes on quite a different aspect. Dickens did not like his women to be either interesting or dynamic, nor could he allow anything resembling these qualities in his ideal marriages.

A MAJOR PART of Elizabeth Gaskell's achievement as a novelist lies in the way she records, quietly and steadily, the intimate relationship in ordinary life between work and the home. When we read her novels we realize how often this is absent from the writing of the greatest Victorian novelists. She writes most often about people who work, people for whom work is the dominating activity of their lives. Her portraits of marriage and married life are part of this, but it is also important that many of the households she describes in such detail do not contain married couples, but sisters, as in *Cranford* (1853), father and daughter, as in *Mary Barton* (1848) and again in the first part of *Wives and Daughters* (1866), and brother and sister, as in *Ruth* (1853). These households are, too, family life. Mrs Gaskell did not represent marriage, as so many nineteenth-century novelists implied or strongly stated, as being the only useful and fulfilled way of life. It is because she is so careful and explicit in the way she explores just how people live together, whoever they are, that she avoids this emphasis on marriage as the summit of human existence. When she does describe the life of married couples very often she shows, as she does in *Sylvia's Lovers* (1863), the depth and intensity of the problems which a particular kind of intimacy involves.

Mrs Gaskell writes about families as households, as units of hard work and familiarity, of sensitive, sometimes resentful, reaction, and at their best of loyalty. Her families are not, even in *Wives and Daughters* (her most 'middle-class' novel), patriarchal pyramids, because the members tend to share in the work and responsibility, and to be united by a sense of love and common interest. These qualities may not be those that the fiction of the great romance and the climactic marriage celebrates, nor the qualities that the fiction of the domestic haven celebrates, but they seem to me to dramatize the family at its unsentimental best.

Mary Barton opens with the meeting of the two mill-working families on a holiday. They are badly off, not in good health, yet there is a tenderness in their portrayal – 'tender' is a word Mrs Gaskell repeats to describe the attitude of one of the men to his wife and babies – and an understanding of their feelings of interest and loyalty towards each other that prevents the kind of depressed resignation that is present particularly in later writers about working people.

The two families share a meal together in the Bartons' home, and as she describes the interior Mrs Gaskell relates very precisely the objects in the room to the work that the husband and wife do – he is a mill-worker in relatively prosperous times, she a hardworking and proud housewife. We are told how many eggs and how much ham and fresh bread and butter the gathering sits down to, but most important is the sense of pleasure in the midst of hardship in this modest but rather rash treat the Bartons have decided on:

And now all preparations being made, the party sat down. Mrs Wilson in the post of honour, the rocking chair on the right hand side of the fire, nursing her baby, while its father, in an opposite arm-chair, tried vainly to quieten the other with bread soaked in milk.

Mrs Barton knew manners too well to do anything but sit at the tea-table and make tea, though in her heart she longed to be able to superintend the frying of the ham, and cast many an anxious look at Mary as she broke the eggs and turned the ham, with a very comfortable portion of confidence in her own culinary powers. Jem stood awkwardly leaning against the dresser, replying rather gruffly to his aunt's speeches, which gave him, he thought, the air of being a little boy; whereas he considered himself as a young man, and not so very young neither, as in two months he would be eighteen. Barton vibrated between the fire and the tea-table, his only drawback being a fancy that every now and then his wife's face flushed and contracted as if in pain. (Chapter 2)

There is suggested here domestic pleasure, both in the preparation and the consumption of the meal, combined with domestic responsibility, and with a social context and a sense of individual reality. Even in this short quotation a distinction of attitude and preoccupation is apparent, while the impression of a shared occasion is retained. Mrs Barton is pregnant, and shortly she and the baby will be dead after prolonged, agonizing labour. The event is as much a part of the domestic scene as relaxing over a treat. The Wilson twins die of typhoid in the course of the novel. They are already sickly in this scene. Yet without sentiment, or comedy, both of which feature so strongly in Dickens' portrayals of artisan households, Mrs Gaskell conveys a strong sense of mutual human interest, of warmth, of qualities that are in the working-class context basic in making life worth living.

It is never lost throughout the book. During the typhoid epidemic when we see people brought their lowest (Davenport dying on the wet floor of a filthy reeking cellar) during the strike when we see starvation, there is this strong impression of mutual support. It is also present in *Sylvia's Lovers,* where the community react unitedly against the activities of the press-gang. In both novels the portrait of a household widens into a portrait of the community. This is not 'society' as we find it in Thackeray or Jane Austen, not households bound together by slender threads of etiquette and self-interest, but families whose sense of community, even in the sprawling ugliness of Manchester, is vital to their existence. We don't find this in Dickens, who in *Hard Times* and *The Old Curiosity Shop*, loses this kind of response to class and community through his particular methods of emotive impressionism and individual dramatic exaggeration. Even in those of Mrs Gaskell's novels that have serious flaws, and *Mary Barton* has, it is her treatment of the individual's drama as arising out of the community's ills that gives her writing its special quality.

We see marriage in general and marriage in particular as features of a way of life connected with the basic realities of work and subsistence. We cannot separate the marriage of Sylvia and Philip in *Sylvia's Lovers*, or the marriage of Sylvia's parents, from the town and its work, and its relationship to the sea and the surrounding countryside. We cannot separate attitudes to children from the circumstances in which they were born. In industrial Manchester another child is another mouth to feed, with limited chances of survival. In 1833 a survey of Manchester mill-workers showed that 40 per cent of their babies died in infancy, well over twice the rate in the country as a whole. The most significant moment in the life of a Manchester mill-worker's child was likely to be the moment when he or she first went out to work. The Factory Act of 1833 had limited the age at which children could work, and had shortened the hours, but eight- and nine-year-olds were still frequently employed, and couples longed for children who looked older than they were. In healthier Monkshaven, the town in *Sylvia's Lovers*, based on Whitby, a child was more likely to be seen in terms of usefulness at home. The young Sylvia helps on the farm and in the kitchen; from an early age work in and around her home characterizes her life. This acceptance of work as a way of life is closely bound up with family loyalty and a sense of duty. Their livelihood depended on these things. This is important, because it is out of duty, out of a sense of responsibility towards her mother, that Sylvia marries Philip, thus taking on a life she knows cannot be happy.

Mrs Gaskell writes about people whose ties are elemental. When she writes about romantic passion, as she does in *Sylvia's Lovers*, she sets it in a context of closely woven family loyalty and a closely woven community, most of whose members are likely to be affected by any major event. The community reacts as a whole to the press-gangs; Philip isolates himself by accepting them. In marrying Philip, Sylvia has to share this isolation. In *Mary Barton* the community of mill-workers and their families are all affected by strikes and lock-outs and have a radical understanding of each other's experiences. It is interesting also that Mrs Gaskell's frequent use of folk song – she reproduces the whole of 'The Poor Cotton Weaver' in *Mary Barton* in a version earlier than but very similar to that in A. L. Lloyd's *Folk Song in England* – tends to anchor her communities in tradition and continuity. A signal feature of industrial folk song is its communication of solidarity, of predicaments beyond the individual, and Mrs Gaskell's frequent reference to them is surely no accident.

We are used to finding in Victorian novels a picture of working-class life severely curtailed by the middle-class windows through which it is viewed. Mrs Gaskell retains her middle-class view in one very important aspect, her faith that employers and employed *will* find a way of working and living together and respecting each other. But the tendency of what she actually describes suggests something different. The employers are not included in the sense of community. The family values of the rich are not the same as those of the poor. Marriage is quite different, the motives and the aspirations are different. Mary Barton has illusions that if she marries the boss's son she'll solve all the problems of her family, but even while she is hoping for this she knows it can't work, and she feels guilty because consorting with the bosses is a betrayal of class interests, though that is not exactly how Mrs Gaskell puts it. She sees it as a betrayal of her family way of life, but the Barton family way of life has already been identified as a community and class way of life.

The realities of the way people live affect the nature of their love: Sylvia, hard-working but severely confined by her work and responsibilities, nurses her great love for the adventurous specksioneer, as harpooners on whaling ships were called; Ruth the imprisoned seamstress is all too easily enticed by the gay young man who will abandon her; Mary is tempted by Carson. But if a tough and limited life nourishes dreams of romantic escape, it also moulds the kind of love that can work, and the severest criticism of *Mary Barton* must be that we are not allowed to see the marriage of Jem and Mary in the context of their love, and we cannot help feeling that Mrs Gaskell just could not bear the reality of disease, death, and debilitating work that has ravaged the families of both. They have earned something better, she indicates, and rewards them by sending them off to a new life in the New World. We have to look at the older generation for the loyalty and tenderness in the face of grim hardship, and it is there in the crippled and complaining Mrs Wilson or, in *North and South* (1855), in the way that orphaned children are cared for by willing neighbours.

There is another reality, a reality that Mrs Gaskell does not come to grips with although she hints at it. She does not flinch at death or disease, starvation or violence, and she does suggest the degradation, amply documented elsewhere, that a woman could suffer when making any kind of effort without adequate means of support became pointless, but she is not able to elaborate on factory girls and mill-workers as sexual victims, or on prostitution. So that, as in so many Victorian novels, Mrs Barton's fallen sister is inevitably presented as an extreme case rather than a common one. There is no doubt that Mrs Gaskell knew a great deal more than she allowed into her fiction, but she was compromised by convention, by the habits of mind which made possible the censorship imposed by Mudie's, the highly successful circulating library whose refusal of a novel could doom it to oblivion.

Middle-class investigators were appalled by what they discovered about sexual morality in industrial and rural Britain. Factory girls tended to become the legitimate prey of the masters in much the same way as Russian serf girls were the prey of young gentlemen. Prostitution figures are very unreliable, because it is difficult to disentangle casual prostitution, which a girl in a respectable occupation like millinery, Mary Barton's occupation, might engage in when desperate, from professional prostitution. Middle-class opinion tended to place any woman of dubious morality in the prostitute class, which was one of the things, as we see in *Ruth*, which made it so difficult for a 'fallen' woman to redeem herself.

The middle-class viewpoint is a complicating factor. While it is significant that Mrs Gaskell rarely draws her characters from extreme cases of the deprived and dispossessed, it is also worth noting that she does not characterize ugliness and offensiveness by the kind of middle-class standard that operates in the following quotation from a report on handloom weavers of 1840:

. . . an utter absence of grace and feminine manners – a peculiar raucous or rough timbre of voice . . . a peculiarity owing to various causes, a principal one of which is, too early sexual excitement, producing a state of vocal organs closely resembling that of the male . . . limbs badly moulded from imperfect nutrition – a bony frame-work, in many points widely divergent from the line of womanly beauty – a beauty founded upon utility – and a general aspect of coarseness and a vulgarity of expression quite opposed to all ideas of excellencies in the moral and physical attributes of the sex. (Royston Pike, *Human Documents of the Industrial Revolution*, page 22)

A belief that because the working classes were often forced to live like animals they therefore behaved like animals, were promiscuous, prone to sexual irregularities such as incest, and had little respect for marriage, was widespread. There was some truth in this belief – incest was a relatively common occurrence – but it encouraged a very muddled impression of causes and effects. We can see this in the following passage, taken from the evidence to the Factory Commission of 1833:

In congregating so many men, women, and children together without any other object than Labour, there is full scope for the birth and growth of passions which eventually refuse to submit to constraint, and which end in unbridled license. The union of the sexes, and the high temperature of the manufactories, act upon the organisation like a tropical sun; and puberty is developed before age and education have matured the moral sentiments. The factory girls are strangers to modesty, their language is gross, and often obscene; and when they do not marry early, they form illicit connexions, which degrade them still more than premature marriage. (*Ibid.* page 296)

It is very often this impression of sexual licence that grips the imagination rather than the actual conditions under which men and women live and work. Obviously there is prejudice here and even more spurious science – that the heat, discomfort and hard work demanded in the factories would enhance sexual proclivities seems highly unlikely – and a lack of a real understanding of the causes of such facts as illegitimacy, early marriage, and prostitution. The middle classes were horrified at early marriage amongst the poor, for it could only increase the birth rate amongst that section of the population that it was least desirable to reproduce. There was weighty propaganda against early marriage.

Working wives were not liked by the upholders of middle-class Christian morality, though the necessity of employment in some cases was accepted. It was felt that it was a married woman's responsibility to be in the home, caring for her children and making things comfortable for her husband when he returned after a hard day's work. Dreadful consequences were likely to follow from a wife going out to work: children improperly fed and cared for, a disordered house and a lack of hot dinners which might drive the husband to drink, a general disintegration of family life. A weekly magazine of the 1860s, called the *British Workwoman*, is typical in its attitudes. It constantly exhorts women to stay at home, through little moral tales and direct exhortation. 'Wife of the labouring man! Take warning in time. Try to make your home happy to your husband and children. Remember your first earthly duty, and, whatever the temptations to go out to work, STAY AT HOME!' (*British Workwoman*, 1 Jan 1864).

This is supported by continual exaltation of the value and reward of domestic work. 'Drudgery? She doesn't believe in it, if she be a true woman. She may get weary, and vexed, and all that; but she does it for her dear ones, and every act is a love token' (1 Nov 1863).

Motherhood is regarded as the supreme achievement, and caring for the young the most exalted activity:

If she be a mother, still higher, nobler is her mission. If to the weak hands is entrusted the task of rearing the young immortals, for service here, and glory hereafter; if the gem be given to her to polish which shall one day sparkle in the crown of the Saviour, let her walk softly, for angels might envy her high vocation, and the Almighty looks to see how she is nursing the child for Him.

Such an attitude to children and motherhood was a calculated rationalization of the frequent event of death. Elsewhere it is specifically suggested that children are, as it were, on loan from heaven, which means that not only are the responsibilities of the mother very great, but if the children die they are simply returning to where they come from.

It is illuminating that the *British Workwoman* claimed that it was much approved by employers – it advises that working women should 'esteem and value those for whom they work' – for the appeal of this kind of sententious propaganda was clearly to those whose main concern was to persuade the deprived to be content with their lot. Mrs Gaskell found herself in a difficult situation. It was quite clear to her that working people in Manchester had little reason to be content, yet she felt constrained to excuse and justify at some length their actions when they tried to improve their situation. It was quite clear to her also that, for instance, the morality of middle-class and upper-class marriage, in terms of honesty, mutual respect and tenderness, left much to be desired, yet she doesn't criticize the system, certainly not in the radical way that Thackeray does, but looks around instead for 'good' people who will show us the way things ought to be.

Yet if Mrs Gaskell cannot follow the implications of her clear and honest vision, she avoids the curious duality of other portrayers of the working-class family. Disraeli appears to pull no punches in his representation of 'two nations', and his grim little vignettes in *Sybil* (1845) of rural Marney and urban industrial Wodgate are salutary. But his message is confused, as is Charles Kingsley's in *Alton Locke* (1851) and *Yeast* (1848), by the introduction of, as it were, noble savages, keenly intelligent, dedicated and gentlemanly representatives of the underprivileged, with a tendency to become involved in romantic love affairs with members of the upper classes. Not only does this blur the focus on working-class life, and weaken it; it separates the 'Blue Book', sociological concern with the underprivileged, from the plot of the novel, as if to indicate that the lower classes cannot really be the proper stuff of fiction.

There is entirely absent in *Sybil*, and in *Coningsby* (1844), the kind of detailed interiors we find in *Mary Barton* and *North and South*, the kind of understanding of the way people live that characterizes Mrs Gaskell at her best. What we miss is the sense of intimacy that is so integral a part of the texture of *Mary Barton* or

Sylvia's Lovers. But something that Disraeli does handle in *Sybil* is the disintegration of the home, and this is a symptom of middle- and upper-class worries about the anarchy of the labouring poor, as well as of changes in working-class life.

One of Disraeli's characters comments, 'I think the world is turned upside downwards in these parts. . . . Fathers and mothers goes for nothing. . . . 'Tis the children gets the wages . . .' (*Sybil*, Book I, Chapter 9). Teenagers are leaving home and setting up on their own. They can earn more than their parents. Wives who go out to work neglect their families. Neglected children in learning to fend for themselves learn all too early adult ways of the world.

Another very different character in *Sybil* condemns working wives without blaming them:

We have removed woman from her sphere; we may have reduced wages by her introduction into the market of labour; but under these circumstances what we call domestic life is a condition impossible to be realised for the people of this country; and we must not therefore be surprised if they seek solace or rather refuge in the beer-shop. (Book I, Chapter 11)

The disintegration of the working-class home was something that worried legislators a great deal. The home was regarded as a vital unit in the political structure. To a significant extent the discontent, the disturbances, the drunkenness, and the volatility to be found in heavily industrialized areas could be explained by the lack of clean, comfortable – the comfort of course to be modest – woman-centred homes. The characterization of the labouring poor in *Sybil* is of a fluctuating mass with nothing to do and nowhere to go outside the working hours. It was just this mass, this potential mob, that the Victorian establishment feared.

There is in *Sybil* a rather sullen, self-interested, Chartist who articulates a highly revolutionary idea about the home, an idea which is never examined further in the novel, and which I have not come across elsewhere until much later in the century:

You lament the expiring idea of Home. It would not be expiring if it were worth retaining. The domestic principle has fulfilled its purpose. The irresistible law of progress demands that another should be developed. It will come; you may advance or retard, but you cannot prevent it. It will work out like the development of organic nature. In the present state of civilisation, and with the scientific means of happiness at our command, the notion of home should be obsolete. Home is a barbarous idea; the methods of a rude age; home is isolation; therefore anti-social. What we want is community. (Book III, Chapter 9)

Mrs Gaskell might have argued that community was precisely what the labouring classes had and the middle class had lost. Stephen Morley, the character here, might have replied that if such a community did exist it was a community of slums and disease rather than of mutual help and development. Clearly Morley himself sees the abandoning of the home as a social unit as a step towards tearing down the barriers between the two nations. Disraeli does not expand or comment, but it is interesting to see even an isolated example of the condemnation of the separateness of the home in an age when precisely that separateness was being glorified.

What is relevant here is the motive behind attitudes to the underprivileged. Throughout the nineteenth century in many different areas there was a careful balance in legislation between amelioration and repression. For instance, factory legislation designed to reduce the hours worked by women was prompted as much by this concern for the home as by appalled reactions to reports of giving birth in coal-mines and so on. The woman in the home was doing what her superiors considered she ought to be doing. Much of Victorian evangelism was designed to reinforce this, to help the deprived to be content with their deprivation, to encourage women to see as God's work the bringing up of ailing children in filthy conditions, to make both men and women humbly and respectfully imitative in their attitudes towards their betters.

Ultimately Disraeli's message – and Charles Kingsley's is similar – is that the mob can occasionally throw up a remarkable individual but it is itself cruel, violent and stupid. The gallant Egremont rescues the humble Sybil from the riot, and the whole business can only be solved, Disraeli suggests, by the Young England belief in benevolent feudalism. It is interesting that the Christian Socialist Kingsley, though his novels are more pessimistic, displays tendencies not very different from Disraeli's.

For Kingsley too the home and woman's traditional functions within it were of prime importance. He saw women as the moral lights of society. He lectured middle-class women on appropriate behaviour to the poor, but warned them that notions of doing good to the underprivileged must not lead them to neglect their own families. 'What you have to do,' he exhorted in his *Sanitary and Social Lectures and Essays* (1880), 'is to ennoble and purify the *womanhood* of these poor women; to make them better daughters, sisters, wives, mothers' (p. 8). Kingsley lectured women on the necessity of thrift and the iniquity of tight stays; fundamentally he could see no other role for them in the state except as educators of womanhood.

There is another attempt to tell us something about life in an industrialized urban society in Dickens' *Hard Times* (1854). But *Hard Times* is concerned with describing a system and, granted that Dickens' main purpose is to show us how the system reduces living people to machines, there is nevertheless a curious lack of life in the environment it depicts. We are shown the relationship between theories and their products, but not between work and living, and this lack does serious damage to the novel. Gradgrind and Bounderby cannot take their place in the front rank of Dickens' characters. There is an absence of living relationship which makes it hard to take the Gradgrind household, or the marriage of Louisa and Bounderby, as demonstrative of the realities of industrial life.

This lack of detail in the environment, this absence of the life of, for instance, all those workers in Coketown who had received *no* education, makes the novel oddly two-dimensional. The glimpse of Stephen Blackpool's life is brief and ambiguous. Louisa Gradgrind is equally ambiguous. Is she trapped because she has been brought up under the Gradgrind system, or because she is a daughter in a middle-class patriarchal household and has nothing to do? We have only to look at some of Dickens' disastrous marriages elsewhere, that of Edith and Dombey for instance, to see how featureless Louisa's marriage is, and how her flight, and especially her father's conversion, are totally unconvincing, in spite of the dramatic assistance of the pursuing Mrs Sparsit and the stormy weather.

Dickens is not very interested in women who are trapped by circumstances, which is one reason why Louisa Gradgrind is unsatisfactory. He is much better at women who are pursued by people. He is the greatest writer of the chase in the English language, whether it be the hue and cry of Bill Sykes, or the sinister closing in of Carker on Edith.

At this point I return to Mrs Gaskell, for she was much concerned, as perhaps most of the greatest women writers of the century were, with imprisoned women, and this inevitably coloured her view of marriage, domesticity and of the family.

Mrs Gaskell herself had a marriage which may not have been entirely happy but was certainly worthwhile. She enjoyed her children, her domestic pursuits, and writes hurriedly but with great pleasure in her letters about a life which was a continual tussle between her children, her domestic tasks, her writing, and her responsibilities as the wife of a Unitarian minister. In comparison with most Victorian women of her class and background she led an exceptionally rich and busy life and most, if not all, of what she did was worth doing. She was not a spectacular woman, not a Florence Nightingale who, in the face of fantastic odds, did and got what she wanted, but it was perhaps this view from her own experience of what a woman could do that led her to be so sensitive, so central, in her handling of young women who wanted more than tradition suggested they should even think of.

It is an underlying theme in her novels rather than an urgent one, but it is present in every one of them. Her heroines are all, in some way, imprisoned. In all of them the knowledge of this imprisonment is significant. The restriction is not just an accident of sex. Class plays an important part in it too. There is a suggestion running right through Mrs Gaskell's novels that the kind of restriction modest means dictate brings a reliance on social artificialities, while the bondage of labour and frugality brings a genuine appreciation of the real values in life. She does not use money, either the lack of it or the excess of it, as a means of moral judgment, but she does use work in pretty much this way. Her heroes work: they don't just have occupations, they work very hard – Thornton, Mr Gibson, John Barton, Philip, the cavalier Kincaid – but even more significantly her heroines work too, and their work is closely identified with their imprisonment.

In the early part of *Ruth* Ruth herself sits with her workmates sewing seams under the strict control of their mistress, and casts longing glances out of the window. She wants to be free, free from the necessity of working with her needle from early morning until late at night in bad conditions, free from constant supervision and criticism, free simply to walk about and look at things and find out something about life. Sylvia after her marriage and her removal to town longs to exchange her new and comparatively luxurious life for the old, hard-working ways of the farm, for there she found freedom in the open air and in her understanding of the use of all that she did:

For her creature comforts, her silk gowns, and her humble luxury, Sylvia did not care; Philip was almost annoyed at the indifference she often manifested to all his efforts to surround her with such things. It was even a hardship to her to leave off her country dress, her uncovered hair, her linsey petticoat, and loose bed-gown, and to don a stiff and stately gown for her morning dress. Sitting in the dark parlour at the back of the shop and doing 'white work', was much more wearying to her than running out into the fields to bring up the cows, or spinning wool, or making up butter. She sometimes thought to herself that it was a strange kind of life, where there were no out-door animals to look after; 'the ox and the ass' had hitherto come into all her ideas of humanity; and her care and gentleness had made the dumb creatures round her father's home into mute friends, with loving eyes looking at her as if wishful to speak in words the grateful regard that she could read without the poor expression of language. (Chapter 30)

Ruth, and Margaret Hale in *North and South*, have also exchanged country freedom for town confinement. Ruth is too young and inexperienced to be able to adjust her vision of life to her new situation; *North and South* is about the way that Margaret Hale achieves this. Margaret is the least confined of Mrs Gaskell's heroines, and she is also the most aware of the nature of her situation, the limitations of a life encompassed by parents of whom she is fond but also critical.

For Margaret marriage is a positive solution. She accepts Thornton not so much because her parents have died and she no longer has a home, but because her parents' death has set her free. She needs to become free first, and then to marry. If on a political and social level this marriage-as-a-solution can be questioned, on a personal and moral level Mrs Gaskell does justice to her heroine.

In *Wives and Daughters*, Mrs Gaskell's last and unfinished novel, the whole question of restriction and marriage is less exposed, less near the bone. It is clothed in gentle satire. There is the impression that less is at risk, less at stake. Mr Gibson makes an appalling second marriage, and tolerates his impossible wife with reasonably good-humoured resignation. Yet she interferes with his work, his household, his way of life and, most seriously, his daughter. She operates contrary to his most deeply held principles, and it is clear that she married only because she could not tolerate having to work for a living. A parallel marriage is that of the Hamleys, a weak but charming woman, a gruff but loving husband, one too tolerant, the other too impatient, but neither with serious moral flaws. Yet as a marriage it is hardly adequate; there is certainly love, absent in the Gibson marriage, but also a great deal of blindness and lack of understanding, especially in the Hamley parents' attitudes to their sons. And like Mrs Kirkpatrick, who becomes Mrs Gibson, the decent old squire Hamley is motivated by a faith in status, blood, tradition and convention.

The story is about the triumph of heart and mind over just this kind of blinkered view. The novel stops short of describing this triumph, but we know it is coming, and we know that Molly Gibson and Roger Hamley, who are going to be united, are uncontaminated by the influences and examples all around them. It is the triumph of children over parents, of the young generation over the established. Molly escapes from the father she adores without quite realizing how much she needs to escape from him, and without his understanding that Molly must discover her independence. She does discover this, but it is in spite of him and, ironically, partly because of his disastrous wife, who provokes a situation in which Molly is able to come to terms with herself.

Molly sees the results of uncritical love, of love enmeshed in pride, and of mere passive love. Her step-sister Cynthia, a very different kind of girl, remarks, 'I don't think love for one's mother comes quite by nature' (Chapter 19). The implied message of the book is that there is no kind of love that comes quite by nature; it must be learned. Mrs Kirkpatrick's social aspirations, Cynthia's romantic passions, Mr Gibson's sense of duty, all these are operative factors in the life of households and communities. They can all be substitutes for love, some more workable than others, and they are substitutes that are very often the stuff of fiction. The union of Molly and Roger may ring a little disconcertingly of the righteous happy ending, but it is nevertheless both attractive and appropriate. They have learned to love each other, and in the process Molly has discovered a great deal about the world she lives in.

Like Jane Austen and George Eliot, Elizabeth Gaskell writes about women who learn, women who change through experience and crisis. The Amelias don't change. In Mrs Gaskell's world love and marriage are part of a larger process. The exception is Sylvia; with the others life expands, for Sylvia it becomes increasingly circumscribed. She is the victim of an idolizing love which she cannot return and which has little relationship with the way life is lived at that time, in that place. The identity of Monkshaven is of the greatest importance in the novel. It is against that that we judge Sylvia and find her less wanting than other circumstances might have suggested. *Sylvia's Lovers* is in many ways Mrs Gaskell's most impressive work of fiction, and like *Wuthering Heights*, with which it has been compared, its situations cannot be assessed in terms of conventional expectations. It establishes its own values.

Sylvia cannot be a devoted wife and she is denied the only role of wife she knows, the working role. Her sense of identity is threatened. Her ageing mother has lost hers. Her father, hanged for his championship of the revolt against the press-gang, was an important link in Sylvia's sense of a community of interest with the people and the life of Monkshaven. Her love for Kincaid belongs to this too, for he shares in the major activity of the town, whaling, and is liked and respected by her father. Sylvia is emotionally and by nature involved in the life of Monkshaven, but is denied the identification she needs, and this is the root of her tragedy.

In *Sylvia's Lovers*, as in all the Gaskell novels, family relationships are profoundly important. Sylvia's relationship with her mother is intense and restoring; loyalty is a ruling motive in her actions, as in Mary Barton's. The less access a household has to social pretensions the more important such qualities are likely to be. Margaret is brought closer to her parents by their reduction in means and move to the North. *Sylvia's Lovers* is much more a novel about family and kinship, though not in the bourgeois Victorian sense, than about marriage as such. Operating in the novel are basic human feelings uncorrupted by materialism and artificial social values. It is what that triumphant union in *Wives and Daughters* is meant to be too, but while in *Sylvia's Lovers* these human feelings are enmeshed in drama and tragedy on a very intimate level, in the later novel they appear to be leading confidently towards quiet happiness and unthreatened fulfilment.

Mrs Gaskell is one of the few major Victorian writers who shows us marriage from a woman's point of view as something other than an escape, a reinforcement of social status, or a utilitarian contract. Dickens was trying to cope with all these versions of marriage and more but, although so much more ambitious in scope and intentions, there were certain things he was not able to handle: a sense of the intimate life of ordinary people which he could not communicate, perhaps had little interest in. It was a lack that is much in evidence in the way he wrote about marriage and families.

EIGHTEENTH-century painters often portrayed family groups. These families tend to be an assemblage of parents and children, dogs and ponies, painted in the open air with a vista of rich acres stretching out behind them, and very often a noble mansion also visible. Such paintings suggest a crucial relationship between generation and property. The eldest son is usually pre-eminent, perhaps seated on a pony. He will inherit. The daughters, even if babies, are pretty and graceful and lavishly dressed. They are useful pawns in the game of expansion and acquisition.

In the nineteenth century this expansive relationship between the family and its possessions appears to narrow, but this is the result of an increasing middle-class focus rather than of any radical change. Trollope in the 1860s was still writing, as Jane Austen was half a century earlier, of entailed estates and the inheritance of titles. But because the middle-class relationship is narrowed, on account of, amongst other things, a physically smaller area of living, there appears in middle-class fiction a more intimate connection between money and aspirations and style of life. It becomes increasingly important for possessions to be a reflection of wealth – this becomes more significant than usefulness or beauty, and partly explains Victorian taste. Life must not just be lived comfortably and constructively, it must be seen to be lived according to the precepts of a commercially conscious style.

A vital element of this life-style was the patriarchal role, for the ideal towards which the middle-class family strove was highly structured and organized, and such an organization required, it was felt, a master at the top. We have seen how women were tutored to be submissive to their husbands and fathers, how their restricted life was rationalized and reinforced by a great emphasis on the joys of self-sacrifice. Throughout Victorian literature, running as a massive, insistent theme right through the fiction of the period, we find the authoritarian husband and father, appearing in numerous shapes and guises, as hero and villain, as righteous man and moral pervert, as pillar of society and destroyer of individual freedom. He is one of the most interesting figures in Dickens, interesting because Dickens himself never quite seemed to sort out his own ambiguous position in relation to this role.

The middle classes achieved, through a large measure of dedication and self-discipline, particularly on the part of women, a union of material and moral interests, which is reflected in a great deal of fiction, attacked by some writers – Dickens above all although he also did his part to exalt it – explored and exposed by others, most impressively by George Eliot. This union operates at the heart of the middle-class family. In Mrs Gaskell's *Ruth* and Dickens' *Hard Times* there are fathers who carefully nurture their sons, ostensibly providing a religious and moral education, but in fact grooming them for business, for making money and winning success. The ideal of middle-class morality, of comfortable domesticity, of patriarchal authority, was impossible without cash.

It was only possible with money because certain aspects of its life-style were inseparable from its morality. Domestic comfort required a relatively spacious house, good furniture, certain amenities and decorative objects regarded as essentials of tasteful living, and, perhaps above all, servants. In the design of Victorian houses the assumption that all the household labour would be done by servants, and that their convenience did not matter, is deep-rooted. When Philip Watt designed The Red House for William Morris in 1861 the provision of kitchens and staff quarters on the ground floor, with windows overlooking a cheerful view, was revolutionary. To see domestic order from a servant's point of view was a rare attribute in a Victorian designer.

Fiction towards the end of the century, Gissing's novels for instance, went to some lengths to show how difficult it was to achieve domestic comfort without space, suitable furniture and servants, especially for those who had been bred to expect these things. For a woman virtually confined to the home, the service and the objects and the comfort money could buy were bound to be of enhanced importance. A middle-class wife would almost certainly be hedged in by children, by domestic responsibilities and by duty to her husband, and anything that could represent worth in her limited perspective was likely to be significant in her eyes.

The husband of course had responsibilities, a major one being to provide the necessary cash, and he liked to see the symbolic value of his wealth solidly represented in his home. He had to provide his sons with a good education and set them up when the time came in some suitable occupation, which could be an expensive business. (It cost Betsy Trotwood £1,000 to start David Copperfield on his career in Doctors' Commons.) He needed money to marry off his daughters handsomely; in fact paternal responsibility was seen very much in terms of money, and ultimately it was in money that the father's authority and power lay. The money was his and only his. He owned the house in which the family resided. He paid for the servants, for the clothes for the dinners, stumped up for the son's debts, bought the ball gowns for his daughters.

But what we see most often in the conventional Victorian novel is the obverse of this authoritarianism. We see women and children tamed and acquiescent in the view of man as the provider and arbiter. Of course there are rebels very often in just those writers who seem to be reinforcing the patriarchal role. Dickens, with all his criticism and biting exposure, attacks not so much the patriarchal pyramid as the irresponsible exploitation of this system. The authority of husband and father meant that he could, all too easily, exploit the system without challenge. Benevolent paternalism was the answer.

An apt reflection of the way the middle-class family lived is found in the kind of house it lived in. Urban expansion and crowding meant that 'respectable' houses became smaller, the four-storey terrace house gave way to the two-story semi-detached villa in the burgeoning suburbs, and by the 1880s blocks of flats were going up in the centre of London – Gissing's struggling couple in *New Grub Street* (1891) live in such a flat – but a desirable residence retained certain essential features. Servant space, however tiny, was one of the most important. The *New Grub Street* flat lacks this, and the fact that they are reduced to having a daily cleaner is barely tolerable.

The mid-Victorian urban terrace house was organized something like this: in the attic lived the servants; in the basement, badly lit and ventilated, they did their work. On the ground floor there would be a dining-room and perhaps a study or library, on the first floor a drawing-room, possibly two connected by folding doors, and on the second floor bedrooms. Bathrooms were rare until the end of the century. For the servants in such a house the arrangement could hardly have entailed more work. In order, for instance, to take hot water or fuel to the bedrooms they had to climb three flights of stairs. Many of those tea parties that Victorian heroines preside over meant carrying trays of heavy silverware up two flights of stairs. For every pull on the bell in the drawing-room a servant had to ascend from the basement.

The mistress of the house would probably herself descend to the kitchen to give orders about the meals and domestic arrangements of the day, but she might remain in her drawing-room and simply ring the bell. There are numerous instances in fiction of the mistress of the house with the keys of the store-room dangling from her waist. At least once a day she would need to unlock the store-room and extract whatever was necessary. But wealthier households would have a housekeeper whose responsibility this would be. Of course, the wife's activities would depend on the number of servants. J. F. C. Harrison, in *The Early Victorians*, reckons that those with an income below £300 would only be able to afford a maid-of-all-work, between £300 and £400 would mean another servant, perhaps a nursemaid if there were children, while between £400 and £500 would mean a cook as well.

A reasonably well-off and well-regulated middle-class household would have at least three servants, and pay them between £30 and £60 a year. These three servants would all be female. The really well-off would have a butler as well, or a footman, or both, and a lady's maid, who was usually rather a genteel creature, sometimes French. Those who could afford a carriage would have a suitable attendant for this. Servants were important not only for the work they did but as reflections of the wealth and status of their employers, and the nuances of this are present in most Victorian novels. Servants' manner, and the way they dressed, and the way they addressed their master and mistress, all this was of great importance.

J. F. C. Harrison remarks on the fact that as the middle class had less space to live in than the older generation of servant employers – the aristocracy and landed gentry – they lived in much closer proximity to each other. Even with extreme discretion, servants inevitably knew a great deal about the private lives of those they served. A lady's maid could often make or break the reputation of her mistress. In *Pendennis* Thackeray analyses splendidly the relationship between master and man in his portrayal of Major Pendennis and his servant Morgan. There Morgan manipulates the Major's total reliance on him very much to his own advantage. He goes through the motions of the discreet and loyal servant, while in fact he is carefully manoeuvring himself into a position where he can reverse their roles. His success is such that even the Major has to acknowledge his skill before he himself turns the tables.

But servants do not often feature significantly in Victorian fiction, and those who do tend to be, as Morgan is, personal servants. A favourite of Dickens is the devoted follower who performs menial tasks for his master and gets him out of difficulties when they arise. Pickwick's Sam Weller is the readiest example; Mark Tapley in *Martin Chuzzlewit* is another. This type of follower appealed very much to the nineteenth-century imagination; it was an appropriate characterization of the lower classes at their best. Peggotty in *David Copperfield* is of the same genus.

It was crucial for the married woman to be able to control her servants: one of Dora Spenlow's failings is that she cannot, and it is dramatized in David Copperfield's eyes as one of her major failings. The woman who was helpless in the face of her servants was a failure. Clearly a married middle-class woman's existence was to a great extent defined by this relationship to her servants – they were in effect a part of the family which circumscribed her life. They were involved in some of the most intimate areas of her life, childbirth and the care of her children for example. And they protected her from some of life's grimmer realities.

The criterion of worth, from a man's point of view, in servants, wives and children was very much the same. In all of them duty and obedience to those in authority were of prime importance. The kind of advice that women's magazines gave to servants – to be cheerfully obedient – was much the same as the advice given to young wives. And indulgence of servants was reprimanded, just as indulgence of children was. The control of children was as important as the control of servants.

In this matter women's magazines were full of advice to mothers, and the general tenor was that discipline was vital, but that firmness should be loving. (There was little suggestion that it should be rational.) Indulgence, it was emphasized, could lead to a loss of respect by children of their parents:

You should teach your children that they must always obey you; that your word must never be questioned; your commands never neglected. Carelessness leads to coldness. Those whom we cease to respect we often cease to love. Do not lose your children's affection by over-indulgence. (*British Workwoman*, June 1, 1864)

If this seems a chilling reflection of the authoritarian family, it is mild when compared to the more ruthless exhortations to be found, for instance, amongst the Wesleyans:

Break their wills betimes. Begin this work before they can run alone, before they can speak plain, perhaps before they can speak at all. Whatever pains it costs, break the will if you would not damn the child. Let a child from a year old be taught to fear the rod and to cry softly; from that age make him do as he is bid, if you whip him ten times running to effect it. . . . Break his will now, and his soul shall live, and he will probably bless you to all eternity. (Quoted in E. P. Thompson, *The Making of the English Working Class*, page 375)

Attitudes towards children were conflicting. Here, there is the attitude that all children were limbs of the devil, and only by breaking their will could they be saved. On the other hand, children were also seen as original innocents, and the mythology of childhood as it developed in the Victorian period reflects this. In fact, what was usually demonstrated in the average middle-class family was a mixture of the two attitudes. In children wickedness and innocence were absolutes. Disobedience was absolutely bad, regardless of circumstances; good behaviour absolutely good regardless of hypocrisy – of which children were not meant to be capable. One of the reasons why children had to be so severely protected from the adult world was that it didn't take a particularly alert intelligence to see how distant such absolutes were from real life.

The sheer severity of Victorian parents, either in God's name or in the name of their own authority, is striking. It was genuinely believed that the hierarchy of authority within the family was correct and must be perpetuated, but there was undoubtedly mixed with this a degree of sadism. We find it illuminated in Dickens in a number of novels. In Murdstone's rule of David Copperfield there is much cruelty and little conscience. Murdstone does not bother to rationalize or justify his treatment of the boy, as Gradgrind does. He is savage in his absolutism, which he maintains for its own sake.

Rigid authoritarianism could be as alarming as the conviction of sin: if the one regarded children as damned until they had been proved otherwise, the other regarded them as nothing until those in control had moulded them in their own image, at best, or denied them any image at all. It was not, on the whole, that Victorians felt that love for children was inappropriate, but they were made uneasy by anything that suggested that children had personalities and wills of their own. Children were a potential threat, a potential challenge to family life and parental authority as much as they were an intrinsic part of the rounded domestic scene. An interesting feature of many of Dickens' parentless children is that they are personalities in their own right; they may be trapped and doomed by disastrous circumstances, but they are not hemmed in by authority. David Copperfield has more personality coping independently with bottles and the Micawbers than he has within the benign domain of Betsy Trotwood and the Wickfields.

Dickens liked to write about parents and children, and brothers and sisters, showing their love for one another. Usually the kind of love that he describes is calm, static and self-denying, the love of Amy Dorrit for her father, of Tom Pinch for his sister Ruth. It often flourishes in situations of weakness, incapability or simple-mindedness. Dickens' novels are full of devoted daughters, but he is not at all good at describing happily married couples. He suggests with powerful, usually sentimental, feeling the love of parents and children, but when he is attempting a happy marriage (unless it is a non-middle-class marriage) he tends to fall at once into the 'doll's house' syndrome. I will come back to this, since it is an inescapable feature of Dickens' writing, inseparable from his more forceful portrayals of destructive middle-class marriages. And it is bound up with the fact that so often, when he is suggesting the sexual character of a marriage, he expresses himself in images of cruelty. The doll's house marriage is generally as sexless as the co-habitation of Tom and his sister Ruth in their little home in Islington. It is more than the restraint imposed by convention. Dickens writes about men and women in a way which irresistibly suggests that sex means cruelty.

In Dickens, as in Ruskin, Charles Kingsley and many others, there is evident the underlying fear of what might happen to the world if there were no longer women pure and separate to maintain an ideal of morality and religion and social behaviour. Over and over again we come across praise of women in terms of their incomparable importance as standard-bearers of morality. It was this that simultaneously placed women on a pedestal and kept them subordinate. They had, at all costs, to be protected from the world because men were only too knowledgeable about human temptation and fallibility. Parallel with this went the age-old belief that in women lay the root of sin, that if it were not for women men would be free from sin, and that any woman was, if not a potential prostitute, at least akin to her fallen sisters.

There was a reluctance to believe that women, apart from prostitutes, could, or should, experience sexual pleasure. Sex was a marital duty, and the strictest view was that it was a duty only to be performed for the purpose of procreation. Thus it was tacitly assumed that a husband could, and even should, go elsewhere rather than impose his desires on his wife too frequently. Acton, who wrote with prim sententiousness on sexual subjects, elaborately explained how a woman who was pregnant every two years could effectively be prevented from any sexual activity other than procreation, and argued that restraint in a man would gradually emasculate his desires. This was his prescription for a respectably happy marriage.

Perhaps at no other time in British history were men so afraid of women as in the Victorian period, hence the elaborate conspiracy of the establishment to hedge them in, and perhaps at no other time did they exploit women to such an extent. A revealing rationalization of this situation is to be found in John Ruskin's *Sesame and Lillies* (1865):

The best women are indeed necessarily the most difficult to know; they are recognised chiefly in the happiness of their husbands and the nobleness of their children; they are only to be divined, not discerned, by the stranger; and, sometimes, seem almost helpless except in their homes . . . (Preface, page xxxiii)

It is hardly necessary to comment. He follows it up with:

So far as she rules all must be right, or nothing is. She must be enduringly, incorruptibly good; instinctively, infallibly wise – wise, not for self-development, but for self-renunciation, wise, not that she may set herself above her husband, but that she may never fall from his side: wise, not with the narrowness of insolent and loveless pride, but with the passionate gentleness of an infinitely variable, because infinitely applicable, modesty of service – the true changefulness of woman. (pages 109–110)

In other words for Ruskin the best woman is the most self-denying and malleable woman. These opinions are echoed throughout the period, but perhaps not elsewhere presented with such self-conceit, such lack of questioning.

Ruskin had decided opinions on the home too, and in them there is a condensation of all that is pre-eminent in the Victorian sentimental ideal:

This is the nature of home – it is the place of Peace; the shelter, not only from all injury, but from all terror, doubt and division. In so far as it is not this, it is not home; so far as the anxieties of the outer life penetrate into it, and the inconsistently minded, unknown, unloved, or hostile society of the outer world is allowed by either husband or wife to cross the threshold, it ceases to be home; it is then only of that outer world which you have roofed over and lighted fire in. But so far as it is a sacred place, a vestal temple, a temple of the hearth watched over by threshold Gods, before whose faces none may come but those whom they can receive with love, – so far as it is this, and roof and fire are types only of a nobler shade and light, – shade as of the rock in a weary land, and light as of the Pharos in the stormy sea; – so far it vindicates the name, and fulfils the praise, of Home. (page 108–109)

The insubstantial language here indicates the weakness of Ruskin's vision. Nevertheless this picture, or something like it, is reflected in innumerable Victorian novels, the best and the worst. Home with a woman in it was cherished as a refuge in a world where the harsh realities of life were becoming increasingly difficult to disguise. It is characteristic of later fiction that this version of the home becomes less tenable. A feature of post-Victorian fiction is that life's battles are brought within the home, in fact life's battles very often become, precisely, family conflicts.

It is perhaps unfair to Ruskin to move at once from his idealization of woman as 'the beautiful adornment of the state' to a consideration of the obverse side of the comfortable middle-class marriage. But it is misleading to discuss the Victorian ideal without in the same breath indicating the underflow of reality upon which it was constructed, the dependence on prostitution. More important than the actual numbers of prostitutes was the fact that they were so much in evidence, openly soliciting and crowding the streets in certain notorious areas, London's Haymarket for instance, and not only in London but in all Britain's growing industrial cities and ports, Manchester, Liverpool, Glasgow and so on. Emerson, on a visit to England during which he met Dickens and Carlyle, was shocked by the lewdness of the after-dinner conversation of London's literary men, and was appalled at the number of prostitutes on the streets of Liverpool.

In 1857 Acton published his famous book on prostitution, and concluded that it was a fact of life that could not be obliterated, although every effort should be made to control it. W. E. H. Lecky's equally famous *History of European Morals* was the first unambiguous statement of the intimate connection between the prostitute and middle-class marriage. He described prostitutes as 'guardians of virtue' because, without recourse to prostitutes, the 'respectable' male would inevitably threaten the respectable female. I have already mentioned Acton's insistence that it was unlikely that a decent woman would have any serious sexual desires – 'a modest woman seldom desires any sexual gratification for herself'. He also felt, like many others, that anything but the most restrained and limited sexual activity was damaging to men and women alike. But although he implies that male sexuality has to be accepted, however reluctantly, he also, like many others, lays the burden of sin on women. The following passage is revealing:

It is a delusion under which many a previously incontinent man suffers to suppose that in newly married life he will be required to treat his wife as he used to treat his mistresses. It is not so in the case of any modest English woman. He need not fear that his wife will require the excitement, or in any respect imitate the ways of a courtezan. (Quoted by Steven Marcus, *The Other Victorians*, page 29)

It is revealing for a number of reasons. First, there is the acceptance of male 'incontinence', which was general though tacit. Then there is the underlying assumption that it is the mistress who makes extravagant demands on the man – 'he need not fear . . .' – as if without sinful women a man could tame, and of course would *want* to tame, his desires. And finally there is the belief that sexuality in a wife is disgusting. In some ways these three sentences of Acton's condense the duality of the Victorian male attitude and all its implications.

Dickens succumbs to this in his work, as he did in his private life. Interestingly, the duller Trollope does not. His later novels are full of women aware of their own sexuality. The temptation for the Victorian novelist was to romanticize the fallen woman as the innocent victim of the predatory male. Of course this was sometimes the case, but more general was a habit of mind and experience of many young women and girls which led them to accept casual prostitution as a legitimate means of fending off destitution. For many of them this was probably no more distasteful and no more damaging physically or mentally than working in the mills or the potteries, or as a sweated seamstress.

During that visit of Emerson's to Britain he recorded in his diary a conversation with Dickens and Carlyle, in which they said that 'chastity in the male sex was as good as gone in our times; and in England was so rare that they could name all exceptions' (quoted by Gilbert Haight, 'Male Chastity in the Nine-teenth Century', *Contemporary Review*, Nov. 1971). If this was indeed true, we must fill in those silences in Victorian fiction as to the activities of unmarried men with visits to prostitutes or perhaps, more discreetly, to mistresses set up in comfortable seclusion in St John's Wood and other tasteful suburbs. Most young men would not be able to afford the latter, and this was one of the great though barely surfacing complaints, that because men were discouraged from marrying until they could maintain their wives in the style to which they were accustomed they were 'forced' to go to prostitutes.

Certainly by the end of the century the dependency of middle-class morality on prostitution was being openly acknowledged and attacked, although earlier feminists criticized the lack of concern over widespread prostitution on the grounds, implied rather than elaborated, of Lecky's comment. In 1871 Josephine Butler battled against the Contagious Diseases Act – an attempt to license prostitutes – on two fronts; first, that the act made no attempt to discourage prostitution (its main concern was the protection of Her Majesty's forces from venereal disease), and secondly that it could subject entirely innocent women to degrading medical examinations, as the authorities were empowered to arrest any woman on suspicion. Josephine Butler's campaign accomplished something very important. It brought into the open a situation which no one could ignore but no one wanted to discuss.

By 1888 Mona Caird, a feminist writer, could discuss what she called 'the twin system of marriage and prostitution' in these terms:

Prostitution is as inseparable from our present marriage customs as the shadow from the substance. They are the two sides of the same shield, and not the deepest gulf that ever held human beings asunder can prevent the burning vapours of the woman's inferno which is raging beneath our feet, from penetrating into the upper regions of respectability and poisoning the very atmosphere. ('Ideal Marriage,' *Westminster Review*, Nov. 1888)

This was part of an attack on marriage rather than on prostitution, and Mona Caird was arguing for free marriage without sanction of church or state. But it is significant that she assumes that the dependence of a rigid marriage system on prostitution is bound to lead to widespread corruption, and that her answer is to loosen the bonds of strict morality.

The reality of this dependence is emphasized by the fact that very little was done to control or diminish prostitution, apart from isolated attempts to 're-claim' small numbers of fallen women, and set them up in suitable institutions where they could be taught to sew and perform other useful tasks. The general belief, which is to be found in Mrs Gaskell's *Ruth* (though she did not herself hold it), was that a woman once fallen was irredeemable. A frequent character in fiction is the prostitute who, like Mary Barton's aunt or Martha in *David Copperfield*, has a horror of her profession but cannot disentangle herself from it. The style of life of a prostitute was not necessarily the grim existence of the Whitechapel streetwalker. Some managed to maintain themselves in quite decent circumstances by their earnings, and there were a few notorious women who, out of a combination of luck, cleverness and charm, did very well indeed for themselves. Among the latter was Laura Bell, who confined her favours to men of wealth and high birth. Ballet dancers and opera girls were generally assumed to be buyable, and a reference in fiction to a young man hanging about a starlet's dressing room would have suggested to many contemporary readers an attempt at a sexual liaison.

Something can be learned about the habits and assumptions of the nineteenth century from a novel published in 1907, which was in fact suppressed, called *The Yoke* by Hubert Wales. It describes with unexpected directness the difficulties of a young man 'stung by the call of sex' – the yoke in question. He is a respectable, well-educated young man, whose taste and conscience lead him to spurn the normal outlet for someone in his position, the opera girls who for the price of a champagne supper were prepared to spend the night with a genteel young man. (His friend is less discerning, and contracts venereal disease, which leads him to suicide.) Hubert Wales' hero, in his personality and profession, the law, could represent countless Victorian heroes. The seduction of Little Em'ly by Steerforth in *David Copperfield* should be seen in the context of what would have been considered the normal sexual activity of young men. We should see David's innocence in this context also.

In the 1840s an American visitor to Cambridge commented thus on the habits of the students there:

There is a careless and undisguised way of talking about gross vice, which shows that public sentiment does not strongly condemn it; it is habitually talked of and considered as a thing from which a man may abstain through extraordinary frigidity of temperament or high religious scruple, or merely as a bit of training with reference to the physical consequences alone; but which is on the whole natural, excusable, and perhaps to most men necessary. (Quoted in Haight, *op. cit.*)

This natural activity depended on the existence of one hundred prostitutes in a community of sixteen hundred undergraduates. The American observer added, 'that shop-girls, work-women, domestic servants, and all females in similar positions, were expressly designed for the amusement of gentlemen, and generally serve that purpose, is a proposition assented to by a large proportion of Englishmen, even when they do not act upon the idea themselves.' Here is Steerforth, not so much the impulsive, Byronic male, which is how he is usually interpreted, but an average English undergraduate.

But behind the sentimental image of domestic comfort that exists throughout Victorian fiction lies not only the reality of the prostitute and her function. There was also a much tougher understanding of the family's purpose. The family was a political unit, a unit of stability and order, a symbol of acquiescence in the hierarchy of authority that rose above it. When the family broke down, as it often did, for instance, under the pressures of factory working and extreme poverty, anarchy, a lack of respect towards the institutions of the state, and chaos would ensue. Legislators were very reluctant to interfere with the idea of the family as a self-governing unit voluntarily perpetuating the *status quo*.

The family was required to exist, 'a little sovereign commonwealth' as O. R. McGregor describes it (*Divorce in England*, page 62), a crucial unit in the operation of the state's authority but independent of it. McGregor quotes W. Cooke Taylor, who was much concerned with conditions in Lancashire and argued in 1874 like this against the limitation of the working hours of children in factories:

The family is the unit upon which a constitutional government has been raised which is the admiration and envy of mankind. Hitherto whatever else the laws have touched, they have not dared to invade this sacred precinct; and the husband and wife, however poor, returning home from whatever occupations or harrassing engagements, have there found *their* dominion, *their* repose, *their* compensation for many a care. . . . There has been a sanctity about this . . . home life which even the vilest law acknowledged and the rashest law respected. . . . But let the state step in between the mother and her child . . . domestic confidence is dissolved, family privacy invaded and maternal responsibility assailed. For the tenderness of the mother is substituted the tender mercies of the state; for the security of natural affection, the securities of an unnatural law. Better by far that many another infant should perish in its innocence and unconsciousness than to be a victim of such a state of things. (Quoted in *Divorce in England*, page 61)

Usefully explicit here is one of the ways the family was seen to operate politically. It was hoped that the family unit would act as a restraint on working-class discontent – when Engels attacked the family ten years later in *The Origins of the Family, Private Property and the State*, he saw it as a weapon of the bourgeoisie. The idea of sanctity encouraged the notion that the family was something private, owned as it were by the members themselves and exclusive of outside forces – of course a ludicrously unreal assumption. The idea that the dispossessed did in fact have something that was their very own, not their employer's, not the state's, separate from the turmoil of the threatening world outside, appealed to the establishment. There was a perfectly sincere desire to reproduce the working-class family in the middle-class image, suitably controlled and on a modest scale. Linked with the family as a unit of private ownership is the idea of protection, the suggestion that however buffeted the individual members of a family may be by the working world, within the family they can exercise their own authority in safety.

The implication of all this is that the family was seen as the only way of making the unspeakable life of the underpaid cotton worker and his wife and children tolerable. Clearly for many cotton operatives in Lancashire the family was the root of their daily life, which made it all the more desperate that its survival was threatened by many of the things that the legislators were reluctant to interfere with: poor diet, disease, chronically bad housing and drainage, ignorance, and a hopeless lack of amenities in matters of hygiene and child care, the necessity of working mothers leaving their infants with negligent and ignorant nurses – all of which added up to a high infant mortality rate that W. Cooke Taylor, for one, was complacent about.

Against this image of sanctity writers like Dickens tested their portraits of family life. Dickens was fond of pictures of modest comfort, the sharing of good but unluxurious food in an atmosphere of warmth and good will, and this kind of illustration helped to substantiate a longing for its reality. Yet there were contradictions. A strong belief in the sustaining qualities of the home necessitated a belief in marriage, but early marriage was frowned on as being improvident, especially in the working class. Mingled in the attitudes towards working-class marriage is the threat of what a horrified middle class saw as uncontrolled sexuality on the factory floor. There is no evidence to suggest that there is any truth in the kind of picture illustrated in the previous chapter, although isolated cases of seduction by master or overseer have been documented. But the respectable were alarmed by what was often an exaggerated version of the labouring poor living and breeding together, disregarding the sanctions of marriage and careless about the birth of illegitimate offspring. A strong, Christian family unit, backed by discreet propaganda on the dangers of sexual excesses, was the antidote.

What we see in all this is the reflection of that authoritarian, regulated and disciplined family which is such a dominant image of Victorian life. The family unit, money and influence were inextricably woven together in the process of middle-class self-discipline. Sexual irregularities on the part of the men were outside this particular nexus. The working class needed the discipline, but could not be allowed the money or the influence, so the regulated family became the means not only of checking the underprivileged, but also of persuading them to be content without these. What we find very often described with generous moral approval in the fiction of the period, are contented artisan families who have successfully modelled themselves on the middle-class unit.

Christianity provided the ideal structure for this kind of propaganda; sermons were preached on the blessedness of being content with one's lot. Much of the aid and many of the reforms which affected the labouring classes were a part of the conspiracy to keep the poor content. Cleanliness, homeliness and hot dinners were assets in the life of any working man, but a striking irony emerges when these are seen as the rewards of hard work and decent morality rather than of higher wages.

There is a further aspect of the Victorian family which it is most productive to see in direct fictional terms: the Victorian marriage that preserved a polished shell of conformity but within was rotten. This is what is so savagely exposed in Dickens – it is one of the areas in which Dickens operates most devastatingly. Money is the culprit most often, and Dickens more than any other commentator on Victorian life unravels the closely knit strands of money and morality. It was the kind of thing that only a novelist could do.

DICKENS WAS always up against the problem of what his characters knew about the realities of life. His novels are full of innocents, men and women who, even when they are allowed to discover unpalatable facts about the ways of the world, retain an island of safety where innocence and purity can prevail. Neither Dickens' rich texture of concern nor his savage stabs of exposure owe their origin to the observation and experience of a single character. Indeed, his writing is often at its very best when a major character, such as Pip in *Great Expectations* (1861), is exposed along with the world around him. It contrasts with *David Copperfield* where the maintenance of David's moral superiority makes him an inadequate vehicle of understanding.

Very few of Dickens' characters are allowed to have a full and varied experience of the world that is so richly presented as teeming around them. This in itself is a significant reflection of the stratification of Victorian society, but it is also the result of something that reflects a much more personal aspect of Dickens' fiction, which is the necessity of protection. All but the uncompromisingly evil and ruthless – and these are generally those who 'know' most about the world they operate in and can exploit the ignorance of others – need moral, psychological or physical protection. Sometimes they need all three. Not only in *Little Dorrit* (1856) is Dickens' fiction full of prison walls. Throughout his novels characters are, voluntarily or by force, placed in restraint.

There are a number of forms the prison walls can take: businesses, or domestic households, or particular obsessions, or social aloofness, or social deprivation. Dombey and Mr Merdle are trapped, as are Miss Havisham and Miss Wade. Jo is trapped, and so is Lady Dedlock. One of the less obvious ways in which Dickens constructs protective barriers around his characters is by depriving so many of them of what we would normally think of as an adult awareness. The innocent, the simple-minded and the child-like are scattered generously throughout Dickens' fiction, but *Bleak House* (1853) is probably the novel most liberally and variously stocked with such characters.

Bleak House contains a superbly controlled multiplicity, a closely woven structure of qualifications, a refusal to deliver any easy moral answers. The dull and the virtuous are represented in the placid tones of Esther Summerson so that they do not interfere with the kernel of the work. We are not allowed to see innocence solely in the form of the virtuous, self-immolating Esther. We are forced to look at it in the 'child' Harold Skimpole, whose self-professed simplicity only briefly disguises his true role as irresponsible sponger: and as worse than that as the novel progresses, as an active collaborator in destruction.

There is also Grandfather Smallweed, childish in quite a different sense. He is small in size, is carried about everywhere, and behaves with the obsessive, spasmodic truculence of a very spoilt child. He too is venomously destructive. If these two children are placed alongside two genuine children who are having to cope with the adult world, Jo and Charley, we can begin to see as a striking feature of the novel the inversion of the normal parent-child relationship. Charley and Jo are children whose childhood is denied. Reflections of this theme spread throughout the novel: in the Jellaby household for instance; in the way Caddy Jellaby refers to her fiancé as 'my darling child'; in the fact that Esther is being constantly referred to as if she were middle-aged; and in the way that the relationship between Esther and Jarndyce has such an odd duality, Jarndyce being both father and lover, and sometimes child, and Esther being both daughter and motherly housewife.

Bleak House is a texture of wholly unconventional family relationships. Miss Flite talks to her birds as if they were children; the Lord Chancellor is a father figure; Esther is discovered as a daughter, Mr George as a son, and so on. And each relationship implicates others. Caddy's respect for old Mr Turveydrop echoes Esther's regard for Jarndyce: they both accept the duty owed to middle-aged gentlemen. The orphaned Charley, up to her elbows in soap suds, is a silent reflection on the busy and patronizing Esther with her basket of keys. The one is a child whose sense of care and hard work is a matter of life and death, the other a protected little woman who must be busy and kind and helpful to guard herself from redundancy.

This aspect of *Bleak House* is the core of the novel's achievement. The major point is this: only with Esther's marriage and her final consignment to the doll's house does a conventional picture of marriage and family life emerge, and significantly it has very little to do with the meat of the novel. The rest of the book is wholly concerned with inverted, fragmented, butchered versions of family life and relationships, which are in their turn reflections of a ruthlessly stratified society which only fog, disease and Bucket can penetrate.

Generally the knowing in Dickens are also morally dubious, usually in ways involving money or sex, often both. The worldly-wise Steerforth, who mocks David's innocence, is the seducer of Emily. The mysterious Merdle, so knowing about money, is a crook. Dickens constructs few bridges between innocence and experience. David Copperfield is intended as one, but ultimately his moral aloofness removes him too absolutely from the corrupt world. Arthur Clennam, in *Little Dorrit*, is another, but is dulled by the weight of his own moral sense and a corresponding lack of vitality. Often Dickens tries to use the wholly innocent, always a young girl, as a redemptive messenger between good and evil – Little Nell, Little Dorrit, Agnes and Esther, and others – but his vision of innocence is severely limited by his lack of imaginative apprehension of the potentialities of young women.

The evil and the experienced also try to erect prison walls, sometimes to protect themselves from the consequences of what they know, sometimes to fend off an encroaching society which might expose them. Mrs Clennam, mouldering away in her decaying house, is an example. But there need to be some who are entirely beyond the pale, like Rigaud in *Little Dorrit*, who can move freely and without respect for traditional authority, like the smallpox in *Bleak House*, and transmit their evil. From these, as from less potent carriers of taint and disease, most of Dickens' characters are protected. Esther is infected by the smallpox, but she does not have to face the logic of the society that Dickens exposes. She is shielded from the full impact of reality.

Most of Dickens' childlike adults are men, whether they are morally negative, morally pernicious, or morally radiant in the most sentimental fashion, like Tom Pinch. In women, childishness, or simplicity, or purity, is absorbed into the general characterization of femininity. They do not need to be simple-minded as a protection from reality: the fact that they are women is sufficient. Dickens' women tend to be more than usually withdrawn from the rigours of real life, although they do not always appear to be. Little Dorrit, for instance, whose experiences with the Marshalsea and the underprivileged, followed by her elevation to polite society, we might expect to provide with some kind of insight into economic stratification and exploitation: but precisely the point about her is that she does not change. She is the same admirably humble and sincere little woman at the end as she is at the beginning. She is 'good' because neither prison nor high society has spoiled her, and she retains her capacity for caring for others. Insight, a more thinking reaction to what she sees and experiences, might damage care as an adequate response.

The image of care is crucial in Dickens' portraiture of women. All the women he wants us to admire look after others, particularly men. Little Nell cares for her grandfather, Agnes cares for her father, until he is replaced by David: Esther cares for Jarndyce until he is replaced by Woodcourt; Little Dorrit cares for her father, until he is replaced by Clennam. In each of these cases the attitudes and actions of the girl in respect of her husband are essentially the same as those in respect of father or father figure. The ideal bride is a daughter. Filial duty and respect couples with paternal authority and kindness: this is the image that dominates the marriages of Dickens' heroines.

Again, this is about the protection of the female. In characterizing his brides as dutiful daughters, Dickens is blotting out the sexual side of marriage. He does not just ignore it, which is what we might expect; he positively suggests an asexual relationship. Esther's role is that of devoted daughter to Jarndyce, and she retains it as the devoted doctor's wife. But she has another role, that of 'Dame Durden' as Ada and Richard call her, the middle-aged housewife. She herself refers to Ada, who is her contemporary, as if she were her daughter, calling her 'my darling', 'my dear one'; 'they gave my darling into my arms' she says in the final chapter, referring not, as one might expect, to her own first baby, but to Ada. Ada and Richard are both mothered by Esther, and Esther's own marriage is focused as significantly on her relationships with Ada and with Jarndyce, that is as mother and daughter, as it is with her shadowy husband.

There is something similar in *Little Dorrit*. There Arthur Clennam refers to Amy Dorrit as 'my child' and is always emphasizing their difference in ages, while the retarded Maggie calls her 'Little Mother'. Amy herself insists on retaining the adjective 'little' and gently reminds Arthur every time he forgets to use it. It is like Dora's insistence that David think of her as his 'child bride'.

It is not difficult to trace in Dickens' own life convincing reasons for his attitude towards the role of wives and daughters. He considered that his own mother did not provide the care for him that he needed, that she was irresponsible and inefficient, and he at least partly blamed her for that disastrous episode in his life when he was sent out to work at the blacking factory and shortly afterwards left to fend for himself when his parents were imprisoned for debt. As an adult he insisted on the proper regulation of domestic affairs, and one of the reasons for the break-up of his own marriage was that his wife failed him in this. It was his sister-in-law Georgina who ran the Dickens household with its many children, while Catherine, his wife, became increasingly disinclined to take part in domestic responsibilities, and produced more and more children, to Dickens' professed dismay. It is hard to say whether Catherine's lack of a proper grasp of her duties was the cause or the effect of Georgina's presence in their home to perform them with a devoted admiration of the master of the house, but it is quite clear that Dickens considered this kind of selfless sense of duty, the willing and unrewarded care of others, to be an ideal of womanhood.

His last complete novel, *Our Mutual Friend* (1865) has a heroine, Bella Wilfer, who learns the true value of uncommercial love. After she has been happily married, and is settled in a comfortable little cottage, she says that she wants to be more than 'the doll in the doll's house'. What she means here is not a rejection of the doll's house, but a wish to be more than merely ornamental. She wants to be tested, she wants to show that she is up to anything life or her husband might demand of her. She is not going to be a Dora, but a useful and busy housewife, making life as comfortable as possible for her husband, and a loyal support to him through his troubles. But Bella is not asked to *share* her husband's troubles; she is safe from the grimmer events with which he is connected.

There is no doubt that Dickens' limited view of women's fulfilment seriously damaged his novels, which is all the more regrettable as he created so many powerful and memorable women. But the more forceful these women are the less are their chances of ordinary happiness. The Edith Dombeys are beyond the pale of domestic bliss, or any kind of creative function. The devoted little housekeeper carries the day:

Pleasant little Ruth! Cheerful, tidy, bustling, quiet little Ruth! No doll's house ever yielded greater delight to its young mistress, than little Ruth derived from her glorious dominion over the triangular parlour and the two small bedrooms.

To be Tom's housekeeper. What dignity! . . . Well might she take the keys out of the little chiffonier which held the tea and sugar; and out of the two little damp cupboards . . . and jingle them upon a ring before Tom's eyes when he came down to breakfast! Well might she, laughing musically, put them up in that blessed little pocket of hers with a merry pride! For it was such a grand novelty to be mistress of anything, that if she had been the most relentless and despotic of all little housekeepers, she might have pleaded just that much more for her excuse, and have been honourably acquitted. (*Martin Chuzzlewit*, Chapter 39)

What we have here, in the modest household of Ruth and her brother, is a surrogate marriage. Ruth's cheerfulness in her duties – she goes on to mend and cook, though even the Pinches have a skivvy to do 'the mere household drudgery' – her conviction of their importance, combined with the patronizing yet rhetorical way in which Dickens describes all this, are the signal features of this passage. Like so many Victorian men Dickens is able to patronize and to admire simultaneously, and we find this ability summed up in the character of David Copperfield. For all his valuing of Agnes, his Ministering Angel, he sees her all the time as outside the main business of life.

In all Dickens' portraits of bustling housekeepers, the household keys are a significant image. The first time David meets Agnes, still a small girl, he notices the basket of keys which she carries about with her, and which indicates her domestic responsibilities. As soon as Esther arrives at Bleak House she is presented with the housekeeping keys; it is an event regarded by all concerned with great seriousness. They are an important symbol, for they suggest the merging of two dominant expressions of the 'good' qualities of women, as daughters and as mothers. It reinforces the argument that Dickens saw his good women as daughters, as mothers, as housekeepers, but not as sexual partners.

When David graduates from Dora to Agnes, he loses a child bride and gains a mother and an efficient housekeeper. Agnes has mothered her father and run his house, and we can see exactly what kind of a wife she will be. David's love for Agnes is contained in his recognition of her as a good woman just as, in the same novel, Annie Strong's love for her husband is contained in her understanding of his good qualities. In neither case has love anything to do with sexual passion. But David's love for Dora has, and this is what Annie Strong's solemn phrase, 'the mistaken impulse of an undisciplined heart', is about. David succumbs to a physical attraction for someone unworthy, and it is very important that the sexuality of the marriage should be made respectable by hard work on his part and efficiency and care on Dora's. It doesn't work, and Dora is struck down by the palpable result of their union, the birth of a dead child.

In the Dora and David episode a juvenile romantic aura, connived at by Dora's aunts and Julia Mills and Traddles, disguises the nature of their attraction. But their life-style after marriage cannot sustain it, and Dora, unsupported by those who had originally encouraged her, is rapidly exposed as a failure. She has been treated as a plaything before her marriage:

Dora seemed by one consent to be regarded like a pretty toy or plaything. My aunt, with whom she gradually became familiar, always called her Little Blossom; and the pleasure of Miss Lavinia's life was to wait upon her, curl her hair, make ornaments for her, and treat her like a pet child (Chapter 41).

Dora, as David himself is aware, is a creature on much the same level of existence as her dog Jip. How could she be anything but a failure when it came to the serious business of keeping house? And she also fails as a mother. Her inability to produce a live child is dimly seen by Dora herself as a moral inadequacy, a judgment on her.

There are several contradictions in the David and Dora episode. While it seems quite clear that their relationship can only be seen as one of youthful sexuality, with the added feature that David, aware of his superiority, finds in Dora ideal sustenance for his ego, there is a reluctance to see it in this light. It is significant that Annie Strong talks of the 'undisciplined heart' in reference to her predatory cousin Jack Maldon. It is clear that she is talking of sexual attraction, and David immediately applies this to himself – has he preyed on Dora as Jack Maldon does on Annie? But he never quite puts this question to himself. He and Dora want to see their love as innocent and childlike, the love of 'boy and girl', as Dora puts it – there is surely a suggestion here that she is afraid of sex just as she is afraid of adult responsibility – and Miss Trotwood refers to them as a 'poor little couple', as 'two pretty pieces of confectionary'

which certainly does not suggest any kind of physical vitality. So we are simultaneously invited to see them as two pretty ornaments in their doll's house, and
as youthful lovers, and the two images don't unite very successfully. Dickens
never sorts any of this out; Agnes is David's reward for hard work and applica-
tion, not for a matured understanding of human needs and impulses.

It is appropriate that David gains a mother, for his own mother was a child,
one of Dickens' childish adults who radiate not innocence but defeat. Like Dora
and Mrs Dombey, David's mother cannot make an effort. Dickens does not
intend us to rest our moral approval with Dora and Mrs Copperfield. At the
same time he maintains the conspiracy to protect the innocent, even when the
innocent are inadequate. Everyone wants to protect Dora, to shield her from
the kind of influences and experiences that might have taught her something.
There is a general reluctance to spoil things for these innocents.

Dickens' difficulties here arise from the depth of his inclination to sustain
innocence and protect women, either physically or spiritually, or ideally both
together, spiritual protection *earning* physical protection. There is another aspect
of this in his portraits of prostitutes. These are always fallen and repentant innocents, fully conscious of what they are and sickened by it. They are victims,
dramatically presented, but never associated with a life of pleasure, and very
rarely seen with the men who buy them. Martha in *David Copperfield* is a lone
outcast who wanders the streets on the brink of suicide. Dickens does not even
briefly indicate the men who might have made use of her services, without
whom she would not be what she is. So that even his prostitutes are in a way
protected, seen always in the light of self-condemned victims, never operating
in their profession. Em'ly is ruined, but is saved from the consequences of her
disaster. We do not see her situation as part of a normal world of lusts and
weaknesses, because Dickens has carefully isolated her and Steerforth as
uncommon people.

Of course this can be said about most of Dickens' characters. His inclinations
towards the grotesque and the dramatic and the exaggerated do not lend themselves to the depiction of an ordinary world. The whole tendency of his fiction
questions whether normality exists. Yet he is forced to employ certain conventions of normality, conventions sustained by a traditional Christian point of
view, because the alternative is to accept an anarchic and destructive world.
Dickens relishes the anarchy, the grotesqueries, he has a passion for the freakish
in character and incident, but is he perhaps afraid of their implications? He
must always balance these extremes with a version of solid normality, and most
often solid normality means a domestic marriage, a limited, serving role for the
woman and a kindly, protective role for the man.

Critics tend to acclaim those novels of Dickens where the balance is at its most unified. *Little Dorrit* is perhaps the best example. In this novel everyone is enmeshed in the same web of influences. The prison symbol contains everyone. The influences of money and snobbery stretch everywhere. It has been pointed out that it is the most static of Dickens' novels, the most concentrated in its exploration of its major theme, and there is also a lack of vitality in the book. Apart from the stagy Rigaud its villains are dulled and immobile. Mrs Clennam does not move, Mr Merdle does not eat. Gestures are truncated, conversation almost unnecessary. Only one or two minor characters escape this heavy feeling of repression.

The unity of balance is achieved because Dickens does not, or cannot, provide an image of normality with which to contend against the forces of repression and destruction. Pet Meagles is not rescued from her unhappy marriage to Henry Gowan, nor is Amy's sister Fanny absolved from her association with the Merdles. And although Amy Dorrit and Arthur Clennam walk hand in hand into their 'modest life of usefulness and happiness', 'inseparable and blessed', it seems to me that nowhere else in Dickens is it so positively indicated that the reward of the doll's house for the hero and heroine represents, not a victory over the real world, but a withdrawal from it. The last phrase of the novel reminds us that 'the noisy and the eager, and the arrogant and the froward and the vain, fretted and chafed, and made their usual uproar', but Amy and Arthur, in their union, are beyond all this. In fact, they have made no impression on reality, and reality has made little impression on them.

As we have seen, Little Dorrit was never a part of this reality. She has carved her own modest, untouchable route through the streets of London – even the anonymous prostitute she encounters is remorseful at having touched her – and her greatest asset is that she is not contaminated, not involved, not drawn into what she witnesses. She is constrained in her emotions; care and kindness for her father, her brother and sister, Maggie, Arthur, are all that she can manage, and although Dickens would like us to believe that care and kindness are powerful and redemptive qualities, Little Dorrit emerges as an example of someone whose feelings have been narrowed by her experiences. She has preserved herself from the consequences of the life she has been forced to lead. The alternatives are, it is suggested, the passion of Miss Wade or the repression of Little Dorrit. Miss Wade may be perverted, but Little Dorrit, small, her figure undeveloped, often mistaken for a child, never quite grows up.

Like Thackeray, Dickens attacks snobbery and the commercial marriage, and it was an attack that became commonplace in Victorian fiction. Although money was so crucial in marriage strategy, few Victorian writers would have defended it as the proper basis of a marriage. It was frequently pointed out that love without money was disastrous, but on the surface at least general opinion concurred with Dickens: love with hard work and a modest competency was enough. What Victorian fiction so often offered as an alternative to cash was romantic love, with all its associations of passion, sacrifice and self-denial. But this is not what Dickens is after, although in fact the passions of romance might well have been more in keeping with the heightened atmosphere of his novels than the rather pallid sentiment he tends to suggest.

There was nothing sentimental or pallid about his own marriage. He was an authoritarian husband and father, knew exactly what he wanted from a wife, and was disappointed and, I think, personally chagrined, that he did not get it. Catherine's apparent inability to respond to his requirements, and the fact that most of his nine children tended to fall into the snares that he had so determinedly prepared them against, offended his aloofly rigid ideas of what marriage and parental and filial responsibility ought to be. It is not surprising that the failed marriages in his novels, the destructive, painful entrapped unions, are so much more telling than the successes. His hatred is so much more memorable than his love. It is interesting that Florence Dombey, whose love flourishes in the poisoned atmosphere of hatred and ambition, is the most convincing of Dickens' negative heroines. Unlike Esther or Amy Dorrit, she has no loving father figure to graft her good influence on to until the very end of the book, when she gains her own father. It is as if, surviving in the icy Dombey household, she is conscious that she must provide her own warmth and sustenance: she is self-sufficient.

Angus Wilson, in his irresistibly readable book *The World of Charles Dickens*, argues that although Dickens' wife's importance to his life and art should not be underestimated, he never felt what might be described as passionate love for her. Whether he felt something like passion for the actress Ellen Ternan, who was his mistress in his latter years, is hard to guess at. It was perhaps more likely a need for the stimulus and gratification of youth, beauty and vitality that he satisfied in his relationship with her: whatever it was, it did appear to have some effect on his understanding of women, for after Ellen Ternan he was able to write about women who were conscious of independent personalities. Before this, as Angus Wilson puts it, 'his marriage did not waken in him sufficient understanding of women to give reality to the central emotional relationships of his great novels' (*The World of Charles Dickens*, page 253).

In *Dombey and Son* (1846) Dickens describes Dombey's first marriage, to the lady who is unable to 'make an effort':

Dombey and Son had often dealt in hides, but never in hearts. They left that fancy to boys and girls, and boarding schools and books. Mr Dombey would have reasoned: That a matrimonial alliance with himself *must*, in the nature of things, be gratifying and honourable to any woman of common sense. That the hope of giving birth to a new partner in such a House, could not fail to awaken a glorious and stirring ambition in the breast of the least ambitious of her sex. That Mrs Dombey had entered on that social contract of matrimony: almost necessarily part of a genteel and worthy station, even without reference to the perpetuation of family Firms: with her eyes fully open to these advantages. That Mrs Dombey had had daily practical knowledge of his position in society. That Mrs Dombey had always sat at the head of his table, and done the honours of his house in a remarkably lady-like and becoming manner. That Mrs Dombey must have been happy. That she couldn't help it. (Chapter 1)

Mrs Dombey dies shortly after, and this is all we ever know about her. What Dickens gives us here is an encapsulation (the style is effectively a matter of brilliant punctuation) of the commercial marriage, seen simultaneously from two points of view. As an undertone to Dombey's authoritative voice spelling out what was required of – and therefore, as far as he is concerned, wanted by – the woman who is his wife, is speculation concerning the woman herself, her spirit broken, dying after producing the necessary perpetuation of the family firm. Here, pre-eminently, is woman as material object, as a thing, as a symbol of status, as a decoration in the necessary social rituals. A little later we are told that 'he certainly had a sense within him, that if his wife should sicken and decay, he would be very sorry, and that he would find something gone from among his plate and furniture, and other household possessions, which was well worth the having, and could not be lost without sincere regret' (Chapter 1).

In this is contained the logical inference of the commercial marriage. If you do not marry for love, it is important that you make sure you are valued as an object. The husband is valued to the extent that he appreciates, and sustains with cash, the wife's value as an object. In *Little Dorrit* Mr Merdle buys Mrs Merdle because her expansive bosom makes her a useful edifice on which to display jewels, to display his own wealth. The above quotations are taken from the opening of *Dombey and Son*, and of course they are most important for what they establish about Dombey's character. Looking forward in the novel we can see that Dombey cannot tolerate Florence because she refuses to be an object, a useless and decorative object, the way that Dombey is inclined to see her, that ought to be shut away in a cupboard. We can also see that the marriage with Edith is inevitably destructive because, although she objectifies herself, and this is what Dombey recognizes and appreciates, she will not be manipulated. His first wife was ideal, being both an object, and 'meek and dutiful'.

It is hard not to speculate, knowing, as we do, something but not enough about Dickens' own marriage, that what he himself really wanted in a wife might have been similar; or at least that he regretted its absence. Dombey is only one of a crowded gallery of overweening males that Dickens created. And although Dombey himself is icy and awful, and his treatment of women as pieces of furniture is savagely exposed, most of these, from Quilp to Bradley Headstone, are produced with a gusto and a sense of power that suggest a close reflection of Dickens' own energies. If he was not able to come to terms with women as independent personalities in his fiction, it is also true that he had difficulties with the energies and impulses of men.

THERE IS A great deal of physical violence in Dickens' novels. And there are many characters who radiate a latent aggression as well as those who are more obviously violent. It is a very physical world that Dickens describes, a society represented in terms of objects that can be manipulated, people who can be crushed, houses that can crumble. Where in the hands of most writers the manipulating, the crushing and the crumbling would be seen metaphorically, in Dickens all this is actual. In *Dombey* Carker is literally fragmented by a train; in *Little Dorrit* old Mrs Clennam's house crumbles into dust.

It is not only individuals who are violent, it is society itself, with its structures and institutions, and it is also the natural world. Part of the struggle of humanity was to protect itself from this violent world and, as we have seen, Dickens was preoccupied with this idea of protection, which played an essential part in his version of ideal marriage. He felt not only that marriage should be a refuge, but that it was the only refuge, and if one did not find this in one's own marriage one found it by being an accessory to the marriage of others, as so many of Dickens' elderly parents or unattached brothers and sisters are.

Dickens made some direct statements about marriage and the home; the following appeared in *Sketches by Boz*, a sentimental conclusion to an amiably satiric exercise:

. . . let them cherish the faith that in home, and all the English virtues which the love of home engenders, lies the only true source of domestic felicity; let them believe that round the household gods, contentment and tranquility cluster in their gentlest and most graceful forms; and that many weary hunters of happiness through the noisy world, have learnt this truth too late, and found a cheerful spirit and a quiet mind only at home at last. ('Sketches of Young Couples', Conclusion)

It has become so deeply ingrained in our culture, though it is a relatively recent idea, that home should mean contentment and tranquillity, that although we react against the sentimental emphasis of this kind of writing we generally accept something of what it says. But it is just here, in his insistence that home should be in some absolute way separate from, indeed protected from, society, that Dickens is at his most vulnerable. It is not just a question of sentimentality. It concerns a profound need in this author – and in many others, but not in all Victorian novelists, not in George Eliot, for example – to retreat from just the world that he is so busy encountering and analysing and attacking, and in his fiction creating.

When Dickens attacks marriage he attacks it as an instrument of society, often trying to beat society at its own game. When he praises marriage, he praises it as a refuge from society, an island in a nasty world. The sterile social gathering of the Veneerings in *Our Mutual Friend*, and the Podsnaps and the Lammles in the same novel, and the Dombeys, and the Merdles in *Little Dorrit*, are playing to win, according to the rules society has dictated. When people play society's game they become dehumanized, because it is not human values that count any more but the liveries that the servants wear, the dinner service that the guests eat from, and the price per yard of the curtains in the drawing-room. Marriage is both the means and the end of society's game. It is significant that Dombey as a widower is not 'in society'; when he marries, one of his wife's most important functions is to act as hostess. It is when Edith refuses to do so that the crisis in their marriage becomes blatant.

The reverse of marriage as a refuge from a threatening physical world is marriage as a contract, a collaboration with this world. And inevitably such a collaboration means that individuals take on the characteristics of the society they are co-operating with. Thus the language of contempt and threat, which Lady Dedlock uses, and the Dombeys, becomes natural, as does the language of trade and acquisition which surrounds the Merdles and the Lammles. In society marriage is a matter of trade, and the marriage contract is a commercial one.

Dickens portrays this contamination most relentlessly in *Our Mutual Friend*. It is a novel about commerce in human beings, about people translated into objects for the purpose of buying and selling. He draws his net so tightly around his characters that even those whom he obviously intended to escape are enmeshed. And this is just as well, for the redemptive aspect of the book is not convincing, and is even at times tedious.

The variety and the ramifications of the trade are consistently explored throughout the book. It begins with the activities of Gaffer Hexam and Rogue Riderhood, fishing bodies out of the Thames, which they then rob before turning over to the police. They are perhaps responsible for the bodies being in the river in the first place. Then we are introduced to the Veneerings, archetypes of the vulgar *nouveaux riches*, who collect social acquaintances with the money that has given them their new status. We meet the Lammles, newly married, each under the illusion that the other has money, and prepared, when they discover that neither has, to collaborate in order to exploit and manipulate others.

The trade becomes most explicit with the introduction of Silas Wegg and his friend Venus. Venus has a shop which deals in skeletons, pickled babies, and parts of human bodies. Wegg has a wooden leg, and sold his amputated limb to Venus. And although Wegg says, 'You can't buy human flesh and blood in this country, sir; not alive, you can't' (Book II, Chapter 7), that is just what most of the characters in the book are doing. This is what the cannibalistic marriage is about. Bella Wilfer declares that she won't be bought by John Harmon, yet insists that she must 'marry an establishment', which is as much to say that she is for sale. The Lammles try to sell Georgiana Podsnap to Fledgeby. Jenny Wren makes and dresses dolls which she then sells: the inference is clear.

No one is free from the trade. Fledgeby has bought Riah. Bradley Headstone has, in effect, bought Charlie Hexam. Eugene Wrayburn has it in mind to buy Lizzie, for that in social terms is what that kind of seduction amounts to. In Venus the two ideas of commerce and manipulation are brought together, and the manipulation, the rearrangement of people as if they were things, the using of people as if they were pieces of machinery, is elemental in the novel. Venus not only sells his skeletons, he puts them together, articulates them. He can make them move in any way he wants. Twemlow is articulated by the Veneerings. Georgiana is articulated by the Lammles. Neither really exists until these people have put them together. And it is just where these twin themes of commerce and articulation become blurred, just where the book is most seriously flawed, that it becomes in some ways the most revealing.

This occurs in the episode of the Boffins, Rokesmith and Bella Wilfer. The Boffins are intended as an example of truly loving, unselfish, unambitious humanity, beyond the contamination of money and the manipulation of society. Yet they take part in a piece of deception which, in spite of the worthiest motives, is closely akin to the manipulations that we see other less admirable characters practising. They deceive Bella in their attempt to engineer her into a genuinely moral outlook, while John Rokesmith not only collaborates in this deception, but also is himself not what he seems. Bella is in fact manipulated into reform, and is then doubly rewarded, for she marries John Rokesmith thinking with pleasure that she is embarking on a life of modest, housewifely usefulness, and then discovers that he is after all John Harmon and a wealthy man. It is odd that in a book that is so much about the corruption of money the rewards are, precisely, monetary – could it be that Dickens could suggest no alternative? – and the rewarded, the Boffins and John and Bella, are left to lead wealthy and comfortable lives.

But another aspect of the plot, which weighs a little against this, concerns Eugene Wrayburn and Lizzie Hexam. Eugene has to cast off society, and can only live humbly, for with his marriage to the inferior Lizzie society has rejected him. They are not rewarded with moneybags. We leave them on rather a sombre note, for the last words on their fate are shrilled by the condemning voices of society, while Bella and John are, as Boffin puts it, 'a pretty and promising picter', 'as if his [old Harmon's] money had turned bright again, after a long rust in the dark, and was at last beginning to sparkle in the sunlight' (Book IV, Chapter 13). Money does not have to be bad, but it comes as a disappointment that Dickens cannot avoid this, on his own terms, soft conclusion.

In most of Dickens' fiction marriage is inextricably linked with the most sinister aspect of a violent society, with mystery and murder and sudden disappearance, but until *Our Mutual Friend* he is always able to isolate certain characters from the taint of these connections. It is true that Bella is, in the end, protected, but she has to earn that protection. Little Dorrit maintains her original innocence throughout. No one in *Our Mutual Friend* is wholly untainted and, this being so, the character of Lizzie Hexam is particularly interesting. She feels the contamination of her background, yet she does not reject it in the way her brother Charlie does. She respects her father, although she hates his trade, and she maintains an independence of mind and action that is unusual in Dickens' females, apart from those whom we are intended to condemn. She is no innocent Little Em'ly, easy prey for a seducer, but a woman who knows what Eugene is after and, more, is aware of her own response to him. She is a woman who understands the risks and the threats of the world she lives in, and undertakes a marriage that is consonant with those risks. The last word on the marriage of Eugene and Lizzie is the daring vindication at Society's dinner table on the part of the timid Twemlow, but they are left in an ambiguity that is much more artistically satisfying than the padded happiness of the Harmons.

Lizzie Hexam, though, is not one of Dickens' passionate women. We see her finally conforming to Dickens' favourite image of the caring woman, looking after the damaged Wrayburn – reduced, like Rochester at the end of *Jane Eyre*. In both cases the overweening male is cut down to size in order to smooth the way for compatibility. The hint of *Jane Eyre* is relevant. In that novel Charlotte Brontë describes how Jane's aunt condemns her as a 'passionate child'. Passion is wicked, and Dickens shares Mrs Reed's disturbance at it. Edith Dombey is passionate when she is at her most aggressive. Miss Wade, in *Little Dorrit*, is passionate, Tattycoram sometimes so. Estella, in *Great Expectations*, has an icy, repressed passion. Here are Miss Wade and Tattycoram:

It was very curious to see them standing together: the girl with her disengaged fingers plaiting the bosom of her dress, half irresolutely, half passionately; Miss Wade with her composed face attentively regarding her, and suggesting to an observer, with extraordinary force, in her composure itself (as a veil will suggest the form it covers), the unquenchable passion of her own nature. (Chapter 27)

Passion in *Jane Eyre* amounts to sin. For a child to have strong feelings and to express them is wholly inappropriate, a challenge to the correct order of things. There is a great deal of the same attitude in Dickens' portrayal of women. Charlotte Brontë wrote a novel about a woman of strong feelings who insisted on her right to express those feelings, in pictures, actions or words. In Dickens passion means aggression, or self-destruction, often self-contempt. Passionate women are profoundly discontented. They cannot win happiness; the comfort of hearth and home with which the good women are rewarded (even those who do not marry, or who, like Ada in *Bleak House*, lose their husbands, usually get this) cannot be theirs. They destroy themselves – Lady Dedlock in death, Edith Dombey in lonely expulsion – as if their passionate natures exiled them from a normal life. For normality, in Dickens' version of what normality should be, is too evenly and comfortably regulated to have room for the heights of passion.

These women tend to be at their most passionate when they are despising or repulsing men. Edith Dombey reaches her peak first when she defies Dombey, then later when she rejects Carker:

She had better have turned hideous and dropped dead, than have stood up with such a smile upon her face, in such a fallen spirit's majesty of scorn and beauty. She lifted her hand to the tiara of bright jewels radiant on her head, and, plucking it off with a force that dragged and strained her rich black hair with heedless cruelty, and brought it tumbling wildly on her shoulders, cast the gems upon the ground. From each arm she unclasped a diamond bracelet, flung it down, and trod upon the glittering heap. Without a word, without a shadow on the fire of her bright eye, without abatement of her awful smile, she looked on Mr Dombey to the last, in moving to the door; and left him. (Chapter 47)

This is highly theatrical, and strongly reminiscent, with the heap of jewels on the floor, of the unforgettable scene in *Vanity Fair* in which Rawdon discovers Becky with Lord Steyne. The gestures are the stylized gestures of melodramatic passion, but they surmount a scene during which more truth has been spoken concerning the real nature of the Dombey marriage, and Carker's relationship to it – employed, 'being an inferior person, for the humiliation of Mrs Dombey' – than at any previous point in the novel. It is Edith's passion that has brought the truth to the surface, and for which Dickens seeks to find an outlet in these symbolic actions.

When Edith rejects Carker she elaborates on the subject of her marriage – 'I suffered myself to be sold, as infamously as any woman with a halter round her neck is sold in any market-place' (Chapter 54) – and makes it quite clear that in allowing him to be the instrument of her escape she is acknowledging no attraction:

. . . if I tell you that the lightest touch of your hand makes my blood cold with antipathy; that from the hour when I first saw and hated you, to now, when my instinctive repugnance is enhanced by every minute's knowledge of you I have since had, you have been a loathsome creature to me which has not its like on earth. . . .

It is hard to imagine any of Dickens' heroines speaking thus in response to unwelcome attentions, Little Nell to Quilp, for instance, or Agnes to Uriah Heep. We are told what Lizzie Hexam said to Bradley Headstone, and it was nothing like this. Only the passionate are allowed to utter the language of repulsion, just as only they are allowed to utter the language of aggression. Dickens' passionate women are cold, and it is consistent with this that they should be at their most powerful in rejection, in essentially negative actions.

Edith, and the other women like her in Dickens' novels, have no use for their energy but to destroy themselves. Dickens, like most other Victorian men, could not conceive of a genuinely creative woman. He cannot translate Edith's passion into love, for he would then have something so powerfully sexual that he would have been reluctant to cope with it. When Dickens does suggest a potentially adulterous situation, as in the case of Annie Strong, or Louisa Gradgrind, the man concerned is wholly unattractive and something of a cad, so we are bound to see the affair in the worst light. In the case of Edith and Carker we are only too aware that Carker is evil: we think he has Edith under his spell, as he has Rob the Grinder under his spell, and then we discover otherwise.

Carker's motives are to destroy the house of Dombey and to get his own back on Dombey himself. But he certainly intends to claim the sexual rewards of the escapade and has no doubt, until Edith confronts him, that she will succumb. This conjunction of evil with sexual rapacity occurs frequently in Dickens. Power over men means power over women too. The ability to win on the bloody battlefield of business appears to contain victory in love also. What this suggests is an interpretation of sex as violence, and it is true that throughout Dickens' fiction, with few exceptions, whenever he indicates sexuality in a man he suggests violence, and often deceit and scheming also.

This is present in several of his early characters, in Quilp, for example, and in Jonas Chuzzlewit, who both bully and torment their patient and subdued wives. In fact, they physically attack them, and violence is an essential part of their characterization. Quilp is especially fascinating as we see him ill-treating his wife (who by virtue of this treatment scarcely exists as a human being but appears to love him) and gloating over the unformed body of Little Nell. This, with his deformity, makes his sexuality particularly repugnant, and yet there is such energy in it, such vigour and cleverness, that it is hard not to believe that Dickens thoroughly enjoyed his creation.

I think Dickens liked to write about men totally dominating women, just as he liked to write about physical violence. There is another instance in the case of Murdstone, where the vicious clarity of style in the descriptions of the way in which Murdstone treats Mrs Copperfield and David seems to betray Dickens' own convictions in the matter. Not that intellectually or morally he approved of this behaviour, but he had a great respect for power, and for male superiority.

In *Martin Chuzzlewit*, there is the wooing of Mary Graham by Pecksniff. Here Dickens portrays the physically abhorrent with absolute finesse. Throughout the proceedings Pecksniff is making love to Mary's hand – 'examining the rings upon her fingers, and tracing the course of one delicate blue vein with his fat thumb':

'Ah, naughty Hand!' said Mr Pecksniff, apostrophising the reluctant prize, 'why did you take me prisoner! Go, go!'
He slapped the hand to punish it; but relenting, folded it in his waistcoat to comfort it again.

And finally:

They were so near [Mr Pecksniff's house] that he stopped, and holding up her little finger, said in playful accents, as a parting fancy: 'Shall I bite it?' (Chapter 30)

In Dickens' male characters sexuality emerges either as lust or as violence, and the first is repulsive while the second is destructive. We have seen how the marriages of Dickens' heroes and heroines tend to suggest the relationship of father and daughter, or brother and sister, rather than of man and wife, but I don't want to suggest that there was anything abnormal in Dickens' emphases. Like most Victorian writers he was prepared to make great dramatic use of the rapacious male. Innumerable plots in nineteenth-century novels are concerned with seduction, elopement, forced marriage, adultery and potential adultery, in spite of the fact that it was considered a breach of taste to write about sex. That renowned piece of Victorian melodrama, Mrs Henry Wood's *East Lynne* (1861), turns on adultery. But what is tantalizing, interesting, and irritating about Dickens is that sex plays a very important part in his analysis and exposure of society, but it does not play the most accepted role of all, within the confines of married love.

The violence of the male predator is emphasized by the helplessness of his victim. Mary Graham has no defence against the unctuous advances of Pecksniff, nor Agnes Wickfield against Uriah Heep. A woman must be weak in the face of this kind of aggression, however strong in spirit she may be, and however worthy, for if the male were preying on an equal the whole effect would be lost. This is an important ingredient of romantic fiction: the female *must* be weaker than the male, whether the male is authorized lover or would-be seducer. The essential ambiance of romantic love would be lost without it. Dickens plays on the expectations of his readers, when he makes Pecksniff so revolting. His starting-point is what he knows about readers' expectations of romantic courtship, the standard situation, the accepted phrases employed, and the accepted responses.

Dickens' legitimate courtships are very dull, and are often simply a slight intensification of an already existing relationship. Clennam and Little Dorrit as father and daughter, for instance. Nothing takes place that could be called courtship. The same is true of Florence Dombey and Walter Gay. They have called each other brother and sister over many years, and step into marriage as if it were the most natural thing for innocent childhood friends. And Dickens very much wants us to believe that it *is* the most natural thing, that what is unnatural is not just the commercial unions of such as Edith and Dombey, but the importunate wooing of lustful men and the agonized disquiet of impassioned women.

In the character of Dombey Dickens draws together the authoritarian, latent violence of the domineering male and the chilling dedication of mercenary ambition. Money and violence have been closely linked in earlier novels – Quilp and Jonas Chuzzlewit are both after money – but in Dombey there is an added feature, that of status in society. *Dombey and Son* is not just about money and power, but social status and, enmeshed in all three, inheritance. Dombey marries for a second time because he wants an heir. Interestingly, the full quality of his authoritarianism, his violence, does not emerge until after he has established a sexual relationship, and the object of that violence is the woman with whom he has established it. However, Edith is more than a match for him, and it is his daughter, Florence, who receives his physical attack. She is the weak and helpless victim, the necessary object of the aggressive male.

Another type of male character bears a close relationship to Dickens' impassioned women. We find it in Steerforth, and the closely related Eugene Wrayburn. Steerforth is a playboy with plenty of money, talents and energy, but nothing to do with any of them. He too is a bully, as can be seen in the way he behaves at school, and in his treatment of Rosa Dartle, herself close kin of Miss Wade. He is like Dickens' passionate women because ultimately he can do nothing with his energies but destroy himself, leaving destruction in his wake, but he is unlike them to the extent that he performs this destruction in an adventurous, daring and attractive manner which is quite different from the bitterness and sterility of the women. The manner comes from the privilege and power to which he has been bred; he is expected to behave like that. He is, more or less, expected to seduce young girls. Like the mother of the seducer of Mrs Gaskell's Ruth, Steerforth's mother cannot see her son's actions as reprehensible. He has been bred to ignore the consequences of his actions, and it is this that allows him to be carefree and daring – and this that his friend David finds so attractive.

Steerforth is the attractive predator, not the repulsively lustful, not the violent. Eugene Wrayburn is this too, but with the significant difference that he is poor, and to be poor in a novel that is so much about the dirtiness of money is bound to weigh in his advantage. At the beginning of the book this factor alone suggests to us that Eugene is redeemable. But he is specifically characterized as a predator, and specifically linked with the others who share that identity: Gaffer Hexam, Rogue Riderhood and Bradley Headstone. The first two are called 'birds of prey'. To ensure that Eugene too is thoroughly involved in this terminology Dickens uses the bird analogy when he describes the part Eugene plays in the discovery of Gaffer's body, and its aftermath. When he returns after spending the night comforting Lizzie on her father's sudden death, his friend Mortimer greets him like this:

'Why what bloodshot, draggled, dishevelled spectacle is this!' cried Mortimer.
'Are my feathers so very much rumpled?' said Eugene, coolly going up to the looking-glass. 'They *are* rather out of sorts. But consider. Such a night for plumage.' (Book I, Chapter 14)

There is no doubt that Eugene is of the bird species, and that his prey is Lizzie. And he, unlike Gaffer Hexam and Venus, is attempting to deal in live flesh and blood.

Lizzie's protection of herself from the predatory Eugene is convincing, but Eugene's redemption is less so. At the end of the book he is reduced, he is less of a threat and thus more acceptable to Lizzie, but there is little to suggest that he is essentially changed. There seems nothing to indicate that his near death by water has had a purifying effect on him (though this has been argued by some), first because, if there has been a change, it has occurred before this and it is Lizzie's strength of purpose that has accomplished it, and secondly because his rescue from the river links him as closely with Rogue Riderhood as with the 'good' John Harmon. It is possible that Lizzie marries Eugene because now he is weak and she is strong, in which case Lizzie is the only one of Dickens' respectable women who retains a dominant role. Lizzie has proved herself the stronger both in decisiveness and in strength – it is she who pulls Eugene out of the water – and so there is no question of submission. There is a hint of Dickens' old habit in that Eugene has to be virtually robbed of his manhood before he can marry, but Lizzie's vitality is not damaged, and the marriage is not cushioned by intimations of domestic bliss.

Ultimately it is neither the Wrayburn marriage nor the Harmon marriage that is most memorable, but that of the savage Lammles. Dickens operates the Lammles like a pair of fiendish puppets, which is very much how they try to operate each other. They are as bad-tempered and vicious as Punch and Judy. They represent the logical but inhuman extreme of the commercialization of a human institution. Here they are, on their honeymoon, having discovered the truth about each other, the only important truth, which is that they are both penniless:

Mr and Mrs Lammle have walked for some time on the Shanklin sands, and one may see by their footprints that they have not walked arm in arm, and that they have not walked in a straight track, and that they have walked in a moody humour; for, the lady has prodded little spirting holes in the damp sand before her with her parasol, and the gentleman has trailed his stick after him. As if he were of the Mephistopheles family indeed, and had walked with a drooping tail. (Book 1, Chapter 10)

We follow the Lammles in their honeymoon walk, reading their characters and their situation in the sand. There is a combination of inference here, suggesting animals (the tracks), the devil, and a calculating antagonism which is summed up by their different uses of parasol and stick respectively. Their icy conversations emerge in a series of wickedly glinting sentences, under which we can sense Dickens' delight in composition.

The Lammles do not operate on their own, they are riveted into the general theme of commercial manipulation. They are its most extreme representation, but their close connections with other manifestations are clear. Towards the end of the book Dickens comments on their manner of talking to one another:

Was it the speciality of Mr and Mrs Lammle, or does it ever obtain with other loving couples? In these matrimonial dialogues they never addressed each other, but always some invisible presence that appeared to take a station about midway between them. Perhaps the skeleton in the cupboard comes out to be talked to, on such domestic occasions? (Book III, Chapter 12)

The mention of the skeleton, and the extraordinary picture it suggests, not only confirms their lack of humanity, it immediately reminds us of Venus and his articulations. It is an appropriate reminder, as the Lammles are the prime articulators.

If there is anything unsatisfactory in the characterization of the Lammles it is the change of heart allowed to Mrs Lammle, who rescues Georgiana Podsnap from the plot she herself has instigated to wed her to Fledgeby – another bird of prey, as the name suggests, though not yet arrived at his full maturity. Mr Lammle is made more of a villain than his wife, and it is clear early on that he too is cast as a bird of prey, and his wife is one of his victims:

So, the happy pair, with this hopeful marriage contract thus signed, sealed, and delivered, repair homeward. If when those infernal finger-marks were on the white and breathless countenance of Alfred Lammle, Esquire, they denoted that he conceived the purpose of subduing his dear wife Mrs Alfred Lammle, by at once divesting her of any lingering reality or pretence of self-respect, the purpose would seem to have been presently executed. The mature young lady has mighty little need of powder, now, for her downcast face, as he escorts her in the light of the setting sun to their abode of bliss. (Book I, Chapter 10)

The intimation here is of positive sadism. It is more than the insistent authority of Dombey, more sinister, more corrupt – the two have just made their bargain to maintain their union in order to make money, by fair means or foul, out of others – more directly suggesting that Mr Lammle's subduing of his wife is the significant intimacy of their marriage. The invocation of a romantic picture of newly wedded bliss in that last sentence, with the woman stripped of her power to deceive and the man declaring his sadistic purpose, adds a final, brilliant, razor-sharp edge to the whole scene.

Dickens spreads his birds of prey right across the social arena. Venus and Wegg must share the term, along with the more obviously disreputable Gaffer and Riderhood, and to bridge the gap between the low and the relatively high there is Bradley Headstone, the ambitious and apparently decent schoolmaster. But Bradley is in a class by himself, for his violence is born of madness, obsession and jealousy, rather than direct greed or lust, although the latter motives play their part. He is a murderer who does not kill for a livelihood, as the birds of prey on the river perhaps do, and a lover who does not indulge his emotions in search of idle pleasure, as Eugene does. The feelings that he has for Lizzie certainly are not those of ordinary love, nor of ordinary lust:

'I love you. What other men may mean when they use that expression, I cannot tell; what *I* mean is, that I am under the influence of some tremendous attraction which I have resisted in vain, and which overmasters me. You could draw me to fire, you could draw me to water, you could draw me to the gallows, you could draw me to any death, you could draw me to anything I have most avoided, you could draw me to any exposure and disgrace. This and the confusion of my thoughts, so that I am fit for nothing, is what I mean by your being the ruin of me.' (Book II, Chapter 15)

And she is the ruin of him. She draws him to attempted murder, potential disgrace, and death by water. There is no suggestion of anticipated pleasure or happiness in Bradley's proposal of marriage, no outline of domestic bliss, no real awareness of the object of his love as a personality. He sees Lizzie only as a force which he cannot resist, and which his pride assures him he need not resist. As if to emphasize the masochistic tendency of his obsession, Dickens describes him grinding his bare hand against a stone wall until the knuckles are bleeding.

Eugene is Bradley Headstone's prey, not Lizzie, and while Eugene hunts Lizzie, Bradley hunts Eugene, and Rogue Riderhood hunts Bradley, so that a curious imitation of the natural order of animal predators occurs. But there is nothing natural in murder, greed and lust operating in a highly artificial society, and this is just Dickens' point. On the one hand, human beings imitate the savagery of the untamed animal world; on the other, they imitate humanly constructed, unreal and artificial standards which have nothing to do with the true potential of humanity. But money and social aspiration have a great deal to do with both.

In all this, marriage is ideally an island. No man is an island, but man and woman joined in holy matrimony should be. To operate according to the rules of society is dangerous. The standards of society are destructive of true human values. To operate according to the rules of commerce and trade is also dangerous; if it is necessary to work for a living – and Dickens shared the feeling of Mrs Gaskell and many Victorians that to work with decency and dedication was itself a kind of moral victory – the battlefield of toil should not be brought within the home. And profound human feeling is dangerous, whether it is love, or ambition, or sorrow, or regret: all of these Dickens fends off, diffuses, except in those characters who are allowed to sink in a stormy world rather than find refuge on a matrimonial island.

Yet Dickens' novels are full of badly organized, unhappy, unsatisfactory marriages, as well as destructive and cannibalistic ones. In effect he opens an immense abyss between the happily united hero and heroine with their, at least, modest competency, and superfine awareness of bliss, and the rest of the world, who at best muddle along and learn to tolerate the Mrs Wilfers and the Mr Micawbers, if they do not actually savage each other. The men hunting their prey and the women bitterly nursing their defeats are firmly shut out of the domestic abode. And that is the reward of the just, to be able to close the door.

By 1859, WHEN George Eliot's *Adam Bede* and George Meredith's *The Ordeal of Richard Feverel* were published, there had been two significant pieces of legislation that had had some effect on Victorian marriage. The first was the Infants' Custody Act of 1839, which gave the Court of Chancery power to allow mothers custody of their children under the age of seven in cases of separation. The second was the Matrimonial Causes Act of 1857, which extended the possibilities of divorce. After 1857 women, if they could afford it, could divorce their husbands on grounds of cruelty, desertion or rape, but it was not until 1923 that they could obtain a divorce on grounds of the husband's adultery. Both these Acts had the effect of diminishing a little the legal authority of the husband and father. But divorced women were considered socially beyond the pale, and it was still assumed that children belonged naturally to their father.

Such legislation was symptomatic, if not radical. Women were more aware of the anomalies of their position, even if they still accepted them. This can be detected in the mainstream of fiction: so much of it, especially novels written by women, consciously sets out to illustrate the value of the woman's role, although usually emphasizing that the traditional role is the only satisfactory one. Eliza Lynn Linton, a prolific writer of the 1860s and '70s, is a revealing example of an alert and intelligent woman, commenting on a changing world and changing assumptions, severely critical of extremes, of women who demanded too much, who imitated men, or who were loose in their morals. Yet she understood that without, for instance, more economic independence, women could find themselves in a desperate situation.

Among the more famous of Mrs Linton's products were her essays on 'The Girl of the Period', initially published in the *Westminster Review* in the 1860s, and reprinted in book form. In these she criticized the 'fast' woman impatient of traditional restraints and making a noise about women's rights. But there is a revealing ambivalence in her writing. She saw women entirely in terms of what she thought men wanted them to be, but recognized the dangers of women being entirely at men's mercy, with no redress and no escape. She acknowledged that society was changing, yet felt profoundly that the essential activities of women were to be the devoted wife, the instinctive mother, the efficient housekeeper. 'What we would urge on woman is the value of a better system of life at home before laying claim to the discharge of extra-domestic duties abroad.' She emphasized that women had lost many of their traditional skills and cares, and argued that it was partly this, a weakening of responsibility, that was leading to undesirable changes. She failed to note the fact that these 'traditional' domestic responsibilities had grown only with the middle class itself; the feeling that, for instance, mothers should spend time with their children if they did not have to, was relatively new.

On one point, however, Eliza Lynn Linton was able to focus clearly. She showed how women often tried to have their cake and eat it too. They wanted to keep their pedestals, and enter the fray at the same time:

If they demand either mystic reverence or chivalric homage they must be content with their own narrow but safe enclosure, where they have nothing to do but to look at the turmoil below, and accept with gratitude such portions of the good things fought for as the men to whom they belong see fit to bring them. They cannot at one and the same time have the good of both positions – the courtesy claimed by weakness and the honour paid to prowess. If they mingle in the *mêlée* they must expect as hard knocks as the rest, and must submit to be bullied when they hit foul and to be struck home when they hit wide. If they do not like these conditions, let them keep out of the fray altogether: but if they choose to mingle in it, no hysterics of affronted womanhood, however loud the shrieks, will keep them safe from hard knocks and rough treatment. (*The Girl of the Period and Other Social Essays*, Volume I, pages 83–84)

Mrs Linton was herself a robust and energetic woman who coped with an odd and unsuccessful marriage, and took on the world and her career with great energy. She and George Eliot met on several occasions, but did not like each other. Eliza Linton disapproved of George Eliot's irregular liaison with G. H. Lewes, and envied her success. While she made some money out of her writing and received some popular fame, George Eliot made a lot of money and was an object of homage in the literary world. In fact, George Eliot was precisely a woman who 'had the good of both positions'. She ultimately received both courtesy and honour, and Mrs Linton, struggling honestly with the process of change, found this unacceptable.

This gives us a clue as to the remarkable qualities of George Eliot as a woman and a writer. She kept aloof from causes, but her commitment to a moral outlook that comprehended the difficulties of women and the anomalies of marriage gave her a natural sympathy with the women's movement. Barbara Bodichon, a leading figure in the movement, was a close friend. George Eliot disliked Eliza Linton, but it is probably true that the latter's grasp of the practical issues that faced women, married and unmarried, during this period was greater than George Eliot's. It was the larger issues that always concerned the greater writer.

George Eliot, or Marian Evans, came from a background of solid Warwickshire farmers who were concerned with life on a more fundamental level than that of London society. Only one of her novels, apart from the historical *Romola*, moves out of a small, enclosed, individually characterized and apparently self-contained area, and this is *Daniel Deronda*, her last. During the years that she was writing, the most widely read fiction was set either in London or in the middle- to upper-class range of social living, so that love and marriage was almost always seen in terms of money and artificial status and standards. Mrs Linton's own novels were examples, although she continually wrote against the mercenary marriage. The people she wrote about were just the sort most likely to marry for reasons other than love. They were people who, in spite of owning land and property in a particular area, had no real identity with it. They were the kind of people for whom marriage was most likely to be a transaction.

George Eliot, on the other hand, wrote about marriage in a context of work, a closely identified way of life, community, and the emotional and practical needs of ordinary humanity. If her approach was rather different from that of Mrs Gaskell, her concerns were similar. Of course her major characters, Maggie Tulliver, for instance, did not necessarily find what they needed within the context that nourished them: in such a situation lies the drama of fiction. Marian Evans herself had early developed a scepticism about marriage. She comments somewhat drily on the marriage of her brother: 'my Brother Isaac . . . seems to have a suitable partner as far as similarity of taste and domestic habits are concerned, and I think we have reason to hope for his worldly prosperity' (*Letters*, Volume I, page 112). In her early twenties, Marian Evans had no illusions as to promises of marital bliss. At the age of thirty she was reading with great admiration the works of George Sand, who pronounced marriage '*une des plus barbares institutions*'.

Until the death of her father in 1849, when she was in her thirtieth year, George Eliot was intimately involved in family life. Her father had married twice, and she had a brother and sister of her own and, much older, a stepbrother and step-sister. Their families, wives, husbands and children she cared about a great deal, and one of the great sadnesses in her life was their rejection of her when she and Lewes made it known that they were living together. But though she enjoyed her sister Chrissey's children, she clearly thought it a mistake that she had so many, and although she valued her relationship with her brother Isaac, she was not particularly impressed by his marriage. Family life in itself was not attractive to her, certainly not as demonstrated in the mid-

Victorian ideal, but kin and companionship were profoundly important. Her novels are very much about this.

Through her friendship with Charles and Caroline Bray, who lived in Coventry and were in touch with the literary and intellectual world, George Eliot came to London early in 1851. She lived at the house of the publisher, John Chapman, who was publishing her first literary work, a translation of David Friedrich Strauss's *Leben Jesu*. This was her introduction not only to one of the liveliest centres of literary and intellectual life in London, but also to an emotional life which had until then little existence for her. In addition to Chapman himself (who maintained, in a most un-Victorian household, his publishing business, his wife, his children, his mistress, and George Eliot), she was also deeply influenced by the philosopher Herbert Spencer, and finally by George Henry Lewes himself who already had, when she met him, an extensive reputation as a writer and journalist.

In 1854 George Lewes and Marian Evans were united in what George Eliot always referred to as her marriage. Lewes had left his wife before he met George Eliot, she maintaining a long-standing affair with Thornton, son of Leigh Hunt, and producing several children by him. Lewes's acknowledgment of these children as his own, to save his wife's reputation, eliminated what could have been proof of adultery for the purposes of a divorce. It was never possible for Lewes and George Eliot to marry, yet George Eliot always considered herself married, insisted that people should address her as Mrs Lewes, and made it clear repeatedly that she did not advocate extra-marital unions. (A number of advanced women who claimed her as their own because she was not married were repulsed.)

The liaison was in every way successful. Lewes gave her the support and encouragement she needed in her writing. They lived together in a union of trust, loyalty and devotion, through many trials, not the least being George Eliot's outcast state from society, which only the enormous proportions of her literary reputation finally mitigated, until Lewes's death in 1878. They had no children, a deliberate choice as far as can be established, and George Eliot had no time for domestic concerns. She resented the responsibilities that owning a house brought her. As long as they lived in lodgings she did not have to concern herself with housekeeping, but even with servants the ownership of property inevitably meant interruptions to her work, even if only to order dinner.

While George Eliot was virtually ostracized, Lewes moved freely in society. Only when her fame had reached the heights did people find it convenient to forget the irregularity of her position so that they could join in the homage that was paid to her. Those who expected to find her mannish and unattractive were disillusioned, for although she was much too strong-featured to conform to conventional expectations of feminine beauty, and was briskly, often tactlessly, critical of many of the people she met, many friends and acquaintances recorded the attraction of her personality.

When she was very young George Eliot had recognized the fact that she was deeply ambitious, and it worried her. It was contrary to what she was being brought up to consider important in a woman. By the time she was fifty she was acknowledged as a novelist of high achievement and was earning a great deal of money – far more than Lewes ever earned. Their material advancement, which of course helped her social acceptability, was due to her success. Of all the nineteenth century's successful writers, and there were many of them, George Eliot was probably the least compromised by her achievements, the least changed in terms of personality and endeavour. She owed this to a great extent to the depth of her moral and personal commitment, a quality that in her earlier life had brought her pain – she found it difficult to cope with people who were less committed than herself – but which ultimately triumphed.

In May, 1880, a year and a half after Lewes's death, George Eliot married John Cross, twenty years younger than herself, who had been devoted to her for some years. In December of the same year she died. Her life and her personal strength are a salutary antidote to the usual assumptions about Victorian life and marriage, and to the mainstream of writing about these things. In fiction George Eliot would have been at best a tragic sacrifice on the altar of mistaken endeavour. At worst she would have been an outcast, like Edith Dombey, and would have been rewarded with some suitably grim punishment. It is worth noting this, as so much of Victorian fiction is obsessively concerned with the verdict of society. Society provides the moral force. It shapes lives, it condemns and punishes, it adulates and rewards. And even those authors who try to attack society – and this was happening more often in the 1880s and '90s – found it almost always impossible to free themselves from its ominous force.

Eliza Linton's novel, *The World Well Lost* (1877), is an example. In it an eminently respectable woman stands by her weak husband, who has served a long prison sentence for fraud. But although she stands by him, she has kept the truth from her children, who throughout his fifteen years' absence have believed that he was 'abroad'. Inevitably the truth comes out, on his return, and the children are exposed to the horror and scorn of society. It is all the harder for them to bear, as they have been brought up by their mother well protected from the realities of life and with the highest moral attitudes. In other words, the mother has conformed to the demands, not of what society is, but of what society pretends to be in the upbringing of her children, and the children have to pay for this. Their father is completely beyond what their mother has taught them to respect.

The novel is not centrally about this. It is about the marriage prospects of the son and daughter. But it is this aspect that is most interesting. Like so many Victorian writers, Mrs Linton was able to diagnose a social ambiguity, an example of injustice and rigidity and hypocrisy, but did not know quite what to do with her diagnosis. She shows very cleverly how the most powerful social forces twist morality to suit a materialistic outlook and, like Marie Corelli and other late Victorian women writers, is all for true love. One of her characters, who has breeding but no money, castigates the penniless girl who is in love with her son:

You are a shameless young woman . . . Your love is as immodest as it is selfish. Love! It is not in the nature of a good girl to care for any man in this frantic manner, and I am more than ever against the marriage, seeing what an undesirable person you are in yourself. Poverty, obscure birth, doubtful history – all are nothing compared to this shamelessness, this want of maidenly dignity and reserve! (Volume II, Chapter 6)

Lady Machell converts her insistence that her son must marry money into a moral weapon. The girl is selfish because she won't give him up, and shameless because she reiterates her love. The reader is intended to condemn Lady Machell and to sympathize with the loyal and loving heroine.

One of the most striking characteristics in all Eliza Linton's writing is her inability to commit herself. She can isolate the fault, but has no consistency of purpose in suggesting a cure. At the end of *The World Well Lost* there is a flurry of reconciliation, and all in all the characters get their just deserts according to a very conventional, social moral standard. There is no scope for individual morality. Where difficult choices have to be made, events, or other people, help to make them less difficult. Either things just happen to them, and they are martyrs from incapability rather than from choice, or outside forces opportunely assist in solving the difficulty.

If we look at George Eliot's life, and at her novels, we can see that this kind of thing just does not happen. The same weapons are in operation as in Mrs Linton's fictional society, but the protagonists either have to stand up and fight, and be prepared to lose a great deal in the process, or retreat. There is nothing else at hand to fight the battles for them. If it seems that in George Eliot's novels the ultimate answer is very often retreat and compromise, whereas in her own life she did neither, this may reflect her own very intimate understanding of the difficulties. Social and moral pressures disadvantaged women. In George Eliot's novels it is her heroines who have to compromise.

George Eliot's place in the growing awareness of injustice to women is difficult to pinpoint. We might have thought that on specific issues, such as divorce, or property rights, she would have had something to say. But she never questioned Lewes's continuing acknowledgment of his wife – he supported her and her legitimate and illegitimate offspring until his death, after which George Eliot continued the job – or his use of her money. She paid her earnings into his account in spite of the fact that, being unmarried, they were legally hers. Until 1873 if she had been his wife they would have been his.

But her general attitudes are clear. She was genuinely dubious about most women's abilities to cope responsibly with political and social ideas. For her personally a loving, happy and successfully union with a man, combined with a rewarding profession, obviated the need for women's rights. Of course, she was scarcely typical. Her own identity as a separate individual with a name of her own (George Eliot rather than Mrs George Lewes, in spite of her insistence) was unchallenged. She could be economically independent whenever she chose. She had at various periods lived on her own, and travelled on her own, and though she acknowledged her need for other people she was not wholly dependent on them. She was impatient of domestic tasks, yet she had run a house and cared for her father during several years of ill-health, and was well able to look after herself. She did not appear to need those rights that she felt other women did not deserve. She did not care enough about property to want to campaign for the right to own it: to her it was as much a burden as a pleasure. Even if she had had the vote she would most likely have remained outside party politics, and the principles involved in the feminist movement did not seem to concern her.

Yet her profoundest interests lay with women who had hopes and aspirations beyond the conventional, women who wanted to achieve things, however vague, who were impatient of the aims usually attributed to them. She wrote about women who are singled out because they are unusual, untypical, unrepresentative, too much so perhaps to be allied to a cause, but who are nevertheless symbolic of the deeper stirrings and frustrations of women's life in general. Her heroines, Dinah Morris, Maggie Tulliver, Dorothea Brooke, Gwendolen Harleth, are all women who want more than conventional attitudes would be ready to grant them. But they are not rebels, let alone revolutionaries, though there is a touch of the rebel in Maggie Tulliver. They are not like Meredith's heroines, who strike out for themselves against immense pressures to conform and submit, and carve out independent lives. It is as if George Eliot wished to anchor her heroines in 'normal' society – and almost always she characterized that normality very carefully – for the purposes of demonstrating that, if they were unusual in terms of conventional assumptions about what women ought to do with themselves, they were not unusual in terms of humanity, history and the needs and wants of women in general.

There is a continuity in the society that George Eliot describes. Like Scott, whom she greatly admired and whose influence on her writing is readily detectable, she is historically specific in terms of place and time, while suggesting continually that what she is describing has both a past and a future, that she has chosen a moment in a process, a development, a movement. So that Hetty Sorrel, so specifically rooted in the context of the year 1799 in a particular kind of farming community in a particular part of middle England, is a representative figure also, both socially and historically. In fact, it is interesting to see Hetty as a re-interpretation of Scott's Effie Deans in *The Heart of Midlothian*. Hetty combines both Effie and Scott's heroine, her sister Jeanie: she, like Jeanie, makes a journey to the centre of government, not precisely to see the Queen, but to Windsor, which is suggestive. If Hetty's journey has more of the pathetic than the epic about it, it does, like Jeanie's, accent and isolate her. Hetty, like Effie, is a victim almost unaware of the part she herself has played in that victimization.

George Eliot was interested in the way that society, and specific communities, threw up potential heroes and heroines, and the way in which these people interacted with the communities that tested them. An explanation of her popularity as a novelist may lie in the fact that she went so far beyond and beneath the artificial structure of society that dominated most fiction. She allows her characters no easy successes. Her heroes and heroines are almost all potential rather than fulfilled. She brings them to the moment of crisis, but then does not, or cannot, force them through to the far side of the great test. Adam Bede, Maggie Tulliver, Dorothea Brooke, Dr Lydgate, are all like this. These characters are all primed for heroic achievement, but are then evened out, cut down to size, or, in the case of Maggie and, virtually, of Lydgate, they are destroyed. In a number of ways most of George Eliot's fiction is a re-enactment of the prologue to *Middlemarch*. So many of her heroes and heroines can be seen as potential St Theresas, who find in the end no outlet for their passions and talents. Adam Bede, so much admired and respected, fails the test of his love for Hetty Sorrel. Dinah Morris is forbidden to preach – her great talent – because the Methodists decide that women preachers do more harm than good. There is nothing for Maggie Tulliver to do with her burgeoning personality, and although we can question the success of the ending of *The Mill on the Floss*, it is only too easy to understand the rationale of a catastrophic death. The remarkable Felix Holt doesn't do anything much, after all. The book is often criticized because of this, but isn't this just what it is about? It seems precisely in tune with the tendencies in most of George Eliot's fiction.

George Eliot carefully establishes situations and contexts, allows character and drama to ferment, and then, as it were, exposes the whole thing to the air, to the reality, of that very context she has so explicitly described. There is a kind of neutralizing effect in this, which is both profoundly impressive, for we think we are seeing a solid, real, complete society at work, and naggingly frustrating. Do we not really want Maggie and Dorothea, even Esther Lyon in *Felix Holt*, even poor Hetty Sorrel, to make more of themselves? And do we not see a little of how this could be done within the terms that George Eliot herself establishes? Are we convinced that it is necessary for them to fail?

In *Middlemarch* she talks about Providence and inevitability, forces which weigh down on human activity. The stage isn't set for glamorous heroics, but for the trials and disappointments of ordinary life, for ordinary failures, ordinary successes. It does seem very extraordinary that George Eliot should have had such success as a novelist at a time when so much fiction, even of the highest order, was concerned with the triumph of heightened individuals. In this kind of fiction the talk is of Fate and Destiny. Heroes and heroines relate, not to an ordinary prosaic community life, but to a world of enlarged challenges and more glamorous rewards. Marriage is not seen as a normal way for people to live together and cope with society, but as a climax, sometimes a crisis, towards which all their expectations have strained. Yet it is perhaps because George Eliot's fiction is not like this that, as I have suggested, so many people wanted to read her.

Like Elizabeth Gaskell, George Eliot makes her marriages out of work and community and limited, sometimes half-blind vision. Neither novelist saw marriage as a function particularly of women, but as a function of society. It is against this that we must set George Eliot's very evident awareness of what marriage meant and did in particular to women – in *Middlemarch* and *Daniel Deronda* she could hardly be more explicit. Unlike Meredith, she did not write about marriage as a sign of lopsided and damaging values; rather, it is the very heart of social continuity. Unlike some of her contemporary feminists, she did indeed believe that in marriage lay fulfilment, and it is in the context of this belief that Maggie's, and Dorothea's, and Gwendolen's difficulties arise. It is when they have to do with men and attempts to come to terms with marriage that these women become confused.

It is not really appropriate to discuss these issues without mentioning George Eliot's irony, for it is at work all the time, and as well as influencing the reader's response it operates as a useful check to ultimate commitment in the writer. I think that George Eliot can be accused of a failure of commitment, and this will emerge in the following chapters. There are times when Providence and an ironic approach, both of which in the hands of George Eliot are skilful aids to a balanced perspective, hold back an element of daring, of taking up the challenge that she herself creates. Her finales sometimes appear to be welded with irony on to a dramatic structure that might be thought to have promised something else.

Yet her public bore witness to the fact that her grasp of human action and aspiration, her strong moral vision, her rooted sense of continuity and human intercourse, nourished the imagination of the period. And that she spoke to women in particular is evident, for women adulated her. Many felt that she wrote just for them, that she illuminated their special problems, that she understood their lives with uncanny exactitude. Was it that her readership included thousands of women who had a vague inarticulate awareness of frustration in their own lives, though they were told that they had what they wanted, and didn't dare confess even to themselves that they wanted more? If we consider the ambivalence of Eliza Lynn Linton, aware of the limitations of tradition yet reluctant to concede to new forces, or the immense seriousness with which women writers in particular were trying to come to terms with what they diagnosed as significant contemporary problems, or the continual exposure of the vulnerability of women and the limitations of marriage, it seems fair enough to suggest a positive reply. Inevitably George Eliot was involved in the questioning about marriage and what women ought to be and do. Because she was not limited and not partisan it was all the more likely that her writing should be taken to heart by very many readers.

LOVE AND THE COMMUNITY

GEORGE ELIOT wrote about men and women bound by close ties of kinship and proximity, struggling to tolerate each other, to slot together in a workable fashion as pieces of a larger and essential entity. Although her heroes and heroines often try to separate themselves from ordinary life they can never achieve separation. They are subject to the forces and fluctuations of a community. In *Adam Bede* Adam is suddenly faced with the consequences of human weakness and thoughtlessness which his distinctive strength could never have considered as a possibility. In *Middlemarch* Lydgate is overtaken by human prejudice which he failed to recognize as a radical characteristic of the community in which he operates. If the hero has traditionally been a character who rises above society to confirm his independence, George Eliot's major characters are not heroic. Only Daniel Deronda, who most readers agree is not an entirely successful characterization, has an awareness of a lack of identity which grows into a kind of independence.

George Eliot's first stories, published as *Scenes of Clerical Life* (1858), are unhappy. They are about failures of understanding and communication. From them emerges an ironic illumination of marriage as providing the roots and nourishment of a community, but also a feeding-ground for individual pain and tragedy. This apprehension of the basic institution of human intercourse as both sustaining and damaging is present in all her fiction.

A year after *Scenes of Clerical Life*, pessimistic in tone but well received, she published *Adam Bede*, which was a great success. Its richness and more positive view of life is very largely due to its setting in an active and productive rural community, where we never lose sight of the operation of natural growth and human effort. This is its vital context. It is against this that George Eliot weighs her assessment of unhappiness and human wastage. It is not some conventional ideal that she invites us to contemplate, but a grasp of the way human beings can co-operate and work together and make the best of an imperfect society.

Early in the novel there is a portrait of discontent in the family life of Mrs Bede and her two sons, and the alcoholic father who will shortly be dead:

Family likeness has often a deep sadness in it. Nature that great tragic dramatist, knits us together by bone and muscle, and divides us by the subtler web of our brains; blends yearning and repulsion; and ties us by our heartstrings to the beings that jar us at every movement. We hear a voice with the very cadence of our own uttering the thoughts we despise; we see eyes – ah! so like our mother's – averted from us in cold alienation; and our last darling child startles us with the air and gestures of the sister we parted from in bitterness long years ago. The father to whom we owe our best heritage – the mechanical instinct, the keen sensibility to harmony, the unconscious skill of the modelling hand – galls us, and puts us to shame by his daily errors; the long-lost mother, whose face we begin to see in the glass as our own wrinkles come, once fretted our young souls with her anxious humours and irrational persistence. (Chapter 4)

Here is the family as a network of frustrations and enmities, all the more intense for 'natural' closeness. No novelist of the nineteenth century described so well the hostilities, jealousies and petty quarrels of family life as did George Eliot. She questions the naturalness of human relations within the most intimate unit of living. This is a very physical passage, 'bone and muscle', 'yearning and repulsion', 'brains', 'heartstrings', 'wrinkles' and the 'modelling hand', as if to remind us that living with people is a physical reality, not just a question of the various members of a family taking their proper places in a hierarchy. Parents and children, brothers and sisters, husbands and wives, live together, simultaneously linked and separate, aware of natural ties and resentful of them, submitting their individuality and protecting it.

In the families that George Eliot goes on to describe, in *Adam Bede* and in subsequent novels, there are qualities of reality that go far beyond the slots of authority and obedience, of polite affection, that are so apparent in so much Victorian fiction.

The striking feature of the Bede family is that husband and wife and the two sons are all so different from each other. They don't seem to belong to a single unit: they 'jar' on each other. The sons have no respect for the father who taught them their trade. Seth can tolerate his querulous mother but Adam barely can. The mother is loving and anxious for her children, but doesn't know what to do to make life better for them. The father, in his alcoholism, has opted out of his responsibilities as husband, father and working-man. This is the context of Adam's severity, his uprightness, which is so much admired, and so unforgiving. Adam is stronger than Seth, more positive, but he has a potential for cruelty which Seth totally lacks.

We move from the Bedes to the Irwine household. Mr Irwine, the vicar, is bland and civilized, in accordance with upbringing and education. He lives tastefully but not wealthily. A clue to the sensibilities of the household can be seen in the remarks of his mother:

Nature never makes a ferret in the shape of a mastiff. You'll never persuade me that I can't tell what men are by their outsides. If I don't like a man's looks, depend upon it I shall never like *him*. I don't want to know people that look ugly and disagreeable. . . . If they make me shudder at the first glance, I say, take them away. (Chapter 5)

For the Irwines, and for others living in comfortable stability, the idea that people might not be what they seem is too disturbing to tolerate. If the outsides are not seen as a reflection of character and morality there would seem to be little importance in appearances, and if appearances are not important, then elegance, and tasteful living, good furniture and clothes and nicely decorated houses are not important. The whole tendency of George Eliot's morality is to see ferret and mastiff in everyone. Her judgment of the Irwines and the kind of society they represent is that, in not being able to do this, they are guilty of a radical failure. It is appearances, Hetty Sorrel's freshness and beauty which *everyone* in the book finds beguiling, that lead Arthur Donnithorne to actions that he knows are contrary to everything he ought to stand for.

It is with the Poysers that we find a standard by which our judgment can operate. We see the Poyser farm in juxtaposition to 'the grey church-tower and village roofs', and also as a kind of natural growth. 'It is a very fine old place, of red brick, softened by a pale powdery lichen, which has dispersed itself with happy irregularity, so as to bring the red brick into terms of friendly companionship with the limestone ornaments surrounding the three gables, the windows, and the door-place' (Chapter 6). This impression of the features of the farm in living relationship to each other is enhanced.

Plenty of life there! though this is the drowsiest time of the year, just before hay-harvest; and it is the drowsiest time of the day, too, for it is close upon three by the sun, and it is half-past three by Mrs Poyser's handsome eight-day clock. But there is always a stronger sense of life when the sun is brilliant after rain; and now he is pouring down his beams, and making sparkles among the wet straw, and lighting up every patch of vivid green moss on the red tiles of the cow-shed, and turning even the muddy water that is hurrying along the channel to the drain into a mirror for the yellow-billed ducks, who are seizing the opportunity of getting a drink with as much body in it as possible. There is quite a concert of noises; the great bull-dog, chained against the stables, is thrown into furious exasperation by the unwary approach of a cock too near the mouth of his kennel, and sends forth a thundering bark, which is answered by two fox-hounds shut up in the opposite cow-house; the old top-knotted hens, scratching with their chicks among the straw, set up a sympathetic croaking as the discomfited cock joins them; a sow with her brood, all very muddy as to the legs, and curled as to the tail, throws in some deep staccato notes; our friends the calves are bleating from the home croft; and, under all, a fine ear discerns the continuous hum of human voices. (Chapter 6)

This is the Poyser community – for it is more than a family, and it is perhaps in this that its suggestion of containing a positive, creative force lies. It is a collection of people bound together, some by kinship and all by a shared purpose in continuous work. Mrs Poyser's qualities are those of hard work and keen responsibility, and she expects both from those who work with her. They are judged by practical standards, as to whether they work willingly, churn good butter, brew good beer, or treat little Totty, the youngest Poyser child, with lively affection. In the Poyser context these are human values which cannot be detached from work and productivity. That they are not fully adequate the subsequent fate of Hetty Sorrel will demonstrate. But they are more adequate than most when measured against, say, the calm neutrality of the Irwines, or the good-natured egocentricity of Arthur Donnithorne, as is conveyed by the energy of relationships, human and otherwise, on Poyser's farm.

Marriage and family life – the whole quality of life – are seen as inseparable from work. The work itself is a way of life. But although rural life is richly conveyed, and the sense of pleasure in natural growth and harvest is profound, there is no idealism in this picture. The fact that such a scene has nurtured the tragedy of Hetty Sorrel would be enough to weigh against such an interpretation, but there is something much more radical than that to suggest that this is a community working continually against difficulties, weaknesses and failures. Mrs Poyser is energetic, and Mr Poyser is benign, but neither of them are of any great stature as people. Removed from the work that they do what would they be? Taken away from their practical understanding, patronizingly praised by the gentry, of good butter and good grain, their humanity would be unremarkable. And Adam himself is characterized in terms of his skill and appreciation as a carpenter. He is not an upright man who happens to be a good carpenter, but a man in whom skill and morality and dedication in his work are inseparable. We can contrast him with Arthur Donnithorne, who has no particular skill or dedication, but birth and status. Both, though, are beguiled by appearances.

The closeness of the Poyser community is underlined when the initial reaction to Hetty's killing of her illegitimate child is to feel that they will have to leave that part of the country. The failure of one individual can affect the whole community. They are all damaged and they must all suffer. Here are the 'heartstrings' in operation. The brain may condemn Hetty and wipe her out, as society tries to do, but the heart will not allow it. Hetty is kin, and they must all take her shame unto themselves.

The tragedy unites Adam with the Poysers, but he never becomes fully a part of the Poyser community. In fact in the larger community he has maintained his own sense of being distinctive and separate, and has been encouraged to do so by others. What he had to learn was that he wasn't above making mistakes about people nor beyond the reach of tragedy. He is a more sympathetic man, and less severe, than he was before Hetty's sacrifice, but if his pride is diminished his self-awareness is not: he *knows* he is a better man. I think there is a failure at the novel's close, for George Eliot does not positively characterize the 'fuller life' and 'higher feelings' that have come to Adam as a result of sorrow, except in showing how he falls in love with Dinah Morris. But he has always understood Dinah's worth, and when they marry she has been deprived of some of her strength and achievement by the fact that she is no longer allowed to preach. The final characterization of Dinah as devoted, gentle wife, accommodating in her household two men who love her – Adam, and his brother Seth who had wanted Dinah as his wife long before the thought occurred to Adam – seems neither convincing nor rewarding. For those aspects of Dinah's personality, her quick and decisive independence, which saved her from an insipid priggishness, have been shorn away.

But the ultimate effect is to even out the levels of humanity. Arthur is brought low. Even Mr Irwine has a salutary experience. Adam is less prideful. The Poysers come to terms with pain. Mrs Bede finds it less difficult to reconcile herself with her unsatisfactory lot. There are no revolutions in status, character or way of life. The old conventions, assumptions and inadequate values are not disturbed. Life goes on as before, and the basic institutions of life go on. It is fundamental to unheroic drama that this should be the case, that neither tragedy nor happiness should have finality.

In *The Mill on the Floss* (1860) there is, if anything, an even more rooted sense of established continuity. In this novel there is a more precise notion of families, in particular the Dodson sisters and their respective husbands, taking a firm grip on life and controlling it, and finding signs of disorder deeply offensive. The Dodson sisters have their own cherished symbols of order and respectability, like Mrs Tulliver's best sheets set aside for the last rites, and these are sacred. Habits of propriety, hats for special occasions that may only be worn once, care with money, all these are pivotal in the Dodson outlook on life. They cope with its anarchy by erecting some sort of camouflage of principles rigidly adhered to.

In the Dodson scheme of things marriage is a question of money, an appropriate household, and appropriate objects to put into that household. When bankruptcy descends on the Tullivers Mrs Tulliver's greatest worry is whether the dinner service and the table linen will stay in the family. As she sees it the greatest act of loyal support that her sisters can perform is to buy up these possessions so that they will not end up in the houses of strangers. Although there is irony in this Mrs Tulliver is a woman of practical sense, and on the level at which life is normally lived this sense would be adequate. There is something to be said for valuing dinner plates, for they are actual, tangible objects that are useful even if the best dinner service is put away and never used. In some circumstances things are more valuable and worthwhile than people.

In the community of St Ogg's and its surroundings – and as always George Eliot's focus on a particular locality is so strong that it moulds our reactions – marriage is a state as unchanging as table-cloths. It can be damaged, but it is an absolute that does not allow for growth or the accommodation of non-conformity. It is in this context that Maggie is presented, in her earliest childhood unable to conform to the requirements of the Dodsons and St Ogg's, and torn by her passionate desire to be acceptable, and her equally passionate longing for more than life seems to hold out for her. Her relationship with her brother Tom epitomizes this. She will do anything to be accepted by him, negate herself to the most drastic extent. At the same time she is aware that she is cleverer and more courageous than he is, and resents the fact that, being a girl, she won't have his opportunities to develop her potential. Only her father enjoys her individuality, and the Dodson verdict on him is not favourable.

When crisis comes George Eliot writes of the 'four widely differing beings' who make up the family and have an increasing sense of their lack of cohesion. The *Mill on the Floss* is a family tragedy, the tragedy of a family dependent on an integral unity which it doesn't, cannot, have. The family is fragmented because it is so vulnerable to outside forces at the same time as being committed to family continuity, family work, family values. So much of George Eliot's writing is suggestive of this kind of failure, the failure of people living together who dare not recognize each other's individuality because they are fearful of snapping the threads that bind them, and losing their identity as family and community.

George Eliot exposes a paradox. She shows that it is the family that provides the continuum, the necessary human context of the larger movements of society and history. At the same time it is the family, and the community that sustains it, that stifles individual endeavour. Of all George Eliot's heroines Maggie is most patently a victim of this. But her father is also. As with Adam Bede, crisis levels him, and opinion provides the machinery for cutting him down to size. There is a kind of tragedy in the levelling; but, George Eliot seems to suggest, art cannot pause to heighten tragedy. It must move on just as life moves on. If the purpose of art is to measure life – and that is what it would seem to be in her hands – it cannot afford to linger and risk destroying perspective and proportion.

Marriage is static. Maggie, like her sister heroines Dorothea and Gwendolen, is not. As a little girl she ranges round her home, in reality and imagination, running away to the gypsies – a preview of her unpremeditated escape with Stephen Guest. The marriages of the different Dodson sisters are each a nucleus of unchanging values, and none of these can accommodate Maggie. She is happiest with the improvident and disorderly family of Mr Tulliver's sister, whose standards of cash and cleanliness do not measure up to the Dodsons'. Amongst the higher society of St Ogg's conformity operates just as strictly. But Maggie doesn't fit in any more aptly with the Deanes and the Guests: in fact Stephen is attracted to her because of her peculiarity, although he declares to Lucy, his fiancée, that she is too 'fiery' for him.

So George Eliot uses an accepted pattern of marriage and family – and she shows just how it is accepted and how it operates – to throw into relief the unusualness and ambitions of her heroine. She does something similar in *Middlemarch* (1871) although there the pattern of marriage and society is much more detailed and more widely structured. In *Felix Holt* (1866) it is not the heroine who emerges from conformity, for George Eliot's attempt to demonstrate the education of the sensibility of Esther Lyon does not work very well, but the hero. What is interesting is that this emergence is so much less striking and meaningful than that of the more arresting heroines. Felix is like Lydgate in *Middlemarch*. He acts with all the privileges and the lack of local conformity of an outsider. Daniel Deronda is akin to these heroes too. He does not identify himself with the society where he takes his place. But George Eliot's heroines do, inevitably, and this sense of identity comes into conflict very often with their restless hankering after a wider scope of activity. Felix Holt's starting-point is beyond the conflict that shapes the drama of Maggie, Dorothea and Gwendolen.

Amongst women only the highly eccentric and the socially unacceptable can come sweeping in from outside and make their mark on an established community. Acceptable women have to be static, and are often victims. Only the Brontës were able to reverse this to some extent, but Charlotte's Jane Eyre and Lucy Snowe, and Ann's Helen Grant, have to run the gauntlet of social condemnation. There is in Maggie Tulliver an evocation, surely deliberate, of Scott's free women, Madge Wildfire and Meg Merrilies. Maggie is tall and dark and fiery. She says what she thinks, unhampered by convention – although she suffers for it. Maggie's meeting with Philip Waken amongst the trees in the Red Deeps, where there is a strong sense of uncanny wildness, is reminiscent of Meg Merrilies in the woods in *Guy Mannering*. Although George Eliot read and admired the Brontës, particularly *Villette*, Maggie Tulliver seems to owe more to Scott's 'dark' heroines. The fact that George Eliot's heroines are physically on a large scale, have an impressive aspect – it does not have to be beauty – and act with more eloquent and extrovert gestures than all but Emily Brontë's Catherine, suggests that she places them on a much wider canvas than the Brontës handle.

The context is historical more than social, for she places this expansiveness in small, introverted societies where there is not scope for it to develop creatively, and where the real test is whether it can operate with any point at all. In *Middlemarch*, of all the novels, this is the crux. Dorothea has her illusions and limitations, but the most striking features of her personality are her directness and her honesty. It is astonishing how quickly she becomes aware of the extent of Casaubon's sterility, even supposing, as I think we must, that the marriage has never been consummated. She does not try to avoid admitting to herself that she was wrong in her expectations. It is her honesty that irks Casaubon. When, hours before his death, he asks her to give a blanket promise not to do anything that she knows he would disapprove of, she cannot bring herself to do it. When she is finally prepared to give the promise – and before she can do this she has to be convinced that she will *keep* the promise – it is too late and Casaubon is dead. Ironically the biggest sacrifice that the heroine who longs to sacrifice herself for others is called upon to make escapes her in the nick of time.

Dorothea's aspirations operate in a compromising world of imperfect marriages and imperfect understanding within families. Yet for all the misunderstanding, mistakes and damage that is done, the people of Middlemarch have little evil in them. Just as George Eliot can scarcely allow heroes, there is no place for villains either. It is not outside forces and personalities that cause the damage in this corner of provincial society, although Lydgate is seen by some as a villainous intruder. It is individual mistakes and weaknesses, and the composite social forces that these generate. Perhaps we could do with more distinct 'badness' in Middlemarch society. Perhaps there is too much benignity, too many good intentions. Perhaps George Eliot's general tendency towards levelling individuals robs her fiction of some of its edge. It is worth noting that in *Middlemarch* the middle-aged households have an air of comfortable tolerance, and even where offspring cause friction they do so where they are offending against this comfortable tolerance. The implication is that the older people get, the older Dorothea herself gets in her marriage to Ladislaw, the more the important things in life become a matter of immediate details, the things that money can buy and good humour can enjoy, rather than of large issues.

Even where there is a profound disturbance, as with the Bulstrodes, or real concern about money, as with the Vincys, the established tenor of married life does not appear to be destroyed. That is partly why Rosamond finds Lydgate's difficulties, and the effect that they have on their daily life, impossible to understand. Such things should not interfere. She has been brought up to believe that marriage means security, a certain standard of comfort and freedom from petty concerns. She expects to be her own mistress, and the nature of that expectation has been moulded by her father's household, where she has been indulged. Her parents and relations have taught her that, with her beauty and her status, she is owed a good marriage, i.e. a financially secure marriage, and she cannot accept that she hasn't got it.

The Lydgate marriage collapses rapidly. In his way Lydgate is as honest about its failure as Dorothea is about her own delusions, and he is as ready to bear the consequences. But although Lydgate and Dorothea are clear parallels, one of the reasons for the failure of the Lydgate marriage is that Lydgate and Rosamond are very much alike. Lydgate is ambitious and arrogant. He cannot seriously contemplate the possibility of failure. He would scorn to have a wife who was not both decorative and accomplished:

. . . that distinction of mind which belonged to his intellectual ardour, did not penetrate his feeling and judgment about furniture, or women, or the desirability of it being known (without his telling) that he was better born than other country surgeons. He did not mean to think of furniture at present; but whenever he did so, it was to be feared that neither biology nor schemes of reform would lift him above the vulgarity of feeling that there would be an incompatibility in his furniture not being of the best. (Chapter 15)

Dorothea too is above a life of thinking of furniture, which is I suppose how Celia's life with Sir James could be described. At the same time, although she does not share the 'vulgarity' of Lydgate in having an instinct towards the best in 'things', she is quite certain that she must have the best in minds. Where we find Rosamond resembling Lydgate is in her ambition, which equals his. She is as acute in her determination to make an admirable marriage as he is to have an admirable career. And she is as ready to present herself as decorative and accomplished as he is to assume that that is what he requires a wife to be. For Rosamond marriage is 'a prospect of rising in rank and getting a little nearer to that celestial condition on earth in which she could have nothing to do with vulgar people, and perhaps at last associate with relatives quite equal to the county people who looked down on the Middlemarchers' (Chapter 16).

There is snobbery in Dorothea's idealization of Casaubon just as there is in Rosamond's romanticizing of the well-born Lydgate. But more pertinent to the Lydgate marriage itself is that word 'vulgar'. George Eliot has already used it to describe a tendency of Lydgate's. When the crisis comes he behaves in a way which to Rosamond seems disgustingly vulgar. Rosamond works hard in her initial relationship with Lydgate to put herself beyond all suspicion of vulgarity, although it is a kind of industry that Lydgate himself was scarcely likely to appreciate, and this preoccupation with presenting herself to a man is itself open to accusations of vulgarity. What Rosamond recognizes in Lydgate is that he has a cavalier attitude towards women that requires them to be attractive and undemanding in looks and expression. What neither of them recognize is that this attitude, and the response to it, won't stand up to the realities of married life.

In demonstrating the essential egocentricity of love, or of the marriage urge, George Eliot binds together all the lovers in *Middlemarch*, even Mary Garth whose apparently bland assumption that she can get Fred Vincy if she wants him, and that if she wants him he will reform, has at the very least a lack of acknowledgment of another's individuality. It is difficult to accept her as an ideal, for without falling back on an unconvincing evocation of domestic bliss her marriage to the amiable Fred seems neither gratifying nor instructive. It is no more than the establishment of another static arrangement of human relations with a society that is always on the move.

It is not that George Eliot ever attacks the static quality of marriage, although there are hints in her letters that suggest she found it unacceptable. She recognizes that human inertia will generally prevent a reaction against it. In *The Mill on the Floss* she shows how deliberately the Dodsons have built up ramparts to protect this inertia. In *Middlemarch* the attempts at self-protection go wrong, or don't work. Bulstrode's ramparts crumble because he cannot rid himself of his dubious past. Vincy is threatened because of his struggle to match his style of life to his status. The Garth household remains intact because the individuals within it rely on human loyalty rather than on symbols of strength; they are never threatened as seriously as the others, but it could be argued that this is because they are essentially more modest. They are not tempted to overreach themselves.

If modesty and hard work, which the Garth family represent, are essential qualities for the life of a community like Middlemarch, the failures of Lydgate, the exposure of Bulstrode and the compromises of Dorothea surely do not suggest that the aspirations which these characters represent have no place there. It may be the case that the community can operate successfully on the basis of well-tried values and assumptions, that Lydgate's health reforms would make little difference to the quality of life – it is significant that the threatened cholera epidemic, which might really have put Middlemarch to the test, never materializes – that Dorothea's cottages would have had a minuscule impact. But as George Eliot herself suggests, these are not the only tests of human worth. More important than their success with Middlemarch is their success with themselves. Lydgate retreats from Middlemarch and becomes a fashionable doctor making money out of gout. Dorothea subsides into a happy marriage and sublimates herself in her husband. In both cases their potential seems to escape them.

The marriage issue is most rawly exposed in the Lydgate household. Neither Lydgate nor Rosamond have thought about what marriage might mean as a human relationship. They have seen it as a social arrangement, as a professional arrangement, as a mutually attractive institution, but neither has looked at the other as an individual with individual needs and expectations. Lydgate proposes to Rosamond almost accidentally because he has recognized her as the kind of woman who would make a good-looking, socially acceptable wife for a rising young doctor. Rosamond expects a proposal from Lydgate because he appears to be going through the motions of an upper-class lover. Both of them see their wants in terms of the performance. But what Lydgate really wants has nothing to do with women.

Lydgate is at once at his worst and at his most sympathetic when the façade of the marriage openly cracks. He relies on what he considers Rosamond's duty to obey his authority as a means of salvation. Because it does not occur to him that Rosamond might ignore his commands – and they are commands – he is at a loss when she exerts *her* authority directly against his. Of course he is right and reasonable in his attempt to save their financial situation, but to become suddenly the authoritarian husband after the indulgent lover is not reasonable. He did not marry Rosamond for her reason and sympathetic understanding, and his appeals to these non-existent qualities have to fail. The emergence of Lydgate's categorical imperative is highly convincing, for it is when he commands that his weakness and the extent of his responsibility for the state of the marriage become most evident.

There is a balance of sympathy in the Lydgate affair. Clearly Lydgate is a much more worthwhile man than Rosamond is a woman. But his lack of understanding of her needs, his cavalier indulgence which reflects his low opinion of female status, draws sympathy to Rosamond. It is understandable why Rosamond protects her right to act independently, while we can appreciate that she is doing it for the wrong reasons. Dorothea has the same problem. Where does independence fit in to her marriage with Casaubon? But from the start she wanted to be married to a man so superior that her individuality would be absorbed in his, while Rosamond wanted a husband whom she could manipulate if necessary. Rosamond openly fights against her secondary position in Lydgate's busy professional life. Dorothea is forced to admit that to take a secondary position in the life of a man whose professional pretensions are not worth it is deeply disturbing.

In the lives of these two unhappily married women Will Ladislaw plays a similar role. Rosamond casts him as an admirer whose business it is to make life more interesting, and perhaps to indicate to her husband that she deserves more attention. 'How delightful to make captives from the throne of marriage with a husband as crown-prince by your side – himself in fact a subject – while the captives look up for ever hopeless, losing their rest probably, and if their appetite too, so much the better!' (Chapter 43).

This is Rosamond's vision of power. Dorothea's frank liking for Ladislaw is just as dangerous. Her husband is jealous, and in the minds of others there are hints of intrigue. It does not occur to Lydgate to be jealous of Rosamond; Rosamond would probably enjoy his jealousy. He is unaware that he is not all that she hoped. But Casaubon *is* aware that Dorothea is disappointed, and hence his distrust. Will Ladislaw does indeed make life more interesting for both women, representing, although Dorothea is scarcely aware of it, a relief from the realities of their marriages.

Dorothea and Rosamond share more than an interest in Ladislaw. They both have husbands who expect their authority to be absolute, and who assume, respectfully and courteously for the most part, that women are inferior. The ultimate in this kind of relationship is exposed in the marriage of Gwendolen Harleth and Grandcourt in *Daniel Deronda* (1876). Grandcourt's only interest in life is the exertion of his mastery, and it is easier to be masterful over women than men. Except for his curious relationship with the enslaved Lush he opts out of relationships with men that would imply any kind of challenge or conflict.

Grandcourt despises women, but he has to dominate them. His urge for mastery is *the* essential of his character. Like Rosamond, Gwendolen has been encouraged to believe that with her beauty and style it is her privilege to dominate. Marriage to Grandcourt rapidly shatters this assumption:

One belief which had accompanied her throughout her unmarried life as a self-cajoling superstition, encouraged by the subordination of everyone about her – her belief in her own power of dominating – was utterly gone. Already, in seven short weeks, which seemed half her life, her husband had gained a mastery which she could no more resist than she could have resisted the benumbing effect from the touch of a torpedo. Gwendolen's will had seemed imperious in its small girlish sway; but it was the will of a creature with a large discourse of imaginative fears: a shadow would have been enough to relax its hold. And she had found a will like that of a crab or a boa-constrictor which goes on pinching or crushing without alarm at thunder. (Chapter 35)

Gwendolen is more sensitive and susceptible than Rosamond, and her will is broken, which Rosamond's never is. Her fear of Grandcourt is absolute, and his cruelty of course thrives with her fear.

Grandcourt's courtship of Gwendolen is an exercise in bringing a woman to heel, and her experience of marriage is all the more shattering for the fact that she is aware of this. She does not realize that he is fully conversant with the indignity of her motives. Grandcourt is George Eliot's only evil character, and it is significant that this evil emerges as male cruelty over women. He is the logical extension of all assumptions about male and upper-class authority (his habits and *longueurs* and mode of speech are characteristically upper-class), so conclusive that even the radical Felix Holt's instinctive anti-feminism is reflected in it. The whole aspect of the upper-class society George Eliot is describing in this novel (it is George Meredith's fictional world, and he deals with similar tendencies) in spite of the fact that it contains such benign good fellows as Sir Hugo Mallinger and other harmless males, confirms the logic, the inevitability of Grandcourt.

There are times in *Daniel Deronda* when George Eliot's asperity and her direct confrontation with hopelessness and injustice almost submerge her irony. The result is that there is less levelling, more singling out of individuals as separate beings who cannot be saved by sharing their mediocrity with others. The Jewish theme enhances this, though I think it is a mistake to see that as the centre of the novel. Her fascination with Judaism is part of a fascination with 'separate' people, people who don't fit in to class and community, and the novel is at its weakest when she tries to intellectualize and explain the Jewish situation. The novel is about two people, Gwendolen and Deronda, who for different reasons are so separate that they are beyond reconciliation with ordinary, conventional society.

In this context marriage becomes an intensification of distance and differences. Gwendolen has no symbols of propriety, of the maintenance of tradition and continuity, that she can hang on to. Her only reality is her suffering as an isolated individual, and her realization of the mistake she has made. Marriage is not a safeguard, it is not stability, it is certainly not fulfilment. It is in fact none of the things that George Eliot has indicated keep people and families and communities jogging along, reining back the over-eager and spurring on the slow.

One of the reasons for this is that *Daniel Deronda*'s world is beyond community, beyond the recognized anchors of life. There are no solid values to support Gwendolen if she stumbles. George Eliot tries to suggest that good, strong, human values are to be found amongst the Jewish people in their strong sense of racial allegiance and family loyalty. But this is of no help to Gwendolen, although perhaps she gravitates to Deronda partly because she sees in him a response to this. She is totally on her own.

The communities in the early novels at least provide an established pattern and a well-tried set of expectations, and these mean that even not very well-assorted couples can find marriage sustaining within that community. When women have work to do the perspective changes. Dorothea wants to work, and her want arises from her experience of the community in which she lives as much as from her own personal requirements. It does not occur to Rosamond or Gwendolen that useful activities would be either feasible or appropriate. I don't think it is too much to read into this a message about the anomalies of Victorian womanhood, but I shall consider this in greater detail in the next chapter.

GEORGE ELIOT uses the word 'passion' frequently in her novels, and in her vocabulary it has not the expected flavour of disapproval, as when Jane Eyre's aunt describes her unacceptable niece. She uses it of women who feel deeply and cannot find the right outlet for those feelings, and she uses it with the full awareness of the predicament of such women. Passion in women baffled Victorian society. It suggested at best irregularity and nonconformity, at worst, sin. Yet passion in women like Maggie and Dorothea, that could possibly be channelled into selfless achievement, society could not afford to ignore. Their creator suggests that women have a great deal to offer, but not only does society blindly reject what they have to offer, seeing their freedom of action as dangerous and offensive, but the women themselves don't really know what their potential is, and cannot, or will not, find the commitment and understanding that they need.

Maggie is a girl who needs love and needs to love. It is apparent in her relationship with her brother Tom, on one level simple and basic – they fondle each other like young animals and have a kind of instinctive mutual generosity – but on another, social, level it is complex. Tom is aware of the power he has over Maggie and is very ready to exploit his superiority in being both male and older, and to take advantage of Maggie's 'hunger of the heart'. Maggie knows she is being exploited, resents it, yet cannot bear to be deficient in her love. A perfect instance of this is the shared jam puff. Tom gallantly allows Maggie the jammier half, and then reproves her for not insisting that he should have some of it:

Maggie turned quite pale. 'Oh, Tom, why didn't you ask me?'

'*I* wasn't going to ask you for a bit, you greedy. You might have thought of it without, when you knew I gave you the best bit.'

'But I wanted you to have it – you know I did,' said Maggie, in an injured tone. (Chapter 6)

Maggie is not at all happy that she got the best of the bargain, but distressed at the lost opportunity of giving something up to Tom. This, and the directness, the complete lack of artificiality and self-consciousness in her response, are characteristic of the adult Maggie also. She cannot accept Stephen Guest, for however much she wants his love she knows that she is taking him away from her cousin Lucy. She does not want to damage anyone, although of course she does damage most of the people who matter to her, through their deficiency as well as through her own difficulties.

It is very important that there is so much of Maggie's childhood in *The Mill on the Floss*, but it is not Maggie's *development* that is interesting, for she does not really change as she grows from child to young adult. It is her situation. She has a powerful personality as a little girl, and finds ways of expressing it, although in the process she causes distress to herself and to others. But it does find outlets. Although she is desperate for love and approval she is not hedged in by an adult, restrictive awareness of convention and polite behaviour. Above all she has freedom as a child, and the only significant change that growing up brings her is the wearing away of this freedom.

Other features of Maggie's life as a child are also intensely operative. George Eliot talks about the 'bitter sorrows of childhood', the 'illusory promises of our childhood', 'the conflicts of young souls hungry for joy': the depth, the pain, the hope in Maggie's feelings and responses are powerfully communicated. They last into her adult life, and she is forced to feel that they must be disciplined. As a child the intensity of Maggie's feelings are life itself. As an adult she grasps that they shouldn't be: but what can replace them?

When bankruptcy descends on the Tulliver family Maggie's response is drastic. She can find nothing to salvage her from a totality of disaster and misery in her emotions or her imagination: 'no dream world would satisfy her now'. Not only has an unimaginable financial disaster occurred, Maggie feels that she has lost all the resources that characterized her life:

She wanted some explanation of this hard, real life: the unhappy-looking father, seated at the dull breakfast-table; the childish, bewildered mother; the little sordid tasks that filled the hours, or the more oppressive emptiness of weary, joyless leisure; the need of some tender, demonstrative love; the cruel sense that Tom didn't mind what she thought or felt, and that they were no longer playfellows together; the privation of all pleasant things that had come to *her* more than to others: she wanted some key that would enable her to understand, and, in understanding, endure, the heavy weight that had fallen on her young heart.
(Book IV, Chapter 3)

She thinks that learning might cure this impotence. Tom has had an expensive education and is able to work and earn, to contribute towards the demoralized household. She has always been told that she was brighter than Tom, and has always cherished this praise.

But George Eliot reminds us of her 'illusions of self-flattery', her absorption in herself, and gives us a clue to her next step in self-discovery. She stumbles on Thomas à Kempis, and has a sudden and complete vision – this impulsive total immersion is characteristic of Maggie – of a life of 'self-humiliation and entire devotedness' (Book IV, Chapter 2). She decides that the 'miseries of her young life had come from fixing her heart on her own pleasure'. There is a suggestion of Dorothea in this, and it indicates a specific way in which Maggie and Dorothea share in 'the common yearning of womanhood' (*Middlemarch*, Prelude). They both feel the necessity of being something more than passive receivers of experience, and translate this need at some point in their lives into a vision of doing good for others.

As with Dorothea there is an element of self-gratification in Maggie's sacrifice:

From what you know of her, you will not be surprised that she threw some exaggeration and wilfulness, some pride and impetuosity even into her self-renunciation: her own life was still a drama for her, in which she demanded of herself that her part should be played with intensity. And so it came to pass that she often lost the spirit of humility by being excessive in the outward act; she often strove after too high a flight and came down with her poor little half-fledged wings dabbled in the mud. For example, she not only determined to work at plain sewing, that she might contribute something towards the fund in the tin box, but she went, in the first instance, in her zeal of self-mortification, to ask for it at a linen-shop in St Ogg's, instead of getting it in a more quiet and indirect way; and could see nothing but what was entirely wrong and unkind, nay, persecuting, in Tom's reproof of her for this unnecessary act. (Book IV, Chapter 3)

The irony is double-edged here. Maggie's sense of self-dramatization is obviously in operation – but it is the fastidious Tom who judges her. It is his sense of superiority – '*I'll* take care that the debts are paid, without you lowering yourself in that way' – that seems to expose her. But what it in fact exposes is his sensitivity about the Tulliver status and the way in which Maggie's actions are bound to be circumscribed by convention. However moral her instincts are it is not proper for her to fulfil them. Dorothea has the same problem.

Her father, too, is unable to see a role for Maggie. He is 'bitterly preoccupied' with the knowledge that it will now be impossible for Maggie to make a good marriage, and he cannot bear the thought that she might marry 'down in the world'. Thus we see the limited horizons of Maggie's life. The misfortunes of the Tulliver family narrow her possibilities; they certainly throw her imaginings into sharper relief against reality. But while George Eliot exposes Maggie's self-dramatization she also demonstrates the physical qualities of Maggie that heighten our sense of her as a dramatic figure:

With her dark colouring and jet crown surmounting her tall figure, she seems to have a sort of kinship with the grand Scotch firs, at which she is looking up as if she loved them well. Yet one has a sense of uneasiness in looking at her – a sense of opposing elements, of which a fierce collision is imminent: and surely there is a hushed expression, such as one often sees in older faces under borderless caps, out of keeping with the resistant youth, which one expects to flash out in a sudden, passionate glance, that will dissipate all the quietude, like a damp fire leaping out again when all seemed safe. (Book v, Chapter i)

We have seen her sitting over her sewing in a depressed and demoralized household. Now we see her fully expanded, measuring herself against trees and rocks and wild flowers, 'an amphitheatre of the pale pink dogroses', where she and Philip Waken will enact their relationship. Here Philip tells her she is beautiful and we sense in her an unrestricted power. But at the same time what she is saying to Philip is that 'our life is determined for us'. Her response to Philip is equivocal. Her accidental meeting with him renews the conflict she thinks, but we have not been deceived, she has tamed. He offers her the love she has been longing for, a means of escape, but she is trying resolutely to accept her present life.

By this stage in the book is has been made quite clear that sexual response will be crucial to Maggie. Unlike Dorothea, whose sexual response is awakened only after her experience of its lack, Maggie has made us aware of it at a very early stage. She has a much more physical personality than Dorothea. In her relationship with her father and her brother physical contact and caresses have been very important. I am not trying to suggest anything of incest here, just that for Maggie physical contact is an essential means of self-expression. It makes her lack of response to Philip, and the strength of her response to Stephen Guest, that much more meaningful.

When the scene changes to the drawing-room of the Deanes' house at St Ogg's, Maggie reveals a natural dignity but no understanding of drawing-room rules, and will meet Stephen, an excellent match in terms of local wealth and status. When the introduction takes place George Eliot focuses on those qualities that were heightened in the Red Deeps scene, as if to emphasize the incongruity of Maggie in a drawing-room setting:

For one instant Stephen could not conceal his astonishment at the sight of this tall, dark-eyed nymph with her jet-black coronet of hair; the next, Maggie felt herself, for the first time in her life, receiving the tribute of a very deep blush and a very deep bow from a person towards whom she herself was conscious of timidity. This new experience was very agreeable to her – so agreeable, that it almost effaced her previous emotion about Philip. There was a new brightness in her eyes, and a very becoming flush on her cheek, as she seated herself. (Book VI, Chapter 2)

Admiration brings out the best in Maggie. Not only is she a striking physical presence in the formalized world of Lucy and Stephen, she behaves with such natural directness that she inevitably draws attention to herself. Like Ladislaw in *Middlemarch*, she is not concerned with conventional responses, but unlike Ladislaw it is not because she on principle has no use for them, but because she is not acquainted with them.

This is important because it heightens this first meeting with Stephen. While he, though taken by surprise, is able to disguise his feelings with easy talk, she takes everything to heart, and it does not occur to her to pretend otherwise. Stephen without too much difficulty maintains his role as a well-bred young man by nature polite to ladies, while Maggie in her impolite honesty unknowingly reinforces the powerful impression she has made on him.

The quality of their mutual response emerges strongly in this first meeting. Everything that happens afterwards is an extension of what we already understand. Lucy, 'the dearest little creature in the world', presides politely, unconscious of passion in herself or others, quite confident that she is destined for a highly appropriate marriage. The three of them go rowing, and the awakening of Maggie becomes associated with physical action, as Stephen teaches her to row, and in this her superior physical qualities are enhanced. But she is not so superior that she does not require looking after. When her foot slips and Stephen prevents her from falling her reaction is this: 'It was very charming to be taken care of in that kind of graceful manner by someone taller and stronger than one's self. Maggie had never felt just in the same way before' (Book VI, Chapter 2).

Psychologically the analysis of Maggie's susceptibility in a forbidden relationship is totally convincing. She meets someone who heightens both her strength and her vulnerability, through whom she might find self-expression, if not self-fulfilment. That she draws back ultimately, though too late as far as her reputation is concerned, is also consistent with her character. Although the ultimate disaster, the flood that sweeps both Tom and Maggie to their deaths, is dubious, its preview, the journey down river with Stephen, in its sense of events having a drama of their own which is beyond the control of individuals, works. It also suggests an element that is missing from *Middlemarch*. Like Maggie, Dorothea is never given the chance to fulfil our expectations, and if we felt that Ladislaw was a part of a dramatic situation that pulled Dorothea inside a sphere of moving influences we might find more in her marriage than the essentially static encounters with Ladislaw suggest.

Maggie suffers, as she has throughout her life, the consequences of her impulsive behaviour, and although she returns without consummating the relationship with Stephen, St Ogg's condemns her. This condemnation is akin to that of her aunts and uncles when she was a child. In the end her passion and energy are destructive, for she is trapped by the double barriers of a narrow provincial society and conventional attitudes towards women. She is a kind of outcast, like Gwendolen in *Daniel Deronda*, but in a different way. What is disturbing is that, having established her heroine as an outcast, George Eliot cannot allow her, or any other person in the novel, to come to terms with the situation. Her sensitivity and her hunger prevent it but, relieved of the bondage of womanhood, which is how Gwendolen Harleth sees *her* situation, these same features of her personality might have enabled her to escape.

In Dorothea we find a woman with a more conscious and articulate idea of what she is after than Maggie has. Yet she shares the same essentials:

Her mind was theoretic, and yearned by its nature after some lofty conception of the world which might frankly include the parish of Tipton and her own rule of conduct there; she was enamoured of intensity and greatness, and rash in embracing whatever seemed to her to have those aspects; likely to seek martyrdom, to make retractions, and then to incur martyrdom after all in a quarter where she had not sought it. (Chapter 1)

She shares Maggie's rashness, her intensity, her totality. The form that these take is different, but the motives are similar. She wants an identity other than that prefigured for her. In *The Mill on the Floss* it is mainly the image of flood and water that suggests Maggie's fate, a sense of threat against which she will be powerless, but in *Middlemarch* Dorothea's lack of the kind of success she wants is verbally explicit in the opening chapters, where there is a clear indication of how we should interpret her eventual marriage to Ladislaw. We are told that Dorothea is likely 'to incur martyrdom after all in a quarter where she had not sought it', which seems to refer to her second marriage – in her first she *did* see martyrdom – and to suggest that we should not interpret Ladislaw as a realization of Dorothea's ideals. She does not get, and could never get, George Eliot firmly tells us, what the early chapters indicate she aspires to.

The initial characterization of Dorothea is placed against a background of what most people expect a woman to be. The idea of a St Teresa in their midst would be formidable to Middlemarch society, but although her oddness is noticed, her individuality is not. First she is compared with her likeable sister Celia: Dorothea has ideals, highly inappropriate in a woman, and self-consciously lofty, while Celia has common sense, a useful feminine quality and a great aid to happiness. For Mr Chichely Dorothea is not concerned enough with pleasing men, which is what he looks for in women. He prefers Rosamond Vincy.

Lydgate's verdict is similar, though he dresses it up:

To his taste, guided by a single conversation, here was the point on which Miss Brooke would be found wanting, notwithstanding her undeniable beauty. She did not look at things from the proper feminine angle. The society of such women was about as relaxing as going home from your work to teach the second form, instead of reclining in a paradise with sweet laughs for bird-notes, and blue eyes for a heaven. (Chapter 11)

He prefers Rosamond also, 'polished, refined, docile' as she appears.

Everyone considers Dorothea's interests and inclinations misguided, except Sir James Chettam who is in love with her and, unlike Casaubon, respects her opinions. It is significant that Sir James who, in spite of his limitations at the outset of the book, understands Dorothea better than anyone else, so weightily disapproves of Ladislaw. It is partly because of the implications contained in Casaubon's will, but it is certainly also because he feels that Ladislaw does not deserve her. She is operating in a situation of implicit, if not open, disapproval. No one is very happy about her marriage to Casaubon, but this would seem to her a part of the same situation. She is aware of herself as an un-ordinary woman, much more so than Maggie, and to be judged by the standards and expectations of ordinary women and ordinary men has little influence on her. This is an important moral centre of the novel. Dorothea has to come to terms with the fact that the respect owed to her as an individual does not exempt her from the criteria applied to the mass.

Dorothea marries Casaubon as an embodiment of all that she has been wanting. 'Now she would be able to devote herself to large yet definite duties; now she would be allowed to live continually in the light of a mind that she could reverence' (Chapter 5). Through Casaubon she thinks she can articulate exactly what it is that she does want: Maggie never finds the means to do this. Her disappointment is intense. In those brilliantly suggestive passages (in which 'light' is a crucial word) that describe their honeymoon, the quality and depth of that disappointment is fully revealed. Yet it is much more difficult for her to represent to herself what has gone wrong, for it so intimately involves the recognition of her mistake:

Yet Dorothea had no distinctly shapen grievance that she could state even to her-self; and in the midst of her confused thought and passion, the mental act that was struggling forth into clearness was a self-accusing cry that her feeling of desolation was the fault of her own spiritual poverty. She had married the man of her choice, and with the advantage over most girls that she had contemplated marriage chiefly as the beginning of new duties: from the very first she had thought of Mr Casaubon as having a mind so very much above her own, that he must often be claimed by studies which she could not entirely share; moreover, after the brief narrow experience of her girlhood she was beholding Rome, the city of visible history, where the past of a whole hemisphere seems moving like a funeral pro-cession with strange ancestral images and trophies gathered from afar. (Chapter 20)

Casaubon is a part of the funeral procession. The words that George Eliot uses to describe Rome are suggestive of their relationship: 'ruins', 'the vast wreck of ambitious ideals', 'signs of breathing forgetfulness and degradation'. They apply in different ways both to Dorothea and to Casaubon.

The use of light imagery in association with the triangle of Dorothea, Casaubon and Ladislaw has been much discussed. Casaubon is in the shadows and unresponsive to sunlight, Will surrounded by 'sunny brightness', Dorothea discovered by him standing in a pool of light. The imagery can be traced right through the novel. It has a dimension in respect of Will's artistic activities which is revealing. He sees Dorothea in the Vatican in a pose like that of a statue. Throughout the novel it is her beauty he is interested in, and there is a stronger suggestion of the response of an enthusiastic painter than of sexual passion. There is little indication that he understands Dorothea's personality or is interested in her ideas, which again undermines any picture of their marriage as one of idealistic fulfilment. When Will sees Dorothea posed in a pool of sun-light he sees her as a figure in a Renaissance painting. The light does not suggest life, it suggests static beauty, and there is a static, almost negative quality in Will's response to Dorothea throughout the novel. Whereas it seems quite clear that Dorothea, in the midst of the first intensity of disappointment with the impotent Casaubon, is awakened to a much more live and physical response to the attractive Will.

We are reminded of Lydgate. His vision of Rosamond is also essentially static, posed: '. . . his old dreamland, in which Rosamond Vincy appeared to be that perfect piece of womanhood who would reverence her husband's mind after the fashion of an accomplished mermaid, using her comb and looking glass, and singing her song for the relaxation of his adored wisdom alone' (Chapter 58).

It is that sea creature putting in another appearance, although more benign here than in *Vanity Fair* and *Shirley*. If this is an essentially more vulgar pose than that of the statuesque Dorothea in the Vatican, the association is clear, and it refers to Casaubon as well as to Ladislaw. All three men have their vision of the ideal woman, and the way that the three respond to women illuminates their view of the uses of femininity. Lydgate, as he continues to ponder over the failure of his marriage, reflects that 'his superior knowledge and mental force, instead of being, as he had imagined, a shrine to consult on all occasions, was simply set aside on every practical question' (Chapter 58). Dorothea before her marriage envisaged Casaubon as 'a shrine to consult on all occasions': that was what she wanted. For some time Casaubon himself maintains his uncritical view of himself as husband: 'he had no idea of being anything else than an irreproachable husband, who would make a charming young woman as happy as she deserved to be' (Chapter 20). Ladislaw's attitude to Dorothea implies that she requires the hand of the artist, himself, to give her an identity. Each of them displays a different version of male egotism, which the novel partially challenges.

Dorothea's marriage does not shatter her ideals, but it closes the gates with a resounding clang on the avenue she has chosen for their realization. Her reaction is, after much depression and confusion, a decision to dedicate herself unquestioningly to Casaubon in a manner that, if it were successful, would amount to an obliteration of her own personality. But Casaubon has been shaken by Dorothea's signs of independence, which is how he interprets her inability to disguise her distress, and he is distrustful. Ironically he is correct in his interpretation of Dorothea's response to Will, but although he is aware of his wife's susceptibilities he underestimates her intellect, in which he has had no interest, and when at last he finds himself able to make use of her assistance in his work, assistance which in her idealization of marriage she was desperately eager to give, she knows that his life's work is entirely sterile.

Does Dorothea achieve anything? She interests herself in the new hospital and in the problems of others. With the money Casaubon leaves her she can contribute financially to the hospital, but there is no scope for her ideas. She helps to repair the ruptured marriage of Lydgate and Rosamond, but she cannot make it a happy one. She has complete independence financially, need obey nothing but her own conscience, but then she marries Will Ladislaw, and she loses her money, her independence, and, it is hinted in that gently ironic, and ironically titled, Finale, her identity as well.

George Eliot delicately balances the life that Dorothea has chosen. That she is aware that she has lost something by her marriage is made clear. 'Dorothea herself had no dreams of being praised above other women, feeling that there was always something better which she might have done, if she had only been better and known better' (Finale).

She has lost her dreams of martyrdom, yet, as we have seen, has achieved it after a fashion. There is a suggestion of the acceptance of her fate in the phrase, 'if she had only been better and known better'. She does not blame circumstances, but nor does she seem to blame herself: she could not help not being and knowing better. And what has she gained? 'No life would have been possible to Dorothea which was not filled with emotion, and she had now a life filled also with a beneficent activity which she had not the doubtful pains of discovering and making out for herself' (Finale). In narrowing the scope of her life, in giving herself up to her husband and children, she solves the problem of what exactly she is to do with herself, and if she has to modify the scale of her vision, if she has fallen into a conventional role, this avoids that crucial and challenging difficulty of establishing some other kind of identity.

The final touch to the picture rests with others. Perhaps we should be seeing her through the eyes of the happily married Sir James: 'Many who knew her, thought it a pity that so substantive and rare a creature should have been absorbed into the life of another, and be only known in a certain circle as a wife and mother. But no one stated exactly what else that was in her power she ought rather to have done' (Finale).

George Eliot mildly exposes not only the predicament of the yearning Dorothea, but of women in general struggling to make sense of an adverse situation. 'Substantive' is a word she uses several times, and it gives us a clue to what she felt women – and men – ought to be. Rosamond Vincy is not substantive. Dorothea is. It is the essential difference between them.

Gwendolen's yearning is of a different kind, although it can be traced to similar sources. She is a more sophisticated version of Maggie in many ways. She is more calculating in her passion, more fully committed to escaping the life she leads: Maggie never thinks of rejecting her family. Gwendolen does, but discovers that she needs them. Dorothea in having only a sister as her immediate family is freer emotionally, which surely contributes to her personality (it is important that she is free of parents) and its tendencies, as does her class. We have only to look as far as Mary Garth to see a young woman performing usefully within a large, not very well-off family, and to see how this uses up energies that in a higher social sphere would have no immediate outlet.

Gwendolen has no outlet at all. When we first meet her she is gambling, and the picture of her at the roulette table is wonderfully suggestive:

She had gone to the roulette-table not because of passion, but in search of it: her mind was still sanely capable of picturing balanced probabilities, and while the chance of winning allured her, the chance of losing thrust itself on her with alternative strength and made a vision from which her pride shrank sensitively. (Chapter 2)

Maggie is passionate; Gwendolen wants to be so. She is calculating, ready to take risks, but can't face the thought of losing. She does of course gamble on her future when she marries Grandcourt, and loses, but because of her pride it is only to Deronda that she admits her loss. And it is only Deronda who, in this early scene, knows that she has lost at roulette and has had to pawn her necklace as a consequence.

In the early part of the book Gwendolen toys with visions of adventure and grand gestures. Spoilt as she is by her family, used to a petty kind of power, she likes to see herself in a more expansive role, removed from the pettiness and narrow scope of the household where she can only exert her influence over her mother, her sisters and the servants. 'Passion' is not quite the same as when it is applied to Maggie. There is no suggestion of physical passion in Gwendolen's ambitious nature. When her cousin Rex declares his love for her she reacts with disgust. 'The perception that poor Rex wanted to be tender made her curl up and harden like a sea-anenome at the touch of the finger' (Chapter 7). It is a striking image. George Eliot comments, 'now the life of passion had begun negatively in her. She felt passionately averse to this volunteered love' (Chapter 7). It is partly her contempt for Rex that provokes this, but there is no suggestion of passion in her relationship with Grandcourt either. At best, she tolerates him for what he represents.

Maggie's imprecision and Dorothea's intellectual ideals mean that marriage is not an absolute symbol of their ambitions. But Gwendolen is much more limited in her vision, and it is assumed by her and by everyone that marriage will be the making of her. That is the object of her existence as a beautiful woman. Her mother, who has been through two negative marriages herself, has no thought but of Gwendolen married to the 'right' man: 'For whatever marriage had been for herself, how could she the less desire it for her daughter?' (Chapter 9). Gwendolen is prepared to collaborate in the marketing of herself to the right man, although her ideas of a suitable mate do not necessarily coincide with her mother's.

She is not a cold-hearted adventuress, not a Becky Sharp, and her sensitivity is revealed in interesting and testing ways. It is more than her reaction to the discovery of Grandcourt's mistress, for that can be read as an offence to her sense of propriety as well as to her pride. It emerges in her reaction to a number of different men. Lush, Grandcourt's amanuensis, offends her pride by making it so clear that he has no regard for her, and she has a 'physical antipathy' to him. We have seen how she reacted to Rex. On the other hand she admires Klesmer, who also delivers a shattering blow to her pride, operating as a kind of understudy to Deronda. There is a specific point made of the fact that she does not like men, and the fact that Klesmer and Deronda (both Jewish) are physically acceptable to her suggests the entanglement in her of moral, intellectual and physical attractions.

Apart from Grandcourt, they are the only exceptions. She accepts Grandcourt because he is not 'disgusting' like other men, but of course here his wealth and his class have a great deal to do with acceptability. His physical characteristics are emphasized. He is handsome, but languorous; fit, but will not condescend to employ his fitness even to the extent of speaking more than is strictly necessary. George Eliot says, 'it was perhaps not possible for a breathing man wide awake to be less animated' (Chapter 11). His characteristic gestures, smoking a cigar, stroking a lapdog, are undemanding. But there is a complicated illusion being built up, an illusion which deceives Gwendolen, and which contributes towards the reader's reaction to him as a representation of evil.

For in all this languor there are hints of latent power which will later come into the open. His dominance of Lush is absolute, though he commands without any exertion of himself at all. We have been prepared for his dominance of Gwendolen. She thinks she is marrying a man she can manipulate, but she has also been aware of a sense of adventure, or risk, as the gambling scene suggests, in entering a new life, and the fact that Grandcourt's courtship is so much linked with riding and hunting has added to her exhilaration. She says:

'We women can't go in search of adventures – to find out the North-West passage or the source of the Nile, or to hunt tigers in the East. We must stay where we grow, or where the gardeners like to transplant us. We are brought up like the flowers, to look as pretty as we can, and be dull without complaining. That is my notion about the plants: they are often bored, and that is the reason why some of them have got poisonous.' (Chapter 13)

This indicates her vulnerability to such as Grandcourt. At the same time she wants to choose where she is to grow. Choice is important to her. Briefly she cherishes the illusion that she might become a great singer, an idea that pleases her theatrical sense and has a further attractive feature. 'The inmost fold of her questioning now was whether she need take a husband at all – whether she could not achieve substantiality for herself and know gratified ambition without bondage' (Chapter 23). 'Without bondage'; she sees marriage as trading freedom for material advantage. Klesmer is so important because he disabuses her of the belief that she might have both comfort and freedom. In fact Gwendolen literally sells herself to Grandcourt, and half of his power lies in the fact that he knows it, and he knows the degrading circumstances of the deal.

Gwendolen nurses her illusions, in spite of her appreciation of bondage, right up to the day of her wedding. 'For what could not a woman do when she was married, if she knew how to assert herself?' When Grandcourt comes to propose to her she looks out of the window and sees 'the two horses being taken slowly round the sweep, and the beautiful creatures, in their fine grooming, sent a thrill of exultation through Gwendolen. They were the symbols of command and luxury, in delightful contrast with the ugliness of poverty and humiliation at which she had lately been looking close' (Chapter 27). But the horses belong to Grandcourt, and later on, after their marriage, Gwendolen reflects bitterly, 'He delights in making dogs and horses quail' (Chapter 35).

Gwendolen, who dislikes men, is exposed through the eyes of men: Rex, Lush, Klesmer, Deronda, and her husband. Their attitudes differ, but nothing can rescue her from her husband's ruthlessness, and it is worth looking at his attitude at some length, for it tells us objectively so much about Gwendolen and the cruelties of society:

It was characteristic that he got none of his satisfaction from the belief that Gwendolen was in love with him; and that love had overcome the jealous resentment which had made her run away from him. On the contrary, he believed that this girl was rather exceptional in the fact that, in spite of his assiduous attention to her, she was not in love with him; and it seemed to him very likely that if it had not been for the sudden poverty which had come over her family, she would not have accepted him. From the very first there had been an exasperating tricksiness with which she had – not met his advances, but – wheeled away from them. She had been brought to accept him in spite of everything – brought to kneel down like a horse under training for the arena, though she might have an objection to it all the while. On the whole, Grandcourt got more pleasure out of this notion than he could have done out of winning a girl of whom he was sure that she had a strong inclination for him personally. And yet this pleasure in mastering reluctance flourished along with the habitual persuasion that no woman whom he favoured could be quite indifferent to his personal influence; and it seemed to him not unlikely that by-and-by Gwendolen might be more enamoured of him than he of her. In any case she would have to submit; and he enjoyed thinking of her as his future wife, whose pride and spirit were suited to command everyone but himself. He had no taste for a woman who was all tenderness to him, full of petitioning solicitude and willing obedience. He meant to be master of a woman who would have liked to master him, and who perhaps would have been capable of mastering another man. (Chapter 28)

Gwendolen is a reflection of his own ego. His attitude to her is like that of an adventurous rider towards a horse – and the simile is doubly appropriate. There is no pleasure in riding a docile animal. The satisfaction comes from controlling a potential rebel. This is psychologically deeper than, for instance, the authoritarian Mr Dombey who has, however mistakenly, a moral purpose, or the physical cruelty of some other fictional husbands. Grandcourt can dominate because he understands Gwendolen rather better than she understands herself, or him, or the pressures to which she is subject. As a way of dealing with her situation Deronda's recommendations of optimistic stoicism (though the optimism dwindles as he finds out more about Grandcourt) seem entirely inadequate.

The only character who stands up to Grandcourt is Lydia Glasher, and although she gains nothing by it but a grain of personal satisfaction, it has its effect on him. At the end of the scene in which she gets her own way, 'the effect that clung and gnawed within Grandcourt was a sense of imperfect mastery' (Chapter 30). Again, the physical potency of the image is striking. The hints of violence extend to Gwendolen, as she contemplates her marriage with a sense of terror. 'That white hand of his which was touching his whisker was capable, she fancied, of clinging round her neck and threatening to throttle her; for fear of him, mingling with the vague foreboding of some retributive calamity which hung about her life, had reached a superstitious point' (Chapter 35). The calamity does materialize, in the drowning of Grandcourt and her inability to save him. Fear of the living Grandcourt overcomes the instinct for preserving life, and we have been well prepared for this too.

'Why could she not rebel, and defy him? she longed to do it. But she might as well have tried to defy the texture of her nerves and the palpitation of her heart. Her husband had a ghostly army at his back, that could close round her wherever she might turn' (Chapter 36).

The drowning of Grandcourt seems to me much more acceptable than the drowning of Maggie, and this is much more than a case of poetic justice. The episode is genuinely shocking, while the end of *The Mill on the Floss* is melodrama, but it is meticulously prepared. There is a marvellous impression of the English couple in Genoa, seen simultaneously from contrasting angles, their view of each other, the view of the Genoese of the upper-class, faultlessly dressed couple going out to row, the objective admiration of Grandcourt's physique, and Deronda's sight of them as he meets them on the stairs. If there is manipulation here it is so careful, so precise, has such emotional and psychological unity, that it is appropriate. And of course Gwendolen gains nothing from her husband's death except for a negative commitment to the narrow life from which, before her marriage, she had with such hope and daring longed to escape.

It is clear that George Eliot means us to believe that Gwendolen is a better person, that experience and her contact with Deronda have improved her. Her hasty note to Deronda, which he receives as he himself is about to marry, is a sign of acquiescence to her fate. But there is no lingering impression of calm after storm. Deronda is setting out for a new and adventurous life; this is action. Gwendolen is last seen 'solitary and helpless', and her hysterical insistence to her bewildered mother, 'I shall live. I shall be better', is not a convincing indication of a possible, active regeneration. Dorothea is rewarded by fulfilment in conventional female activity. Gwendolen's fate is much more severe: she is forced to accept exactly the life she had so ambitiously rejected.

There is a footnote to this. When Daniel Deronda rediscovers his mother he finds a woman he cannot love, and who cannot love him. Deronda's mother had rejected him as a young child because he was in the way of her career. 'Had I not a rightful claim to be something more than a mere daughter and mother?' she appeals. The question is not answered. Daniel himself returns to England and marries an ideal woman, with beauty and well-tested talents, but without ambition. But the question is continually present throughout George Eliot's fiction, and both negative and affirmative answers are suggested. Those admirable women who make a success of marriage and motherhood are the least interesting of her creations. Does Mary Garth command our lasting interest? It is the rebels, Maggie, Dorothea and Gwendolen, however inadequate their rebellion, who engage our concern. These are the women who want 'something more', and the fact that their creator does not allow them success does not undermine the point of their efforts.

Sadly, and it is a radical criticism of George Eliot, she does not commit herself fully to the energies and aspirations she lets loose in these women. Does she not cheat them, and cheat us, ultimately, in allowing them so little? Does she not excite our interest through the breadth and the challenge of the implications of her fiction, and then deftly dam up and fence round the momentum she has so powerfully created? She diagnoses so brilliantly 'the common yearning of womanhood', and then cures it, sometimes drastically, as if it were indeed a disease.

FROM A CHILD, a man has seen women debarred by law from the exercise of those functions to which he is to be admitted at the outset of manhood; and he has too often, furthermore, seen his father treat his mother's judgment about business of all kinds, as if he were condescending to let her talk on matters of which the ultimate decision must always rest with the nobler sex. The very same men who will indite most affecting things in prose and verse about the sacred influence of a mother, and tell us that that of a good mother over her son is something quite divine, those same men do their worst, by incessantly snubbing and setting down their wives and treating their opinions as of no consequence, to reduce this 'sacred influence' to a minimum.

This was written by Frances Power Cobbe in *The Duties of Women*, published in 1881. The book was a plea that women should be treated as 'responsible human beings', and its author was representative of the many alert and intelligent women who were much aware of the shortcomings of their own lives, and of the situation of women in general. She was not a militant feminist, arguing that the areas of activity for women should be widened while maintaining that the 'making of a true home is really our peculiar and inalienable right'.

In the 1860s women were beginning to translate their yearnings into active campaigning. That was the decade in which they made considerable gains on the educational front. But in spite of the fact that, by the 1870s, most women knew more, had read more books worth reading, and had seen more with their own eyes than their counterparts thirty years before, a majority of women had unshakeably acquired the habits that had been thrust upon them. Their interests and activities, and sometimes even their responsibilities, were often no more exacting than those of children.

Although Frances Power Cobbe comments astringently on the sacredness of motherhood, at this stage no one seriously challenged the deep-rooted assumption that it was a prime duty of the married woman to produce children. Childless parents were assumed to be suffering a moral and physical lack. Husbands of women who did not conceive blamed their wives, as Dombey blames Edith. Yet by the 1870s ideas about what constituted a family were changing. Families were growing smaller. Economic pressures made it difficult even for a comfortably-off middle-class family to bring up several children, educate the sons and prepare them for some suitable profession, and marry off the daughters appropriately. The lower middle class, imitating as well as they could the patterns set by the more socially elevated, could only afford smaller versions of wealthier housing. The new housing was not built on the scale of the spacious mid-Victorian terraces and villas. As the cities expanded to accommodate their growing populations quantity rather than space became paramount. Building speculators threw up suburban acres of semi-detached villas with smaller rooms and lower ceilings, and blocks of flats began to rise in central areas.

Many parents ceased to be able to afford large families. It seems likely also, although in general we can only guess at this, that many women wanted to avoid being burdened with large numbers of children. In the middle of the century, although publicly the image of the large domesticated family, with loving mother and firm father, was fostered and approved, it is clear that many women regarded – as indeed some regarded the whole of their function in marriage – pregnancy and childbirth as a grim duty. It was difficult for even the most dedicated mother to accept as a frequent event something which brought with it so much discomfort, ill-health, pain, sometimes death, and often permanent physical damage. In the early years of her marriage Queen Victoria, that monolithic example of nineteenth-century motherhood, wrote of childbirth, 'men never think, at least seldom think, what a hard task it is for us women to go through this *very often*' (quoted in Constance Rover, *Love, Morals and the Feminists*, 1970).

Although many novelists describe the deaths in childbirth of their female characters, few attempt to convey a picture of their snugly married heroines undergoing the effects of repeated pregnancies, some of which would produce dead babies, or babies who would die within their first few years. It was a moral as well as a physical reticence, for so long as motherhood was to be glorified its realities could not be detailed. But we get a glimpse of some of these in the following quotation, taken from a report of the Manchester Statistical Society, 1862–63:

I have known a married woman, a highly educated, and in other points of view most estimable person, when warned of the risk of miscarriage from the course of life she was pursuing, to make light of the danger, and even express the hope that such a result might follow. Every practitioner of obstetric medicine must have met with similar instances and will be prepared to believe that there is some foundation for the stories floating in society, of married ladies whenever they find themselves pregnant, habitually beginning to take exercise, on foot or on horseback, to an extent unusual at other times, and thus making themselves abort. The enormous frequency of abortions cannot be explained by purely natural causes. (G. Greaves, 'Observations on Some of the Causes of Infanticide')

The number of abortions was calculated at being somewhere between one in seven and one in three of all pregnancies.

Information about birth control was available, and some doctors at least, especially the doctors to the rich, were prepared to give advice. As early as 1825 Richard Carlile published, in *The Republic*, a highly controversial article on contraception, in which he advocated the use of a sponge. Robert Dale Owen in *Moral Physiology; or a Brief and Plain Treatise on the Population Question*, published in 1831, also provided some hard facts on contraceptive methods. By 1881 277,000 copies of a pamphlet on birth control by Charles Knowlton, an American, had been sold. This was the pamphlet that caused the famous Bradlaugh trial, for Charles Bradlaugh and Annie Besant were responsible for its circulation in Britain. By this time it would have been hard for a woman to be totally unaware that there were ways of preventing conception. There had been some progress since Malthus' weighty advocacy of abstinence as a means of controlling the population.

A remarkable book by a Scot, George Drysdale, entitled *Physical, Sexual and Natural Religion* appeared in 1855. It is a dense and humanistic discussion of all topics pertaining to sexual activity, full of practical advice and pronouncements that would have scandalized a large proportion of its extensive readership. He held that 'if a man and woman conceive a passion for each other, they should be morally entitled to indulge it, without binding themselves for life', adding that they should not have too many children, and should take 'due care' of those they did produce. He also stated categorically that women could not possibly be 'healthy and happy without a due amount of sexual enjoyment'. Inevitably the result of such beliefs was that he insisted that women should understand and practise contraception, and he discussed the alternatives in some detail. It is impossible to know who read the book, but we do know that it continued to sell steadily to the end of the century and was translated into several languages.

But although the quantity of literature on contraception grew as the century progressed, there was much outraged criticism both of the literature and of those who followed its advice. Birth control was condemned as immoral, disgusting, unnatural, injurious to the health, and damaging to the family and therefore to society as a whole. The full fury of the anti-birth control attack was not to be generally publicized until the trial of Marie Stopes in 1921, but the following morsel from *The Lancet*, 1869, suggests the tone and quality of the opposition:

A woman on whom her husband practises what is euphemistically called 'preventive copulation' is . . . necessarily brought into the condition of mind of a prostitute . . . she has only one chance, depending on an entire absence of orgasm, of escaping uterine disease. . . . As regards the male the practice, in its actual character and its remote effects, is in no way distinguishable from masturbation.

The confusion of moral attitude and physical effect is typical of the medical profession's attitude to sex and women.

However, families were becoming smaller, and opinion had even veered to the extent of suggesting that large families were a sign of irresponsibility. It was politely assumed that the avoidance of conception was controlled by abstinence, but both the means for artificial control and the information were available. Discreet advertisements for 'Secret Remedies' appeared in newspapers. One of the most famous woman characters in the whole of nineteenth-century literature, Anna Karenina, practised birth control, although Tolstoy himself virulently disapproved, as he railed against the whole idea of the New Woman. The publicity resulting from the Bradlaugh–Besant trial perhaps did more than anything else to educate the British public.

By the last quarter of the nineteenth century the unquestioning acceptance of women's fate was crumbling a little. Women wanted, often inarticulately and blindly, more choice and more control. Fatalism was being challenged in every area of women's activity, but the knowledge that it was not necessary to be burdened by large numbers of children was crucial. If politically and socially most women seemed to have gained little by the end of the century, this change in attitude should not be underestimated. The knowledge that motherhood was not inevitable gave a new freedom and a fresh interest to many novelists, even where their preoccupations were much the same as those of mid-century, and where their outlook was not predominantly feminist.

An article of 1895 suggests the situation at the end of the century:

The only woman at the present time who is willing to be regarded as a mere breeding machine is she who lacks the wit to adopt any other role, and now she is the exception rather than the rule. . . . For the first time since her creation woman has begun to doubt the morality of producing children under unfavourable conditions, children who lack the physical and mental stamina to wrest success from an adverse destiny, or the fortune to buy it on easy terms. ('The Maternal Instinct', *Saturday Review*, 8 June 1895)

The limitation of children is presented here as a positive and moral step to human dignity. A hint of eugenics, which was becoming popular at the time, is readily detectable. In 1912 H. G. Wells published his novel *Marriage*, in which the Traffords' decision to limit their family and concentrate their resources on the four they have stems from motives that are practical, moral and economic, thoroughly middle-class. Wells' family, in this respect at least, neatly pictures the results of what in the 1870s were cautiously expressed ideas.

Artificial birth control was a hidden source of strength for the New Woman. The title is suggestive rather than specific. It does not describe the ardent feminist, or the unorthodox intellect trying with a serious dedication to come to terms with her anomalous position, or one of the small number of women who had carved out professional careers for themselves. It has no suggestion of militancy or extremism about it, in spite of the violent condemnation it some-times met with. It describes perhaps more than anything else a young generation of mostly middle-class women who reacted restlessly against the traditional system of over-protection by parents until marriage, followed by over-protection by husband.

The New Woman wanted to walk the streets of London and travel on the railway unchaperoned, as Meredith's Diana of the Crossways does. She wanted a more practical education, more experience of life before having to make major decisions – and she wanted to make her own. She wanted to do more in the open air, take more exercise, ride a bicycle, climb mountains and swim. Meredith's heroines are often hill-walkers and mountain-climbers, and his opinions on the desirability of physical education for girls come across strongly. There was in fact a substantial body of opinion in favour of more exercise and fresh air for girls, and this necessarily involved new ideas about suitable clothes. The cycling craze, which grew in the 1880s, confirmed the beginnings of a revolution in dress, which ultimately was to have far-reaching results. Here is a description of a suitable costume for cycling:

Lined with flannel, it is worn over woollen combinations and flannel body instead of stays, to which knickerbockers to match the dress are buttoned . . . of course these unmentionables do not show, but a lady clothed in this way is better able to face the risk of accidents. (Quoted by Alison Adburgham, *Shops and Shopping*, 1964)

The emphasis here is on propriety rather than freedom, but the unmentionable knickerbockers were hotly discussed in the women's magazines. Some defended them as practical and liberating, while others insisted that they were a tem-porary aberration on the part of extremists. But the issue was taken very seriously.

The Lady's World of February 1887 describes the aims of the Rational Dress Society:

To promote the adoption according to individual taste and convenience of a style of dress based upon considerations of health, comfort and beauty, and to deprecate constant changes of fashion which cannot be recommended on any of these grounds.

To protest against the attempt to introduce any fashion in dress which either deforms the figure, impedes the movements of the body, or injures the health.

To protest against corsets or tight fitting bodices of any kind, and high narrow-heeled boots and shoes, as injurious to health; against heavily weighted skirts, as rendering healthy exercise almost impossible; and all 'tie-down' cloaks or other garments which impede the movements of the arms; crinolettes and crinolines of any kind or shape, as deforming, indecent, and vulgar. To recommend that the maximum weight of underclothing (without shoes) should not exceed 7 lbs.

The wish to cast off restraint in dress was part of the wish for greater freedom in other areas. The variations of heavy, elaborate, exaggerated dress through the period had symbolized female subjugation.

But the New Woman was not typical, even of the younger generation. She was condemned, often in terms of violent disgust, by men and women alike. In a symposium on 'The Ideal Woman' published in the *Lady's Realm* in 1897 the consensus of opinion was distinctly against her. A subsequent issue of the same magazine ran a lengthier attack:

That the opinions of the New Woman are not popular or general is a fact no one will attempt to dispute. She appeared as a sort of unnatural production which existed only for a time; she found neither welcome nor favour; she alienated her friends by the vehemence and want of judgment she exhibited, and delighted her enemies by her unmeasured and indecent attacks on all who differed from her; she shocked, and at the same time amused society by her crude ideas on life, and by her absolutely impossible remedies for its reconstruction . . . (*Lady's Realm*, September 1898)

Elsewhere in the magazine a regular column on 'Incomes for Ladies' refers to the New Woman as 'this feminine Frankenstein' (February 1887). The reference was presumably calculated to guard against the taint of extremism in venturing to discuss such a topic at all.

Although the New Woman was condemned by the conservative press, and often characterized as a Gorgon-like creature, it was now widely accepted that women were and should be more independent. Serious questions about status or the vote did not necessarily arise; it was often simply a case of self-congratulation on the products of 'the modern age', another phrase that was much in vogue in the 1880s. A picture of the modern girl emerges as someone active and full of life, ready to help others, and able to face difficulties without wilting. The view that this independence also fed a greater social rapacity, a more reckless attitude to marriage and status, is something most openly found in the fiction of the period, in the novels of Mrs Humphrey Ward for instance, and in those of a very different writer, George Gissing. The world of much of the fiction of the 1880s and '90s, with Meredith as something of an exception, at least in detail and emphasis, is more akin to the milieu of *Vanity Fair* than to portrayals of mid-century society.

While the media were, with reservations, encouraging the new spirit amongst women, they were at the same time sustaining a heavily and artificially romanticized version of the female role. This is very clear in fiction magazines, which might include simultaneously a serious discussion on rational dress and incomes for ladies, and also a shallow tale of fainting females marrying baronets. While there is much awareness of the fact that there were many more marriage-able women than men, the heroine never fails to make a good match. Escapism, of course, but it acutely emphasized the unmarried woman's predicament. Spinsters could not be heroines. They were at best – and this applies also to more sophisticated fiction – good but limited, or worthy but unpleasant. Interestingly, Gissing is one of the few writers who positively characterizes unmarried women over the age of thirty or so, and he is certainly not unaware of the difficulty of maintaining a positive existence in the limbo to which society cast them.

By the last twenty years of the century, the feminist movement had its established figureheads and activists, and had gained significantly in certain areas, particularly education. Disappointed by Gladstone's Reform Act of 1884, which declined to consider votes for women, women's suffrage was becoming a prominent issue, but it was not until the turn of the century that the movement gained powerful momentum, and there is little reference to women's suffrage in the fiction of the period. But an issue of great significance was being much discussed, and this discussion was reflected and embodied in many novels of those twenty years. This was the marriage debate.

The legal basis of marriage had altered slightly. Divorce was now within reach of the middle class, but it was still very difficult and unpleasant for a woman to divorce her husband. In 1878 a Matrimonial Causes Act had established that the woman who separated from her husband in a case of assault was owed maintenance, and the publicity that this gave rise to fed the flames of the feminists. There was much discussion not only of cases of assault but of marriages that were unhappy for a number of reasons, because of neglect, adultery, or simple incompatibility. Women were warned that there were too many risks involved in marriage for it to be undertaken lightly. And to a certain extent the result was a tightening up of attitudes to marriage.

Alongside this were two contrary tendencies, one insisting that only a love match was justifiable, the other calling into question the desirability of marriage itself. Mona Caird wrote several articles pertinent to this debate. She saw the institution of marriage as being part of what she called 'the established system of restriction' of women. She argued that it was because of marriage, and the assumption that marriage was the object of every woman's life, that the activities of women were so distorted. She quoted Jane Welsh Carlyle: 'I do think there is much truth in the German idea, that marriage is a shockingly immoral institution, as well as what we have long known it for – an extremely disagreeable one.' And she herself described the marriage condition scathingly as follows:

These victims are expected to go about perpetually together, as if they were a pair of carriage-horses; to be for ever holding claims over one another, exacting or making useless sacrifices, and generally getting in one another's way. The man who marries finds that his liberty has gone, and the woman exchanges one set of restrictions for another. She thinks herself neglected if the husband does not always return to her in the evenings, and the husband and society think her undutiful, frivolous, and so forth if she does not stay at home alone, trying to sigh him back again. The luckless man finds his wife so *very* dutiful and domesticated, and so *very* much confined to her 'proper sphere', that she is, perchance, more exemplary than entertaining. Still, she may look injured and resigned, but she must not seek society and occupation on her own account, adding to the common mental store, bringing new interest and knowledge into the joint existence, and becoming thus a contented, cultivated, and agreeable being. No wonder that while all this is forbidden we have so many unhappy wives and bored husbands. The more admirable the wives the more bored the husbands. ('Marriage', *Westminster Review*, August, 1888)

In another article in the same journal Mona Caird argues that the State's position in ratifying and protecting a contract that it acknowledges to be temporary, because of the possibility of divorce, is ridiculous, and uses this as a basis for discussing the desirability of marriage independent of Church and State. She condemns the 'self-immolation' of married women, particularly when they become mothers, and talks of degeneration and 'mental coagulation'. Two years later in a further article the relationship between the inequality of women and the present condition of marriage is made quite explicit. 'If woman's claims were granted, if she could secure a liberty as great as that of men, in all the relations of life, *marriage, as we now understand it, would cease to exist*; its groundwork would be undermined' ('The Morality of Marriage', *Fortnightly Review*, 1 March 1890). She goes on:

In a marriage true to the modern spirit, which has scarcely yet begun to breathe upon this institution, husband and wife regard one another as absolutely free beings; they no more think of demanding subordination on one side or the other than a couple of friends who had elected to live together.

Mona Caird was not alone in questioning the realities of marriage. The reaction against child-bearing was a part of this. Some women were worried about certain aspects of marriage without having any wish to attack the basis of the institution. In 1897 Marie Corelli initiated a discussion of 'The Modern Marriage Market' which went on for several months in the *Lady's Realm*. Her own piece was a passionate attack on the fact that, as she put it, 'in England, women – those of the upper classes at any rate – are not to-day married, but bought for a price' (April, 1897). As we have seen, Bulwer Lytton was saying the same thing sixty years earlier. But though she roundly condemns the way the upper classes marry off their daughters to the highest bidder, she retains her faith in marriage. 'Marriage is intended to uplift – to consecrate – to inspire,' she writes. But the only true marriage is marriage for love:

The passion of love is a natural law, – a necessity of being, – and if a woman gives herself to a man in marriage without that love truly and vitally inspiring her, she will find in time that the 'natural law' will have its way, and attract her to some other than her lawful husband, and drag her steadily down through the ways of sin through perdition.

Her opinion of woman's role in love and marriage is thoroughly conventional. 'In a woman's life *one* love should suffice. She cannot, constituted as she is, honestly give herself to more than one man.' Although her attack is clearly justified, her argument has all the limitations of heightened romance, as we see them also in her novels.

It stirred up a lengthy controversy and brought out the old guard in defence of the *status quo*. Here is one response:

The higher standard of comfort which modern society requires, without any superfluities, makes marriage more difficult than formerly, not because there is not the same capacity for affection and self-denial among us, but because the whole conditions of our life have changed and are still changing, and it must be evident to the most Spartan of us that, however simple and rugged may be our theories, it is an impossibility to carry them out in their entirety. (May, 1897)

In other words, one must have money. The argument is supported by affirmations of the purity of English society and warnings about the dangerous romanticism of marrying for love. In spite of the tendencies of popular fiction it was by no means generally accepted that the love match was to be desired. There was a severely practical attitude, rationalizing its commercialism as above, which weighed against this. A further contribution to the debate stated that to marry for love was as selfish as to marry for money; in both cases the motive was self-gratification. Ideally, the motive for marriage should be a modest desire for a home, children and security. In practice that seems to have been generally, as it surely still is, the way it was.

In this debate the consensus was against Marie Corelli. Prudence was the watchword. But two years later the same magazine tackled the subject, 'Does Marriage Hinder a Woman's Development?', a more daring topic which produced slightly less orthodox views. It was felt in general that marriage was necessary for a woman's fulfilment, but that it should be to someone of understanding and sympathy, willing to encourage the interests and talents of his wife. One contributor, however, stated categorically that a woman who wanted a career 'should make up her mind to stand alone. . . . Matrimony is in itself a career, and if the man happens to be interesting the woman is almost sure to give him her best, and put what is left into any work she attempts' (March, 1899). Orthodox in her views of marriage itself, this contributor's assertion that under some circumstances women should choose not to marry is significant. It reflects a more constructive attitude to the single woman – put usually in terms of how she should make the best of an unpromising situation – and a less submissive attitude to marriage.

Two general features of some interest emerge from the marriage debate. One is that many women were taking the whole question, and its related topics, very seriously. Women's magazines are an excellent guide to well-established issues. Women were thinking and talking about their situation in a general way, as distinct from campaigning for or against particular issues, and were doing so more than they had ever done before. The other is the absence of a male contribution to the argument. Men had little to say directly about marriage. The press scoffed at the New Woman, and ridiculed the blue-stocking, but with one or two exceptions men did not anatomize the institution of marriage in public. But this was not true of fiction. The anatomy of marriage, together with frequent attacks on marriage, was a major activity of novelists towards the end of the century, male and female.

Men, however, did not hesitate to advise on married conduct. In 1882 Job Flower's *A Golden Guide to Matrimony* expressed a sententious and conventional outlook. Five years before, a book by Joseph Shillito entitled *Womanhood: Its Duties, Temptations and Privileges* was published, and this too amounted to little more than a continuous reiteration of his belief that 'the true sphere of woman is *home*, and a grand sphere for her consecration and usefulness it is'. Even at this late date the book embodies all that we find most objectionable in the glowing image of mid-Victorian domesticity:

And is it not a high vocation to make homes, like gardens, bloom in the wilderness of life; to be the centre around which hearts gather, and the fondest affections cling; to strengthen, brighten, and beautify existence; to be the light of others' souls, and the good angels of others' path? . . . And what to be a mother? To give birth to young immortals! To guide and train the opening minds of those who shall influence the coming generation. . . . Sacred, blessed motherhood! is not yours a high and holy mission?

There were many people, men and women, who remained convinced that such a description defined a woman's potential. We find fictional characters who echo it. In Gissing's *Born in Exile* (1892) the hero asserts that he hates emancipated women. His picture of the ideal wife is cosily traditional, and he feels that a woman without good looks is incomplete. In his view women are selfish, materialistic and severely limited, and in spite of the fact that the woman he loves is of superior and sensitive intellect he can only think in terms of dominating his future wife.

As a contrast we find in Grant Allen's notorious novel, *The Woman Who Did* (1895), a woman who is not only against marriage in principle but who condemns the whole idea of setting up in domestic union with a man, even without legal sanction:

The notion of necessarily keeping house together, the cramping idea of the family tie, belonged entirely to the regime of the man-made patriarchate, where the woman and the children were the slaves and chattels of the lord and master. In a free society, was it not obvious that each woman would live her own life apart, would preserve her independence, and would receive the visits of the man for whom she cared – the father of her children? Then only could she be free. (Chapter 6)

Grant Allen presents her aims and principles with great sympathy. But although there is a ring of the present-day women's movement here, she has no desire to blur the distinction between the roles of men and women. A woman should be economically self-supporting, she says, but her 'important and necessary' function remains that of motherhood. Once a woman became a mother, it was the duty of the man – or men in general; it was seen as a collective situation – to provide for woman and child. Then as now the battle for independence foundered on the shoals of maternity.

The Woman Who Did is a fascinating document. Grant Allen made a great deal of money out of it, much to the envy of his struggling friend Gissing. The arguments he was airing were certainly not representative of progressive thinking about marriage, but obviously people wanted to read about them. Specifically, not many would have concurred with his heroine's aims, but they reflected a general interest, and a general malaise. Meredith, though most of his novels were written before 1895, and contained more unusual situations and curious people, reflected the same malaise. His most interesting characters are women who, while not aggressive feminists, or people with theories and objectives, have become aware of their anomalous, directionless lives in a society where marriage is the yardstick of success, and take vigorous action towards change. Meredith was perhaps unique in explicitly exposing the situation of women as the key to a critique of society. He saw marriage as an instrument of restraint. It stifled women, limited men, reinforced class barriers, and inhibited freedom of thought and action. In all his best fiction these destructive operations are at work.

SACRIFICIAL MARRIAGE

13

GEORGE MEREDITH wrote *The Ordeal of Richard Feverel* in 1858 and 1859, and it was in part a reaction to personal disaster. He had married when young and inexperienced the daughter of Thomas Love Peacock, who was several years older than himself and had already been married. He himself was the son of a Portsmouth tailor, and it was only through fortuitous family connections that he had been able to go to London first to study law, then to make a career of writing. In Mary Peacock he took on a woman who was not only older than himself, and more experienced, but also, as the daughter of a remarkable man, used to a climate of class and culture quite foreign to Meredith's own background. His wife had an affair with the painter Henry Wallis, left Meredith, and had Wallis's child. Meredith writes of women with consistent interest and understanding – it is quite clear that he liked women as people, which cannot be said of many eminent Victorians – but he never forgave his wife and refused a reconciliation which she later wanted.

Sir Austin Feverel's wife, Richard's mother, abandons him for a poet, his personal friend. In the novel there is an instrument of reconciliation, Richard himself, but the eventual return of Sir Austin's worn and confused wife to Raynham Abbey is an anticlimax, though not without irony. It is during Richard's long and drastic absence from his own wife that he finds and brings home the wife of Sir Austin. It is a pointless gesture, yet of great importance to Richard. His commitment to the return of Sir Austin's wife and his own mother to her rightful home is intense, as is his vaguer desire to reform females of the *demi-monde*. He wants to see women in their proper place. Women of dubious morals operating independently shock and baffle him, though he falls prey to just such a woman. His guilt at his adultery seems to arise less from his unfaithfulness to Lucy, the young country girl he marries, and rather more from his involvement with a woman who has no fixed position, who is anarchic and unattached and lives according to rules of her own. As a contrast Lucy is established in modest but comfortable domesticity and it is this, her absolute certainty of what and where she is, that protects her from the unwelcome advances of the unscrupulous Lord Mountfalcon.

In his later and most significant novels Meredith looks at men through the eyes of women. In *Richard Feverel* he looks through the eyes of men with a particularly limited, rigid and aloof outlook, yet convinces us that there is a great deal that is typical and symptomatic in them. Sir Austin rules the curious and unreal world he has created at Raynham Abbey. He operates his own System of upbringing and education that will culminate in Richard as the ideal, but inevitably an ideal with no particular purpose other than to perpetuate the System itself by inheriting Sir Austin's property and acquiring Sir Austin's limited vision and function. This is a major theme of Meredith's. He sees men and women living quite pointlessly within a quite pointless environment. The power possessed by the upper-class characters who populate Meredith's novels is dissipated because they cannot relate to any other world. But hope lies with the women. In Meredith's fiction it is the women who make the effort to operate not only outside their sex role, but also outside their class role: the two of course being closely interwoven.

Most of *Richard Feverel*'s action takes place in and around Raynham Abbey, and it is from this vantage point that we are invited to look at the world outside. What constitutes society at Raynham, the society amongst which Richard has been brought up? There is, first of all, nothing that resembles a 'normal' marriage, a 'normal' domestic situation, a conventional family. Richard's mother has disappeared under, to him, mysterious circumstances.

There are curious uncles. There are widowed aunts. There are cousins: Austin, unsuccessfully married, Adrian who is single and whose lack of attachment makes him an essential figure in Raynham society. He acts as a kind of amiable Iago. There is cousin Clare who, after Richard's own marriage, is wed to a man a great deal older than herself and dies from it. There is nothing in Richard's experience to suggest that marriage might be a desirable, useful or comfortable institution.

Only by falling in love independently can Richard escape the fetters of the System, for instinct suggests to him that it cannot control him emotionally. Almost inadvertently he precipitates himself and Lucy into marriage. Yet, though the initial gesture is defiant, Richard cannot see marriage with Lucy as in the long run a break with the System, for Sir Austin controls him financially, and only at Raynham does Richard's existence have any meaning. The predicament illuminates Richard's superfluity. He is unable to see his new status as the establishment of an independent life. His taste of life outside the jurisdiction of Raynham is marred by his obsession with his father. His father must forgive, must approve, must see Lucy as the ideal wife. The irony is that in the end Sir Austin does all this, embraces Lucy into the System and thus destroys her when already Richard's anxiety has so severely damaged their life together.

The pressures of the book deny the possibility of a conventional establishment for Richard and his wife and child. But we do catch a glimpse of romantic happiness in the early relationship of Richard and Lucy, quite free from the artificiality that is so evident elsewhere. Lucy and Richard meet in the open air. Flowers and fruit and trees and water help to characterize their emotions, and they respond to each other freely and naturally. When they first encounter each other Meredith mingles his description of beautiful nature with a description of two beautiful people, and the result is a picture with all the lush, sparkling colour of French impressionism, with flowers and grass and clothes and hair all sharing the same richness:

Above the green-flashing plunges of a weir, and shaken by the thunder below, lilies, golden and white, were swaying at anchor among the reeds. Meadow-sweet hung from the banks thick with weed and trailing bramble, and there also hung a daughter of earth. Her face was shaded by a broad straw hat with a flexile brim that left her lips and chin in the sun, and, sometimes nodding, sent forth a light of promising eyes. Across her shoulders, and behind, flowed large loose curls, brown in the shadow, almost golden where the ray touched them. She was simply dressed, befitting decency and the season. On a closer inspection you might see that her lips were stained. The blooming young person was regaling herself with dewberries. (Chapter 14)

It is reality of a sort, young people at one with nature, responding generously to it and to each other. But Meredith's irony, with its striking quality of being simultaneously dry and light-hearted, hints all the time at another kind of reality, a man-made reality, and as if to reinforce the illusion of this beautiful scene he goes on to make explicit references to Paradise and to Prospero's island. The chapter is called 'Ferdinand and Miranda'. The freedom and naturalness that Richard and Lucy experience is not real in terms of the man-made world, and the System has evolved as Sir Austin's response to man-made realities. When they escape from Raynham they become not free, but helpless.

When Richard goes to London for the first time, his love affair in full flood, he goes on horseback. When he goes for the second time, after his affair with Lucy has been abruptly though temporarily terminated by the usual manipulations, he goes by train. The difference in modes of transport is significant. It is in London, amidst a flurry of railway stations, trains and cabs, lodgings and strangers, lies and deceit, that he is reunited with Lucy. It is no longer a question of spontaneous meetings in natural surroundings.

Richard's ordeal is a discovery of possibilities, with an inadequate understanding of how to assess and select. The manipulated exposure of Richard to London society is intended to prise him away from Lucy. It succeeds disastrously, setting in motion the events that leads to her death. The issue is not so simple as that of the natural being overwhelmed by the artificial: Meredith's fiction is rarely developed in terms of clear-cut oppositions. Sir Austin, for all the Rousseau-esque flavour of his ideas, has created in his son an unnatural man, who is intoxicated by his exposure to the natural world, the countryside around Raynham, and is baffled by his introduction to an artificial world outside the precincts of Raynham. Richard needs to be either totally protected, as most women were, or much more independent. In fact he is closely akin to a number of Meredith's women. Women too were by and large brought up by a System, to which they were expected to conform, and which was intended to protect them from untoward influences and exposures. In general Meredith's heroines are better able to cope with this predicament than Richard.

Richard has courted Lucy in a lush, summer countryside. Whisked from a railway station, in lonely London lodgings, Lucy is tremulous, tearful and anguished. At Raynham she has been smiling, loving and trustful.

The omens for their wedding are not good. The balefulness underlying Meredith's description of London, the discussion of Clare's possible marriage to 'some comfortable old gentleman', provide a sombre accompaniment. Richard's attitude to Clare is unconsciously that of a fellow sufferer. The effect of the System on Clare has been to render her totally negative. 'Clare kept opening and shutting her hand, in an attitude half pensive, half listless. She did not stir to undress. A joyless dimple hung in one pale cheek, and she drew long even breaths' (Chapter 29).

Mrs Doria can see no way of disposing of her daughter except through marriage, which she also considers 'a horrid, sad business'. And she berates the System – Richard 'does not know how to behave like a common mortal' – without any thought that the System has also played a part in producing Clare. Clare's wedding follows close on Richard's. In numb apathy she marries a man more than twice her age, and in anguished apathy she dies. Basking in his own consummated youthful passion Richard cannot tolerate what he describes as the 'sacrifice' of Clare to a middle-aged man propped up by the skills of tailor and hairdresser. It is a common sense marriage, Mrs Doria feels, outraged by Richard's misalliance. 'Let us see which turns out the best; a marriage of passion, or a marriage of common sense,' she says, congratulating herself. Clare, deprived of Richard whom she loves, can only think of obeying Mama. She is too listless to object to the man she weds. About her diary, discovered after her death, Meredith says, 'Even to herself Clare was not overcommunicative. The book was slender, yet her nineteen years of existence left half the number of pages white' (Chapter 40).

Clare is sacrificed on the altar of a foolish, insensitive parent's need for self-satisfaction. Sir Austin is no less insensitive. Neither Clare nor Richard nor

Lucy have the moral stature and experience necessary to withstand the pressures emanating from their parents, backed by systems and traditions and conventions. The parents, over-anxious, over-protective, confining their children to a predetermined pattern, eventually destroy them:

It is difficult for those who think very earnestly for their children to know when their children are thinking on their own account. The exercise of their volition we construe as revolt. Our love does not like to be invalided and deposed from its command, and here I think yonder old thrush on the lawn, who has just kicked the last of her lank offspring out of the nest to go shift for itself, much the kindest of the two, though sentimental people do shrug their shoulders at these unsentimental acts of the creatures who never wander from nature. Now, excess of obedience is, to one who manages most exquisitely, as bad as insurrection. (Chapter 29)

It is Thackeray who, in *The Newcomes*, invokes the image of the child martyrs disobeying their parents. Meredith recommends that the parents withdraw their control before rebellion becomes necessary. The tragedy of *The Ordeal of Richard Feverel* is that the children only half-understand what the parents have in store for them. In such circumstances a revolt cannot be successful. Richard does not react against conventional marriage, because he has no opportunity of witnessing it. Instead, his 'insurrection' involves launching himself into precisely that institution which Sir Austin considers to be the System's crowning achievement. One of the points that emerges from the aftermath is that as long as the System's wife is susceptible to Sir Austin's power, who she is scarcely matters.

In describing the wedding of Richard and Lucy, Meredith indicates the inadequacies and difficulties of marriage itself rather than the insincerity of the major participants:

At an altar stand two fair young creatures, ready with their oaths. They are asked to fix all time to the moment, and they do so. If there is hesitation at the immense undertaking, it is but maidenly. She conceives as little mental doubt of the sanity of the act as he. Over them hangs a cool young curate in his raiment of office. Behind are two apparently lucid people. . . .

Firmly the bridegroom tells forth his words. This hour of the complacent giant at least is his, and that he means to hold him bound through the eternities, men may hear. Clearly, and with brave modesty, speaks she – no less firmly, though her body trembles, her voice just vibrating while the tone travels on, like a smitten vase. (Chapter 29)

It is a group of apparently sane people participating with confidence in the celebration of, it is obliquely suggested, an act of madness. The people are overshadowed by the ceremony, but the vulnerability is unequivocal. Lucy's voice vibrates like a 'smitten vase':

Their hands are joined; their blood flows as one stream. Adam and fair Eve front the generations. Are they not lovely? Purer fountains of life were never in two bosoms.

And then they loose their hands, and the cool curate doth bid the Man to put a ring on the Woman's fourth finger. And the Man thrusts his hand into one pocket and into another, forward and back many times – into all his pockets. He re-members that he felt for it, and felt it in his waistcoat pocket, when in the Gardens. And his hand comes forth empty. And the Man is ghastly to look at!

Yet, though angels smile, shall not Devils laugh! The curate deliberates. . . . Eyes multiply questions, lips have no reply. Time ominously shakes his chain, and in the pause a sound of mockery stings their ears. (*Ibid.*)

The vein is mock-heroic, vital, dry, laughing; the effect is comic. Yet what is happening here? A solemn moment, the crown of romance, surrounded by totems and symbols, the entry into independent reality, but undermined, not just by comedy but by barbed hints of failure. We feel the presence of gargoyles with a life of their own perhaps not responsible for the comic reduction of the prideful Richard but drawing our attention to it. When it is all over, Lucy weeps. 'She has nobly preserved the mask imposed by comedies till the curtain has fallen, and now she weeps, streams with tears.'

For good or for ill, the deed is done. The names are registered; fees fly right and left, they thank, and salute, the curate, whose official coolness melts into a smile of monastic gallantry; the beadle on the steps waves off a gaping world as they issue forth; bridegroom and bridesman recklessly scatter gold on him; carriage doors are banged to; the coachmen drive off, and the scene closes, everybody happy. (*Ibid.*)

We see how important Meredith's chapter heading is. 'The Last Act of a Comedy' does not just mark a turning point in the novel, the next chapter being the first of a tragedy; it emphasizes the theatrical nature, the artificiality of it all. There is a final pantomime scene and everybody is happy. At the close of Clare's wedding the bridegroom expands with self-satisfaction and Richard refuses to congratulate him. Both these bridegrooms in a sense slaughter their brides.

In the subsequent scene it is Mrs Berry, that comic yet shrewd commentator on the vicissitudes of life, who takes up the ominous hints of the wedding scene. Lucy will not relinquish the ring she has been wed with. 'It's like a divorce,' Mrs Berry sobs, as she is refused the ring her faithless husband gave her. Separation is to be the keynote of Richard's and Lucy's married life. The wedding scenes powerfully reflect both the emptiness of life at Raynham, once an intimate relationship with the countryside is interfered with, and also the overwhelming importance of symbolically ceremonial events. The novel opens with such an event, the celebration of Richard's birthday, and in the context of the System they have a special importance. But the triumph of the ceremony is only temporary. Neither Lucy's purity nor the presence of angels will keep the hinted dangers at bay.

Marriage, a particular marriage, is an essential feature of Sir Austin's System. Marriage as an institution is an essential feature of the social system in general. Marriage in particular and marriage in general are not always reconcilable, and this is a continual theme of Meredith's. Most of his fiction carries on, sometimes centrally, sometimes obliquely, an argument about marriage. But rather than demonstrate, through a series of debating points, flaws in the institution, as H. G. Wells was to do later, Meredith always starts with individual circumstances and people, and allows his irony and his criticisms to grow out of his situations. Richard is the unusual product of an idiosyncratic system. Diana Merion, in *Diana of the Crossways*, is an unorthodox woman striding into areas of life in which women are not intended to function positively. Clara Middleton in *The Egoist* is an apparently orthodox and confined woman whose understanding of these limitations is suddenly illuminated by the approach of marriage. Carinthia in *The Amazing Marriage* comes into English aristocracy from a strange, foreign upbringing and tests an unrestricted individuality against the situation she finds. Meredith is not concerned with theories, he is concerned with presenting an ironic critique of society through analysis of oddly individual situations. It is only through the particular that the general can be seen to fail.

Richard's attitude to women, in so far as it existed before he encounters Lucy, is feebly romantic. He idealizes Lady Blandish, the confidante of his father. His love for Lucy is a mixture of devotion and pride in *her* devotion. She is repeatedly referred to as a 'little woman'. Yet Richard's attitude to his wife is more complex. When Lady Judith advises him to humour Lucy and allow her to remain in the Isle of Wight when he sets out to encounter his father – 'You can't drag her like a captive, you know' – his reaction is this: 'It is not pleasant for a young husband, fancying his bride the peerless flower of Creation, to learn that he must humour a little woman in her. It was revolting to Richard

(Chapter 34). Lucy's perfection, as far as Richard is concerned, sets her in a sphere of her own, which is why he does not find it difficult to justify his absence from her – her trust and her love are absolute, she won't react like other women – and why he finds it so difficult to return to her once he has been unfaithful – so perfect a woman could not tolerate his impurity. Of course, so perfect a woman proves totally forgiving, and Richard is utterly confused by his idealism.

As the novel moves to a close Sir Austin is exposed at the expense of Richard's suffering. When Richard returns to Raynham to see his wife, now under the protection of Sir Austin, he is convinced that his marriage has been ruined by his own action. Sir Austin tries to persuade him that his unfaithfulness means little. ' "Vast is the distinction between women and men in this one sin," he said, and supported it with physical and moral citations. His argument carried him so far that to hear him one would have imagined he thought the sin in men small indeed' (Chapter 44). He is rationalizing for his own sake as much as for his son's, but at the same time earlier in the novel he made it clear that he would have found it more acceptable if Lucy had been seduced, not married.

Lucy accepts the reunion in a spirit of total love and reconciliation: '. . . she smiled happily . . . and in her manner reminded him of his first vision of her on the summer morning in the field of meadow-sweet. He held her to him, and thought then of a holier picture: of mother and child; of the sweet wonders of life she had made real to him' (Chapter 44). Richard has seen his son for the first time, the son who will be next in line for the System, already under the watchful eye of Sir Austin. His response is polarized in those two idealized visions: he can only see the 'sweet wonders of life' enhanced by a sensuousness which is bound to divert him from the realities. What Lucy has in fact made real, which he does not understand until too late, if at all, is the worth in her own right of her ordinary qualities, her trust, her commitment to her child, her unselfishness, her simplicity. It is these qualities that make her both lovable and vulnerable.

Richard's attempts at the reconciliation of idealization and reality are what make him a sympathetic character. He is thoroughly trapped, by his better nature on the one hand, and by the System on the other. His instincts are right, his understanding insufficient. We cannot disapprove of the instinct that makes him fight Mountfalcon, especially as he grasps at this duel as a kind of absolution from his own sin, but the fact that he does not understand its pointlessness exposes him. Moral structure cannot depend on instinct and good nature. Moral effectiveness cannot depend on love and loyalty. Neither Richard nor Lucy are adequate, for moral power *can* be the product of rigour and rigidity. Thus at the end of the book we have Sir Austin still able to continue the damage. 'All I pray is that this young child may be saved from him,' writes Lady Blandish to

Richard's cousin Austin. 'I cannot bear to see him look on it' (Chapter 45). Sir Austin maintains his mask. No one can be sure if the experience of seeing his son's wife die and his son altered for life has effected any change in him.

And the novel is, very largely, about masks; about, at best, tangential communication, about the pressures of a man-made society on men to make themselves. Only Richard and Lucy, Ripton (Richard's friend) and Mrs Berry have real faces. The rest of the important characters in the book are theatrical, masked, costumed, acting out roles. But on the last page of the book we understand that Richard too has gained a mask. 'Have you noticed the expression in the eyes of a blind man? That is just how Richard looks, as he lies there silent in his bed – striving to image her on his brain' (Chapter 45).

The book does contain a major flaw, though it is a flaw that is so bound up with the novel's unique quality that it is not easy to isolate. It lies in the character of Richard himself. Most of Meredith's more interesting characters behave at times irrationally, inexplicably; they do things which it is impossible to understand in terms of either plot or psychology. Why is Richard, who is neither stupid nor without considerable courage, so thoroughly fooled by his father? Why is there no real insurrection, only, as Meredith so cleverly indicates, an insurrection in the parent's eyes? Why does Richard remain dangling weakly for so long in London? The answers to some of these questions can be found, but the latter, it seems to me, is provoked by a particularly unsatisfactory part of the novel. Richard does not appear to have any real taste for a dissipated life, which he gets drawn into in London, nor is he so far from either his father, who deliberately keeps out of reach, or his wife, for it to be impossible for him to make contact with them. He is cut off from both, he *has* to be cut off from both, for only thus will he make his fatal mistake and destroy his marriage.

Meredith finds it necessary to provide a dramatic spur for the destruction of the marriage. His difficulty is that Raynham is so much a world unto itself that it might indeed sustain a romantic, highly coloured love between two young people. They would be protected. He needs to destroy Richard and Lucy while they are *young*: that is what the book is about, sterility, the cutting off of potential. And in order to destroy them young drama is required: the slow growth of mutual disillusion after years of cohabitation will not do. It is not something that Meredith concerns himself with in his fiction. Disillusion or destruction comes quickly to his married couples.

The novel was published in 1859 at the height of mid-Victorian self-awareness. Meredith's young people are not destroyed by the obvious social and moral weaknesses; it is not drinking, or gambling, or the squandering of money, or fornication, really, that brings ruin. It is an older and supposedly wiser generation. At a time when attitudes encouraged breeding up the young into the ways and possessions of their parents, when property and inheritance were practically moral virtues, Meredith was undermining assumptions about the relationship of an established generation to the young. Richard's marriage offends against Raynham Abbey, just as his mother's adultery offended against Sir Austin's view of women, which in turn is a part of his attitude to property. We will see this conjunction again, with striking emphasis, in *The Egoist.*

WHEN IN 1870 women were enabled to own money and property in their own names it became more difficult to regard women themselves as property, though in most respects they continued to have little independent existence. As long as they could be persuaded to believe that marriage was their major occupation in life, and as long as there were men who could afford to buy wives, either with money or with social status, ideally with both, it would be possible for men such as Sir Willoughby Patterne in Meredith's *The Egoist* to consider their destined brides as precious items of furniture, tributes to their own good taste. This is one of the reasons why Meredith writes about an upper class in which he himself is an alien. He is concerned with exposing features of upper-class life which traditionally have been lauded, and which are woven into the fabric of upper-class aspirations. Among the wealthier classes a woman is almost inevitably a symbol. A desirable residence needs a desirable woman. Meredith's men tend to woo images embodying their attitudes to land, property, and their place in society. Meredith concentrates on a clearly defined sphere. Like Jane Austen, although for different reasons, he can examine a world in some completeness. He has all the advantages of writing as an outsider, both envious and critical, who is attracted and also repelled by what he has the opportunity to observe. He often uses as an important, sometimes a central, character an intruder into this world: *Evan Harrington* (1861) is about such an intrusion, to a certain extent so is *Beauchamp's Career* (1876). Aminta in *Lord Ormont and his Aminta* (1894) and Carinthia in *The Amazing Marriage* (1895) are intruders. And intruders feature significantly in *The Egoist* (1879). These intrusions are a vital part of Meredith's method of exposure. He cannot rely wholly on either comedy or irony to do this work for him. He must have positive, incisive, disruptive characters who can stir things up, prevent alternatives, refuse to be entirely swayed by the dominant ethos. Vernon Whitford in *The Egoist* is a good example.

But perhaps the most important aspect of Meredith's preoccupation with the upper classes is the question of property. Raynham Abbey and Patterne Hall are commanding centres of their respective novels. As houses and land they have their own profound influence on the plot. It is these things that make Sir Austin and Sir Willoughby much of what they are, and lurk as insistent motives behind their actions. Men of property need wives and they need heirs. It is important that, in *The Amazing Marriage*, Carinthia refuses to take up residence on her husband's property: she does not consider either herself in terms of her husband's possession or her son as heir to his property.

In *The Egoist* the diagnosis of a class situation is central. Mrs Mountstuart, intimate of the family, says: 'Sir Willoughby is a splendid creature; only wanting a wife to complete him' (Chapter 2). Sir Willoughby's splendour consists partly of his ownership, to which he needs to add a wife, and partly of his consciousness of status, which the right wife will heighten. For him personally a wife will enhance his situation in a peculiarly satisfactory way, for he seeks in women a reflection of his own image of himself, and that sums up what he wants to find permanently established in a wife.

Patterne Hall is full of ladies only too ready to admire and obey Sir Willoughby and to enhance his self-image. 'He ruled arrogantly in the world of women.' The world of women is perhaps his proper sphere, and they are mostly ladies without individuality, vague aunts, middle-aged and elderly ladies, whose major interest in life derives from him. The fact that Sir Willoughby has no particular occupation is a part of his class characterization; he is able to devote himself to nourishing the admiration of lifeless women.

Clara, his intended bride, is not lifeless. Her sheer physical vigour commands our respect of her as a heroine. She is too strong, too swift, to be imprisoned even in the copious nest of Patterne Hall. *The Egoist* is about a woman's discovery that she cannot be a prize awarded to a man, whatever the man has to offer, although her youth and beauty conventionally characterize her as this. The egoist we understand to be Sir Willoughby, yet Clara describes herself as an egoist, and it is her 'egoism' that prompts her rebellion, her awareness of herself as an independent, individual woman. This idea of egoism, which runs through practically everything that Meredith wrote, is double-edged. Egoism is on the one hand the core of selfish, limited, self-aggrandizing behaviour; on the other it is the spur to what Meredith calls insurrection. A sense of oneself is vital. An ignorance of self in others is disastrous. Sir Willoughby and Clara demonstrate the two facets of the same idea.

Clara's problem is that in many ways she is the perfect wife for Sir Willoughby. 'With the wit to understand him, and the heart to worship, she had a dignity rarely seen in young ladies' (Chapter 5). Sir Willoughby dwells on her qualities:

Clara was young, healthy, handsome; she was therefore fitted to be his wife, the mother of his children, his companion picture. Certainly they looked well side by side. In walking with her, in drooping to her, the whole man was made conscious of the female image of himself by her exquisite unlikeness. She completed him, added the softer lines wanting to his portrait before the world. He had wooed her rageingly; he courted her becomingly; with the manly self-possession enlivened by watchful tact which is pleasing to girls. He never seemed to undervalue himself in valuing her: a secret priceless in the courtship of young women that have heads; the lover doubles their sense of personal worth through not forfeiting his own. (Chapter 5)

This picture of Sir Willoughby bending to Clara, patronizing, self-congratulatory, calculating, stays throughout the novel. We see them together perambulating the gardens of Patterne Hall, restrained and sedate. We see Clara alone roaming the countryside, running, gathering flowers. We see Sir Willoughby sustained by admiring company, often by the best of food, claret and port as well. Sir Willoughby's dignity renders him ultimately ridiculous because he clings to it so rigidly, but the damage which his dignity receives makes him also ultimately sympathetic. Clara's dignity is voluntarily shed when she insists that, after all, she cannot marry him, and risks the anger, scorn and bewilderment of all who surround her.

The tension is indicated early on. Meredith makes it quite explicit that the superbly polite and well-bred Sir Willoughby's view of Clara is as an oriental slave. The suggestions of the harem are obvious. But Clara has 'a natural love of liberty'. 'She preferred to be herself' (Chapter 6). Yet, 'She has no character yet. You are forming it,' says Mrs Mountstuart, whose function as a misleading interpreter is similar to that of Adrian in *Richard Feverel* (Chapter 5). And, 'You are mine, my Clara, utterly mine,' insists Sir Willoughby.

Meredith maintains the tension by showing us Clara's progress towards freedom. She has nothing to sustain her but her own conscience and instinct: instinct, again – it is crucial in *Richard Feverel* – is important. From these she painfully attempts to rationalize and articulate her compulsion to tear herself away from her betrothal. Her association with Crossjay, the active, free-roaming, truant-playing fourteen-year-old boy, and her literal escape in the rain from Patterne Hall are instinctive. Her gradual understanding that she must have it all out in words with both her father and her intended husband, a battle in which she is at an immense disadvantage as neither believes she has a mind of her own, is an act of conscience.

The novel proceeds by means of groups of images illuminated by almost formally dramatic dialogue. Here Mrs Mountstuart and Sir Willoughby discuss the former's characterization of Clara as 'a rogue in porcelain':

'Why rogue?' he insisted with Mrs Mountstuart.

'I said – in porcelain,' she replied.

'Rogue perplexes me.'

'Porcelain explains it.'

'She has the keenest sense of honour.'

'I am sure she is a paragon of rectitude.'

'She has beautiful bearing.'

'The carriage of a young princess!'

'I find her perfect.'

'And still she may be a dainty rogue in porcelain.'

'Are you judging by the mind or the person, ma'am?'

'Both.'

'And which is which?'

'There's no distinction.'

'Rogue and mistress of Patterne do not go together.'

'Why not? She will be a novelty to our neighbourhood and an animation of the Hall.' (Chapter 5)

This kind of antithetical, dramatically pointed dialogue emphasizes the particular quality of contained controversy that is maintained throughout. No other novel of Meredith's is so carefully worked out and fulfilled as regards this sort of momentum. This, and the clarity and tension of the images, are reasons for the high regard in which it has been held. The impression in this passage is of the energetic Clara rigidified into an ornament. Her wild running becomes 'beautiful bearing', her creative conscience becomes 'a sense of honour', her whole personality is seen in terms of her future as 'mistress of Patterne'.

Clara as an *objet d'art* is one of the central images. She will ornament Sir Willoughby's house and his life. She will be static, at home; Sir Willoughby pictures her awaiting his return from masculine pursuits; it is the classic Victorian male image of the wife. Closely linked with this is the image of possession, of enslavement, which recurs varied and insistent throughout. Words such as 'authority' and 'subjugates' surround Sir Willoughby, for although he is negative in personality he is powerful in status. 'Was it possible he did not possess her entirely?' Sir Willoughby wonders as Clara is beginning to indicate her disquiet. There is a passage in which Meredith explicitly draws together the two images of ornament and ownership:

. . . the possession of land is not without obligation both to the soil and the tax-collector; the possession of fine clothing is oppressed by obligation; gold, jewelry, works of art, enviable household furniture, are positive fetters: the possession of a wife we find surcharged with obligation. In all these cases, possession is a gentle term for enslavement, bestowing the sort of felicity attained to by the helot drunk. You can have the joy, the pride, the intoxication of possession: you can have no free soul.

But there is one instance of possession, and that the most perfect, which leaves us free, under not a shadow of obligation, receiving ever, never giving, or if giving, giving only of our waste; as it were (sauf votre respect), by form of per-spiration, radiation, if you like: unconscious poral bountifulness; and it is a beneficial process for the system. Our possession of an adoring female's worship, is this instance. (Chapter 13)

The ownership of things constitutes enslavement to them. But the possession of a woman's adoration makes her less than a thing. The irony is that she has less life even than a porcelain vase – there is an actual vase in the book which is broken as the result of an accident, thus suggesting the shattering of Wil-loughby's image of Clara. For a woman to worship a man is a denial of being, or so Meredith persuades us in this particular class context, and Clara under-stands this. To be the recipient of Willoughby's 'poral bountifulness' – a memorable and genially ironic phrase, and delightfully apt – is just what she rejects.

A second group of images sharpens the focus. These are images of hunting, prey and sacrifice. Meredith describes Clara running like a hare pursued by hounds. She is also 'a victim decked for the sacrifice'. This particular phrase returns us to the ornament image for she goes on to describe herself as 'the gar-landed heifer you see on Greek vases' (Chapter 16). Sir Willoughby is trying to insist that she wear the family jewels.

The tension surrounding Clara is heightened by the fact that she is the only character in the book who sees herself in this light. Although she turns to Crossjay and Vernon for support, and to a lesser extent to the engaging Colonel de Craye, who misjudges her motives, they do not understand the way she sees herself. Clara does think that Vernon perceives her dilemma – 'A scrutiny so penetrating under its air of abstract thoughtfulness, though his eyes did but rest on her a second or two, signified that he read her line by line' – but he refrains from commitment. It is significant that finally, when it becomes clear that he and Clara will marry, an event which is not fully convincing or pleasing, it is Clara who chooses him.

Education, an important substitute for experience, is something Meredith is much concerned with. Clara has been brought up by an erudite father and is versed in the classics, but Dr Middleton is totally traditional, and although her education has helped her to understand him and other men, his own learning has not enabled him to understand her. The problem of education, Meredith suggests, is a problem of communication between generations. Crossjay can learn from Clara because there is something they share, a pleasure in open-air life. Vernon, Crossjay's tutor, shares this too. It is a theme that crops up again in *The Amazing Marriage* and *Lord Ormont*, and to a certain extent in *Diana of the Crossways*: shared experience of open-air activities aids communication.

The picture of Dr Middleton and Sir Willoughby discussing Clara over their third bottle of port is suggestive. This is the sphere of *their* communication. It is a totally male world in which the idea that women might appreciate the quality of the wine from the Patterne cellars is outrageous. Good wine is linked with a male dominated world, with an established generation and status, with the ownership of property built over 'cool vaulted cellars' (Chapter 20), containing wine laid down generations before. They discuss the mutability of women – 'The choicest of them will furnish us examples of a strange perversity,' says Dr Middleton. 'Choicest' sounds like wine, but wine is more reliable. When Sir Willoughby brings forth another bottle Dr Middleton says, 'I have but a girl to give' (Chapter 20). He fears Sir Willoughby might think it an unequal exchange, yet tries to enhance his daughter's worth. 'She goes to you from me, from me alone, from her father to her husband.'

We cannot for long escape the idea of possession. As Sir Willoughby's wine is his to use as he likes, so is Dr Middleton's daughter. Clara reacts against the idea that women must be 'cloistral'. This means more than the indication of a virgin bride, which is what Dr Middleton is talking about. Clara resents the fact that 'young women are trained to cowardice' when they are faced with problems they have no courage with which to handle them:

For them to front an evil with plain speech is to be guilty of effrontery and forfeit the waxen polish of purity, and therewith their commanding places in the market. They are trained to please man's taste, for which purpose they soon learn to live out of themselves, and look on themselves as he looks, almost as little disturbed as he by the undiscovered. (Chapter 25)

'The undiscovered': this perhaps is the crux. Meredith's fiction is about women making discoveries hitherto beyond their reach. No writer in the nineteenth century anatomized the problem in such psychological depth. Clara gains stature as she sees her own particular problem as symptomatic of a much wider dilemma.

After Clara's attempted escape Sir Willoughby is mortified, and ruthlessly, yet sympathetically, exposed.

We now witness a kind of moral disintegration. He turns to Laetitia Dale, who was once devoted to him and whom he has always used to illuminate his own idea of himself. His egoism makes it very hard for him to believe in Clara's treason; at the same time he feels damaged. He needs to bask in what he assumes is Laetitia's continued worship, and proposes to her: she is colourless, he will be able to make his own imprint on her. She refuses him, and he cannot tolerate the thought that he has been totally defeated by women. He reveals the depth of his contempt:

What are women? There is not a comparison in nature that does not tower above them! not one that does not hoot at them! I throughout my life guided by absolute deference to their weakness – paying them politeness, courtesy. . . . Not merely born for the day, I maintain that they are spiritually ephemeral. (Chapter 40)

So we now see the courtesy and deference of the upper-class male to the upper-class female as, what perhaps we suspected all the time, unequivocally empty. Politeness to women means, simply, a calculated emphasis of their uselessness.

It is Laetitia in fact who puts most succinctly what Clara has for so long felt. She knows that Sir Willoughby will drink her dry. 'She scarcely felt that she was alive' (Chapter 48). Laetitia is the ultimate victim, the last ounce of her resistance used up by Sir Willoughby's prideful demands, and he makes no secret of the fact that he wants her because he cannot bear to face the world without a bride. But if Laetitia is the ultimate victim, Sir Willoughby himself is the most instructive one. 'This hateful world had caught him and transformed him to a machine. The discovery he made was, that in the gratification of the egoistic instinct we may so beset ourselves as to deal a slaughtering wound upon Self to whatsoever quarter we turn' (Chapter 47).

Clara escapes the final sacrifice; Laetitia does not. The book is structured as comedy, and reminds us, in its particular emphases, that Meredith used the word 'comedy' in a very specific way to suggest a strictly limited sphere of action, 'no dust of the struggling outer world' (Prelude) – in other words Meredith rejects naturalism – and the operation of an anarchic spirit within it. In his 'Essay on Comedy' he makes it quite clear that one of the most significant ways in which he saw the anarchic spirit in operation was in reversing the role of women. He writes:

The heroines of Comedy are like women of the world, not necessarily heartless from being clear-sighted: they seem so to the sentimentally-reared only for the reason that they use their wits, and are not wandering vessels crying for a captain or a pilot. Comedy is an exhibition of their battle with men, and that of men with them: and as the two, however divergent, both look on one object, namely, Life, the gradual similarity of their impressions must bring them to some resemblance. The comic poet dares to show us men and women coming to this mutual likeness; he is for saying that when they draw together in social life their minds grow liker; just as the philosopher discerns the similarity of boy and girl, until the girl is marched away to the nursery. Philosopher and comic poet are of a cousinship in the eye they cast on life: and they are equally unpopular with our wilful English of the hazy region and the ideal which is not to be disturbed.

This passage provides many clues to Meredith's work. It emphasizes the crucial significance of Meredith's heroines, and emphasizes similarly Meredith's uniqueness as a Victorian novelist. Was there any other novelist in the century whose most important theme concerned the 'mutual likeness' of men and women? He saw himself, this passage suggests, as a fusion of comic poet and philosopher. Critics have often been concerned with the process of this operation of Meredith's, but not so much with its motives or results. Both seem to me rather important. We can also see how certain subsidiary themes that occur frequently in his novels are of great importance. His belief that boys and girls should be educated together is one.

Inevitably, within the confines of the society Meredith chooses to write about, if women are to achieve male freedom of action and decision, an insurrection will be required (it is no coincidence that it involves that child-parent theme that we see in *Richard Feverel*). Clara rebels against her father and her intended husband and the assumptions of all around her. Later, in *Diana of the Crossways*, his most popular novel in his own lifetime, Meredith deals with a heroine who is free of a restrictive context of family and society. *Diana of the Crossways* begins where *The Egoist* leaves off, yet Meredith demonstrates that the problems of both heroines are closely akin and traceable to the same source.

Meredith's later novels from *The Egoist* onwards are about non-marriages, that is, about marriages that do not take place, or marriages that are formal contracts but not complete relationships. There is a sexual theme here, and although Meredith conforms outwardly to Victorian convention in this respect he is much more suggestive and psychologically explicit than most Victorian writers. Sexual relations are closely allied with property and possession. Clara cannot bear Sir Willoughby to touch her; he deems a kiss a right of ownership. When Carinthia gets over her longing for her neglectful husband she sees him in terms of his possession of thousands of acres of land and numerous properties. She rejects the land, the houses and sexual ownership. When in *Lord Ormont* Aminta marries the elderly general she has admired from childhood, it is clear that the marriage is a sexual failure. She becomes not even a sexual object, merely a decorative thing.

Diana of the Crossways is based on the notorious scandal surrounding Caroline Norton, who after her divorce fought publicly for right of access to her children, certainly influencing reform in the guardianship laws. Meredith has made the story his own; clearly his attraction to it in the first place was its appropriateness to his own preoccupations. His Diana is a woman of beauty and intelligence, a combination, he makes it clear, that most men suspect or fear. We see her first at a ball in Ireland, where her attractions, her vitality and her wit are all on display.

Initially here is a free woman, without ties, with intelligence and verve. She has friends and admirers. She has some positive ideas, political opinions the expression of which makes the men nervous, in spite of which she is surrounded by them. But Meredith from the outset in his portrait of Diana builds up the ambiguities and contradictions. She is free, but she is 'unprotected'. She is intelligent, but she has no occupation. She is attractive, but reflects 'how brutal men can be'. She resists the idea of being dependent on a man, yet she is without financial security. Above all she is sensitive to the prospect of becoming a man's victim:

Her experience had awakened a sexual aversion, of some slight kind, enough to make her feminine pride stipulate perfect independence, that she might have the calm out of which imagination spreads wings. Imagination had become her broader life, and on such an earth, under such skies, a husband who is not the fountain of it, certainly is a foreign animal: he is a discordant note. He contracts the ethereal world, deadens radiancy. He is gross fact, a leash, a muzzle, harness, a hood, whatever is detestable to the free limbs and senses. (Chapter 4)

This is a much more sweeping condemnation of men in marriage than we find in *The Egoist*. We see Diana in a much wider perspective, a more experienced woman than Clara, who has learnt at an earlier stage to distrust men. 'He is gross fact': the word 'gross' is significant as is the word 'brutal' that Diana also uses. Both words are physically suggestive, as we see at once when Sir Lukin, her friend Emma's husband, embraces her, where her reaction indicates the 'grossness' of the advance. 'Half-a-dozen words, direct, sharp as fangs and teeth, with the eyes burning over them, sufficed for the work of defence' (Chapter 4). Diana can look after herself, yet she is profoundly humiliated by this episode, just as she is when much later in the book Percy Dacier, the man she loves, attempts the same advances. She handles the situation with the same articulateness: she has to protect her independence verbally. He can sense her responsiveness, yet she says, 'You drive me to be ice and doorbolts!' (Chapter 31). The offence is the physical assault on her decisiveness. Percy insists, 'But you are mine' – echoes of Sir Willoughby. Diana insists on dictating the terms of possession. 'When I have consented to be your paramour this kind of treatment of me will not want apologies.' For Percy it is enough that he declares his love and she accepts it, but Diana's defence of what she considers her free choice is vital:

'But you know we are one. The world has given you to me, me to you. Why should we be asunder? There's no reason in it.'

She replied: 'But I still wish to burn a little incense in honour of myself, or else I cannot live. It is the truth. You would respect me more dead than alive. I could never pardon you too.' (Chapter 31)

The word 'respect' is the crucial one here, in terms of this scene, of the relationship with Dacier and the entire book. We have seen how Sir Willoughby despises women. Diana's marriage to Mr Warwick has been without mutual respect, which in turn destroys self-respect. The marriage is, to use another important word in the novel, 'degrading'. And Diana is aware of the extent to which her own misjudgment is responsible.

Again Meredith's irony works intrinsically. Diana's vulnerability is increased by her marriage, because she chooses, feels compelled, to live apart from her husband. Such curious behaviour draws attention to herself. She is exposed, ripe to become the victim of scandal, as she does first in her relationship with Lord Dannisburgh, and then in her involvement with Dacier, Dannisburgh's nephew. She is exposed because it is assumed that a woman living apart from her husband, a respectable and substantial man in society, can be up to no good, and it is assumed that comradeship between man and woman is impossible without a sexual relationship. Comradeship is another insistent theme of Meredith's. It is his answer to the sex war. Aminta and Matey, Carinthia and Wythan, Clara and Vernon Whitford, are all examples of it. It is a comradeship born of shared activities beyond the drawing-room, shared ideas above the level of social chit-chat.

The wider sphere in which Diana operates is partly the reason why she is a more ambiguous character than Clara. She is associated with many more people and exposed to many more stimuli. She has to earn her own living; the economic motive in the plot is important. She is ambitious, she likes to be close to men of power, enjoys a proximity to decision-making and likes to manipulate. This is a part of her flaw; the other part is more significant and is revealed in this conversation with Emma. She is talking of Dacier:

'Admit that for a woman to find one who is worthy among the opposite creatures, is a happy termination of her quest, and in some sort dismisses her to the shades, an uncomplaining ferry-bird. If my end were at hand I should have no cause to lament it. We women miss life only when we have to confess we have never met the man to reverence.' (Chapter 30)

Diana reveals herself happy to relinquish her independence if she can find 'the right man', and assumes she is speaking for women in general. It is the tension between her instinct for independence and her feeling that she needs a man to 'reverence' that is responsible for her confused relationship with Dacier. It is in her role as a woman of independent political influence, a woman who needs to support herself, a woman reacting over-sensitively to suggestions that she has no real power, that women *cannot* have any real power, that she sells Cabinet secrets to the press. Yet though it is psychologically comprehensible, this episode is not convincing. We can understand, however, that Meredith could not allow a consummation of Diana's contradictory relationship with Dacier, and had to find a means of resolving it. It is the same predicament he finds himself in in *Richard Feverel*.

Meredith's most sparkling intimations of Diana's beauty, seen always in terms of the animation of eyes and mouth, come when he is conveying Dacier's commitment to her. There is an electric quality in his presentation of these two clever and vital people together, and in part the electricity is generated by Diana's constant provocation of Dacier. She undermines his assumptions, attacks his pride and, while he admires her for her 'brains and ardour', he reveals a vein of resentment at the extent of her domination. From time to time this breaks through to the surface. Finally, like Sir Willoughby, damaged by a woman he can't in the end cope with, he turns to a colourless, long-suffering and painfully abject young female, and we understand that, after all, this was not the man for Diana to reverence.

Meredith does not sentimentalize Diana's toughness, in fact it is the core of her character and his message. A woman on her own, dependent on her own efforts for a means of livelihood, must be tough. In a sense she is not quite tough enough, not ready to take risks, in spite of the hints of scandal, precisely because she knows how vulnerable a woman alone is. Meredith skilfully indicates the anomalies and tensions of her situation. These are set in sharp relief in the scene that follows Percy's advances, when he has also imparted to Diana an important Cabinet secret. She smarts with humiliation at the memory of his embrace.

When the same night she enters the humming world of the presses to sell the secret to Mr Tonans, the newspaper editor, her feelings complement her earlier reaction. 'Men passed her hither and yonder, cursorily noticing the presence of a woman. She lost, very strangely to her, the sense of her sex and became an object – a disregarded object. Things of more importance were about. Her feminine self-esteem was troubled; all ideas of attractiveness expired. Here was manifestly a spot where women had dropped from the secondary to the cancelled stage of their extraordinary career in a world either blowing them aloft like soap-bubbles or quietly shelving them as supernumeraries' (Chapter 32).

This passage crystallizes what is troubling about Diana. She wants to both have her cake and eat it. She wants to retain her throne, not the throne of the sexual object but the throne of the woman of power, and she wants to be a part of the real world, on a level with men. This is the dilemma, even for the women who rebel. We understand how important and how devastating it has been for Diana Merion that she knows herself to be desirable.

The novel does end with a wedding, Diana's second. She marries Thomas Redworth, who has maintained his position throughout the novel as a silent, sympathetic awareness of her difficulties. We have seen him, revealingly, on horseback and playing cricket. He is recognized by Diana as a 'loyal male friend'. She resists the thought of him as a possible husband, yet she acknowledges his worthiness. 'The perpetuity of the contrast presented to her reflections, of Redworth's healthy, open, practical, cheering life, and her own freakishly interwinding, darkly penetrating simulacrum of a life, cheerless as well as useless, forced her humiliated consciousness by degrees, in spite of pride, to the knowledge that she was engaged in a struggle with him; and that he was the stronger; – it may be the worthier: she thought him the handsomer' (Chapter 40). The fact that he has bought The Crossways, which Diana has sold out of financial desperation, and does not like herself for doing so, makes him more suspect in her eyes. Yet we can see the inevitability: Meredith of course deliberately sets it up. Is it indeed the 'perfect mating'? Diana has not lost her cynicism about men and marriage, yet she breaks out of the hard shell of her pride and is thus the better for her battering experiences. But her marriage reads also as a statement of a woman's inability to maintain a fulfilled and influential existence without a man. Part of Diana's merit and attraction is that she does in the end submit to 'the right man' – that is what Meredith wants us to believe. Redworth woos her without damaging her sovereignty, yet in a sense we see her fall.

Redworth is of a pattern with a number of restrained heroes who appear out of the shadows of Meredith's plots and claim the heroines as they emerge from their ordeals. Vernon Whitford, Wythan, Matthew Weyburn (though he is less in the shadows than the others), perform similarly. Redworth is certainly the most positive of these, physically and intellectually robust, progressive in actions as well as in ideas. To win Diana he needs to be substantial in every way.

His most revealing action is his ride across country to seek out Diana lurking alone in The Crossways, preparing to escape from the scandal that arises from her association with Lord Dannisburgh. In the early pages of the novel Meredith uses the image of the hare pursued by hounds (as he does in *The Egoist*) to convey Diana's situation. In this episode we see Redworth riding in pursuit of Diana, just as Vernon pursues Clara when she attempts to flee. In both cases flight is prevented. Redworth is more forcefully the hound than Vernon, and like Vernon he catches his hare. There is no suggestion of rapacity in Redworth's character, yet the image, so strikingly presented and reinforced, lingers to cast doubt on 'the perfect mating'.

Meredith's most independent heroine is Carinthia in *The Amazing Marriage*, which contains perhaps the oddest of Meredith's plots. He brings together a collection of curiously unattached individuals, unites them in situations that verge on the incredible, and has them operating outside conventional assumptions about behaviour. The purpose clearly is to set up situations where individuals can be judged morally quite beyond the preconceptions and conventions with which the social context normally surrounds them. There is more free movement than in many of Meredith's novels, more coincidence, and Meredith's style is at its most elliptical.

Yet what he has to say about marriage, and this particular marriage, is glitteringly clear. Carinthia is abandoned on her wedding day by Lord Fleetwood, her husband. Here is the summit of a husband's contempt; he ignores her totally, for she is an irrelevance to his life (which he proposes to continue exactly as before his marriage), and an embarrassment on account of her odd ways. This is a logical demonstration of what Meredith saw as implicit in many marriages. Carinthia, who has responded initially to Fleetwood's nobility – and we never find him wholly unattractive – suffers first in bewilderment, then slowly learns to make something of the independence her father taught her. With customary irony Meredith shows Lord Fleetwood drawn again to his wife by just the qualities that have enabled her to do without him. The impressive image is of Carinthia striding across country with a staff in her hand and her skirts looped up, while Fleetwood is pinned down by his inherited privileges. Here is an insurrection that succeeds.

The message has impact. Yet unlike *The Egoist* and *Diana of the Crossways*, where the lessons of the particular illuminate the general, there is so much of strangeness, of idiosyncrasy, in *The Amazing Marriage* that it is more difficult to read in it a social critique. Meredith was always in danger of losing the sharpness of his comment in sheer density of language, as he tends to do in *One of Our Conquerors* (1891), or in idiosyncrasy of plot, and sometimes momentarily in both.

Carinthia is in a sense a heroine borrowed from Shakespeare, a girl in boy's clothing putting on with the clothes a licence to speak and act with male decision. We can see her emerging directly from Meredith's response to dramatic comedy, and it is there perhaps that she belongs, along with her fellow-characters, rather than in a work of prose fiction. It would rob her of none of her purpose.

By THE TIME Hardy wrote *Jude the Obscure* (published in 1894) the marriage debate had been going for a considerable time, in journals, magazines and also, directly or indirectly, in novels. Hardy's difficulties in writing this book, highly sensitive to public opinion as he was, were perhaps not justified in so far as they concerned his presentation of marriage, for he was not breaking new ground but operating in territory that had been mapped out by 1890. What gives *Jude the Obscure* distinction in its handling of the anti-marriage theme is the particular savagery with which Hardy binds together the frustrations of class, the tyranny of institutions, and established Christianity into a devastating vicious circle. Aspirations and ideals are self-destructive. But even in this he wasn't alone. For although the framework and precise nature of Gissing's attacks are different, the mood and the underlying frustrations are very similar to Hardy's, and a number of less distinguished novelists shared this. There was a general feeling that the time had come for experiment, but that experiment itself was doomed.

Most of the novelists interested in the anti-marriage theme wrote of a middle-class dilemma. The heroines of Grant Allen's *The Woman Who Did* and William Barry's *The New Antigone* (1887), a novel that also caused some stir when it appeared, are middle-class and unusually well-educated girls, though their backgrounds are rather different. The first is the daughter of an Anglican dean, the second of a well-born revolutionary. Both reject marriage very deliberately, and supply highly rational arguments for so doing. Both have to persuade their intended lovers to share their rejection of what they term 'slavery'. Grant Allen's heroine argues:

... marriage itself is an assertion of man's supremacy over woman. It ties her to him for life; it ignores her individuality; it compels here to promise what no human heart can be sure of performing. (Chapter 3)

William Barry's heroine – his is an inferior novel – puts the case in a more extravagant fashion:

'Were I to do as you bid me, to go with you before priest or registrar, I should degrade myself beyond redemption. This, Rupert, is the woman's protest against the old bad order, her martyrdom if you will. It is for man to renounce honours, wealth, glory, the power which involves dominion over the weak, and is founded on their weakness. What can a maiden renounce? I will tell you. Do not shrink if I say it, conscious of the unsullied life I have led and the innocent love that is breaking my heart. Rupert, she can renounce respectability.' (Chapter 31)

The New Antigone is a coy, confused novel and lacks conviction. The heroine pays for her daring and becomes a nun. Allen's heroine, Herminia Barton, pays too, when her grown-up illegitimate daughter reacts with horror at the discovery of her birth, and condemns and renounces her sinful mother. Herminia kills herself to leave her daughter free to enter into the conventional marriage to which she aspires. Grant Allen's portrait, far from suggesting a bold, unfeminine or even wrong-headed woman, presents an intelligent, committed and highly moral personality. She is articulate about her beliefs and dedicates her life to fulfilling one of the most important, the bearing and bringing up of a child. She says, 'Every good woman is by nature a mother, and finds best in maternity her social and moral salvation. She shall be saved in child-bearing' (Chapter 14).

In fact, by 1895 when this book was published there was a growing feeling that women might be saved by relief from child-bearing. Yet this, the prevention of birth, was a subject which novelists were extremely hesitant in approaching.

Hardy conspicuously ignores the issue. Jude and Sue produce several children in their unsanctioned relationship, and the nature of the burden these children are is explicit. They weigh them down, hamper their movements, are a hindrance physically and economically. Jude and Sue walk the streets of Christminster at a child's pace, bearing in their arms more children. If Little Father Time's solution to the problem by hanging himself and his siblings is an artistic crudity, psychologically it is convincing.

For Hardy marriage is just one feature of an agricultural life simple in its elements yet rendered highly complex by the vulnerability of human nature, human aspiration and human effort. His characters have an edgy passion which bears no relation to the plummy romantic feelings that novelists such as Marie Corelli went in for. Hardy's people are continually, deliberately, misleading each other, laying false trails, breaking promises. They have an inability to speak truthfully and openly to each other. In such circumstances, with natural accidents in league with disastrous misunderstanding and human fallibility, marriage can never be more than a shaky and tentative union. The agonizing frictions that Jude and Sue are subject to are present in most of Hardy's couples.

This restlessness, this nervous passion, is heightened by the fact that Hardy is simultaneously portraying a stable and traditional rural society in which such things as marriage, childbirth and death are both taken for granted and highly ritualized, and describing the relentless working of new and outside influences. While in Meredith the outsiders help to illuminate and bring moral judgment to bear on the inside, in Hardy the outsiders invariably damage a homogeneous society and themselves suffer at the hands of the society they attempt to invade. There are some exceptions, the unshakeable Farfrae in *The Mayor of Caster-bridge* (1886) is one, but generally this is what happens in Hardy's fiction. Marriage is a victim of this. Yet people must marry, and marriage is pivotal in his novels. People must live together and find out the worst about each other: this is the way in which Hardy presents it. At best it can provide a viable unit for coping with a traditional cycle of life and work; at worst it can bring destruction, death and untold hurt.

All this had very little to do with the upper- and middle-class marriages that the more conventional novelists of the period continued to write about. If there was a tendency to move further into the realm of passion and away from the exigencies of common sense, this passion usually suggests indulgence rather than pain. By the end of the century love and romantic passion have changed in character from the romance that initiated the century. The pain and static despondency that, for instance, Mrs Radcliffe's characters suffered, have been muffled in a roseate fog of unspecified feeling. While the 'decadent' poets went in for images of decay the romantic novelists, such as Ouida and Marie Corelli, depicted great loves, sometimes tragic but always ennobling, for the man or woman who was capable of such feeling.

Along with this came a greater degree of sexual suggestiveness, if not quite of explicitness. Ironically, while Gissing was struggling to be more explicit about real life without giving too much offence, Ouida was unhesitant in her descriptions of the exploits of young cavalry officers with married women and the *demi-monde*. We have no doubt at all of the sexual adventures of the hero of *Under Two Flags* (1867 – considerably earlier than Gissing's first novel) yet it is difficult to accept that the hero of Gissing's *Born in Exile* (1892) lives chastely into his thirties, especially when we read what Gissing elsewhere had to say about the habits and inclinations of young men.

Adultery and divorce became subjects of major interest for the 'romantic' novelists, almost always in the context of the upper class and in an atmosphere of wealth, artificiality and something like decadence. For all her lushness, and what some critics dismiss as vulgarity, Marie Corelli wrote about the iniquities of the Divorce Laws with justified fervour, and although her novel *The Murder of Delicia* (1896) overstates the case by making the heroine just too perfect, it pulls no punches in its depiction of the married woman as victim. Delicia, a successful and much-loved novelist, marries a young cavalry officer who lives on her earnings. When he takes up with a dancing girl (the suggestions of adultery are explicit, and it is a reflection of the justness of Corelli's theme that Mudie's Library found nothing to complain of in this, although almost certainly if a woman's adultery had been involved the book would have been unacceptable) Delicia condemns the inequality of the possibilities of divorce:

... notwithstanding the death of love, she, Delicia, was bound to the corpse of that perished passion – bound by the marriage tie and also by the law, which has generously provided that a husband may be guilty of infidelity to his wife every day and every hour of the day, without her having any right to punish or to leave him unless he treats her with 'cruelty', his unfaithfulness not being judged by the so admirable law as 'cruel'. (Chapter 7)

Delicia has no escape and no redress.

Marie Corelli abhorred the feminists: neither sexual freedom nor the vote, she felt, should have any part in a woman's life. But she was concerned about the quality of marriage. As we have seen, she condemned the 'marriage market', and she condemned also social artificiality of all kinds. She approved of the simple and the genuine – the heroine of *Thelma* (1887) is an example. A Norse lady unspoilt by the ruthless competitiveness of high society, with a natural beauty and social grace, she exposes the viciousness and gross artificiality of the upper-class life around her. The great emphasis is on purity and innocence. Thelma maintains her distinctive character while around her there is adultery and deception. Marie Corelli's theme is that the ideal of love is one of almost religious devotion and the total negation of self.

A novelist of strikingly different expression but not altogether different concerns was George Gissing. He too wrestles with problems of the viability of marriage, the consequences of adultery, the growing feminist consciousness. His own two difficult and unhappy marriages, the second an uncanny repetition of the first, certainly did not predispose him to consider the question in the same light as Marie Corelli, and he was often inconsistent and less than honest in his writing. But he does document in his novels the dimensions of new kinds of relationships, unconventional and disturbing, between men and women. He often presents the mutual destructiveness of men and women with something of the savagery of Dickens, yet without the flavour of the grotesque. The tone of Gissing's novels tends to be drab and hopeless, presenting grim situations not only as if they were inevitable but as if they were a part of everyday life, unexceptional.

Gissing does not present a consistent view of marriage, or of feminism, or associated issues. It is difficult to know where his sympathies are changing and where he is trying to put different sides of an argument in different books. In an early novel, *Workers in the Dawn* (1880), he presents a very sympathetic, if somewhat unrealistic, picture of a young girl of independent means trying to live an independent life, which involves rejecting the church and working in the East End slums. While she is in many ways an unusual heroine, she is attributed with conventional feminine characteristics, both in looks and in personality. But there is one particularly striking moment when she says to the man she hopes to marry, 'Have I not passions like your own, the thwarting of which causes me pangs as keen as those you suffer from?' (Part III Chapter 12). She is probably the first well-bred woman in nineteenth-century fiction to admit openly her sexuality. It was to become quite fashionable.

Gissing clearly condemns commercial marriages: he also condemns victim-wife marriages. At the same time he allows the hero of *Born in Exile* – and we are never sure throughout the book what Gissing's attitude to this character is – to want this from his future wife:

Little by little she would learn to think as he did and her devotedness must lead her to pardon his deliberate insincerities. Godwin had absolute faith in his power of dominating the woman whom he should inspire with tenderness. This was a feature of his egoism, the explanation of those manifold inconsistencies inseparable from his tortuous design. He regarded his love as something so rare, so vehement, so exalting, that its bestowal must seem an abundant recompense for any pain of which he was the cause. (Part III, Chapter 2)

There are suggestions of *The Egoist* here, which Gissing would almost certainly have read. Psychologically we can read the importance of dominating to Godwin as being a facet of his insecurity, but it is also a product of the tradition of male mastery, all the more naked here for the indication of a process of deliberate subjection. It is rather different from Sir Willoughby's inability to see women other than in terms of upper-class ornamentation. Not surprisingly, Godwin never marries, but drifts into an untimely end, as so many of Gissing's heroes and heroines do. He was very bad at knowing what to do with his individualistic and suffering creations.

In the same novel Gissing pictures a conventional upper middle-class marriage, and although there is nothing particularly untoward about it – it involves neither cruelty nor self-destruction – we must assume again that this is the kind of thing Corelli had in mind:

Martin Warricombe married her because she was one of a little circle of girls much alike as to birth and fortune, with whom he had grown up in familiar communication. Timidity imposed restraints upon him which made his choice almost a matter of accident. As befalls often enough, the betrothal became an accomplished fact whilst he was still doubting whether he desired it or not. When the fervour of early wedlock was outlived, he had no difficulty in accepting as a matter of course that his life's companion should be hopelessly illogical and at heart indifferent to everything but the small graces and substantial comforts of provincial existence. One of the advantages of wealth is that it allows husband and wife to keep a great deal apart without any show of mutual unkindness, a condition essential to happiness in marriage. Time fostered in them a calm detachment, independent of spiritual sympathy, satisfied with a common regard for domestic honour. (Part III, Chapter 3)

The phrase 'domestic honour' could sum up countless Victorian marriages. This is both sociologically and psychologically convincing, and more revealing than many more extreme versions of marriage. Here is a calm, conventional, tolerable *modus vivendi*, essentially negative, in the midst of Gissing's demanding, aspiring, agonized and resentful men and women.

Gissing seems to recognize that there is something both to condemn and approve in such a marriage. In the terms of life which he himself indicates, and so many other novelists of the period echo, the mere avoidance of pain has a great deal to recommend it. There is no suffering here. Godwin's version of marriage is obviously dangerous. Yet men and women must aspire, and a great creative love fulfilled in a great creative marriage is an essential feature of aspiration. Honest fiction was unable to portray such a thing without falling back on the insubstantialities of inflated romance.

Gissing appears to reject marriage, or at least to regard its possibilities for happiness as being remote. His characters tend to be drawn by a fate as overbearing as Hardy's into disastrous unions. He does try to present a coherent argument against marriage, interestingly, like a number of other novelists, from the point of view of women. This is almost always the case. Not only had women more to gain from a revolution in marriage, but men who professed themselves against marriage as an institution were liable to be condemned as libertines, while women, those of respectable background being invariably associated in the Victorian mind with high moral purpose and also lack of sexual feeling, were more likely to be characterized as simply confused and wrongheaded, rather than licentious.

In *The Odd Women* (1893) Gissing describes women who in their dedication to the feminist cause reject marriage. His women here are simply trying to win a right to independence, to work and live on their own. Their reasons for condemning marriage are not only the inequality of women within marriage but what they consider to be its falseness and artificiality. Most marriages are not based on real love and mutual understanding, yet society, helped by the novelists and the journalists, insists in pretending that they are. The contradiction, present in fiction from its earliest days, waits until the last quarter of the nineteenth century to be consciously expressed. Again Gissing's own attitudes are confused. While he presents the female cause with understanding and sympathy he cannot avoid making – and this is characteristic of him – his central character very unpleasant. Rhoda Nunn (the implications of the name are obvious) is obsessive and dominating in a manner calculated to turn the doubtful fully away from the New Woman. She is a prig and a puritan, condemning the 'sexual instinct' and insisting that women will only win their freedom when they can reject not only marriage but sex as well.

On the other hand Gissing's portraits of ageing spinsters struggling to maintain an existence, living on rice, lapsing into alcoholism, despised by society, exploited by their employers when they are lucky enough to find any, are convincing. Gissing's sympathies emerge most fully in his portrayal of the marriage of Monica, the only one of a family of sisters to marry. She marries to escape the unbearable life of her sisters, and this is what she gets:

Never had it occurred to Widdowson that a wife remains an individual, with rights and obligations independent of her wifely condition. Everything he said presupposed his own supremacy; he took it for granted that it was his to direct, hers to be guided. A display of energy, purpose, ambition, on Monica's part, which had no reference to domestic pursuits, would have greatly troubled him; at once he would have set himself to subdue, with all gentleness, impulses so inimical to his idea of the married state. (Chapter 15)

There is all the more point in Gissing's portrait because he is describing a kind and conscientious man who is nevertheless an autocratic, destructive, and ultimately obsessive tyrant because he cannot accept his wife's individuality. In Widdowson Gissing provides us with a representative summing-up of the Victorian husband as we have seen him portrayed throughout Victorian fiction. It is worth quoting further:

In no woman on earth could he have put perfect confidence. He regarded them as born to perpetual pupilage. Not that their inclinations were necessarily wanton; they were simply incapable of attaining maturity, remained throughout their life imperfect beings, at the mercy of craft, even liable to be misled by childish misconceptions. Of course he was right; he himself represented the guardian male, the wife proprietor, who from the dawn of civilisation has taken abundant care that woman shall not outgrow her nonage. The bitterness of his situation lay in the fact that he had wedded a woman who irresistibly proved to him her claims as a human being. (Chapter 19)

The husband as proprietor. In all the major Victorian novelists we have seen husbands as destroyers, and the two features are inextricably linked. In Thackeray, Dickens, George Eliot and Meredith the destructive husband, who is destructive because he believes he has the right of ownership, is centrally operative in the plot. But it was not until Meredith began to write of the auto-cratic, egocentric male with full awareness of the implications of his power over women, and Gissing and others took up the theme variously and sporadically, that the destructive husband was presented without the protection of an ideal of insulating marriage lurking very close behind the sadness of individual cases.

Meredith alters the ideal of marriage by introducing his rebellious women to working partnerships. These unions are positive and active, although they at times seem anti-climactic, even a betrayal of his women's creative independence. But even if there are hints of betrayal, he manipulates his characters in better and more discerning faith than many of his predecessors. He did believe that men and women could live together and discover the best about each other, not the worst, as Hardy would have it. And he was not in favour of pessimistic endings. On the whole Gissing's outlook on the possibilities of the mutual affection and assistance of men and women remained savage. Meredith is much more strongly a novelist of the feminist upsurge than Gissing, in spite of the latter's specific and detailed analysis of the trend, and his determined social awareness.

The Odd Women was republished in 1908. A year later H. G. Wells' *Ann Veronica* appeared, taking up the theme of the New Woman in her militant turn-of-the-century guise. But Wells' version of revolt is highly romanticized compared with Gissing's. His middle-class young girl is not driven by necessity, but is in revolt against the concept of bourgeois paternalism. Ann Veronica's revolt in itself does not come to much. She lacks conviction. She has an inconclusive brush with the suffragettes, and goes off with a divorced scientist. But they do marry, and the last glimpse of them is as they preside over their comfortable, conventional home, about to be reconciled with Ann Veronica's father:

... Mr and Mrs Capes stood side by side upon an old Persian carpet that did duty as a hearthrug in the dining-room of their flat and surveyed a shining dinner-table set for four people, lit by skilfully-shaded electric lights, brightened by frequent gleams of silver, and carefully and simply adorned with sweet-pea blossom. Capes had altered scarcely at all during the interval, except for a new quality of smart-ness in the cut of his clothes, but Ann Veronica was nearly half an inch taller; her face was at once stronger and softer, her neck firmer and rounder, and her carriage definitely more womanly than it had been in the days of her rebellion. She was a woman now to the tips of her fingers; she had said goodbye to her girlhood in the old garden four years and a quarter ago. She was dressed in a simple evening gown of soft creamy silk, with a yoke of dark old embroidery that enhanced the gentle gravity of her style ... (Chapter 17)

And so on. Ann Veronica here is the conventional woman fulfilled by marriage, a baby on the way. Wells was apparently under pressure to provide the platitudes of the final chapter. Without it the novel would end on a note of high romance rather than of bourgeois comfort. Neither alternative takes us any distance from mid-Victorian ideals, and neither fulfils what Ann Veronica's revolt might have suggested, a genuinely unorthodox way of finding satisfaction in life. The point is that Ann Veronica is in fact revolting not against tyranny but convention, so that the novel lacks the social conviction and the worried involvement that characterizes Gissing.

Wells likes to portray lively and rebellious girls – Isabel in *The New Machiavelli* (1911) is another – but his pictures of married life, in that novel and in *Marriage* (1912) focus on ambitious men whose wives don't understand them, rather than on women struggling for equality within marriage. Marriage is seen as an environment that ought to sustain active men, but should allow them to escape if it doesn't. Marriage is a highly fallible institution, Wells seems to be suggesting, but useful, and acceptable so long as plenty of freedom is allowed and people can make mistakes and start again if necessary.

It is a more quiescent view than Meredith's, certainly than Gissing's, if more honest than that of the majority of Victorian writers, and Wells' novels read now with a curious and arrogant complacency which does not contrast favourably with the difficult anger of Gissing, or the more analytic attempts of writers of a younger generation, Ford Madox Ford, Lawrence, Virginia Woolf, to come to terms with human relations.

Wells was ranging over territory that had been covered twenty or thirty years earlier. He was not really interested in carrying on or enlarging the debate about marriage. In fact, essentially, general interest in it had dwindled. Now the emphasis was on sexual freedom in or out of marriage, and the red herring of sexual unrestraint drew attention away from inequality and the anomalies of the marriage institution, as was to happen again in the 1960s. The profound concern with the nature of marriage, which was much in evidence even in second-rate fiction towards the end of the previous century, was to fade. There were of course other preoccupations in late nineteenth-century fiction, and more dominating factors. There was still a tendency for novels, and particularly magazine stories, to concern themselves almost entirely with the lives of the rich and the socially elevated. In popular fiction marriage remained the happy ending, property and status the rewards for love and virtue. Rebels like Kitty in Mrs Ward's *The Marriage of William Ashe* (1905) were punished. Women who forgot their marriage vows and craved for further dimensions to their lives could not be allowed to get away with it. The demands of convention and society were sustained. Yet people liked to read about rebellion, they liked to read about the exotic and the unusual (Mrs Ward's novel contains a character who is quite clearly based on Byron), as the great success of Ouida's dashing novels showed, so that a taste for the daring, the titillating, a taste in adultery, elopement and illegitimacy, was fostered. As novelists became more adventurous, the demands of Mudie's Library were loosing their hold, naturalism, however much condemned, introduced new possibilities, yet conventional marriage was not shaken as a fundament of fiction. It was always there to provide a staple of plot and action, of assumptions about what people wanted, how they behaved, and what the roots of life were. It was as basic to the thoughts of readers and writers as four walls and a roof.

AFTERWORD: THE KREUTZER SONATA

I COME FULL CIRCLE, or nearly so, for I return to Tolstoy with whom this study began, but Tolstoy thirty years after his story *Family Happiness*. I go back to Russia without apology, for Tolstoy was of all nineteenth-century writers both the greatest celebrator of the family and its main antagonist. In his relentless, detailed, awe-inspiring honesty, which spared neither himself nor his own wife and children, he exposes so much of family satisfaction and family conflict, of marriage as fulfilment and marriage as destruction, as an ideal and as sour compromise, and all the bitter contradictions involved in the whole idea of family living, that he is an essential key to the nineteenth century.

In *War and Peace* (1869) Tolstoy finishes with a picture of family life, with the children of Natasha and Pierre, of Nicolai and Maria, and Andrey's son all under one spacious roof, attended by parents and relatives in an atmosphere of cheerful, disorganized bustle. Natasha, the lovely, charming young girl who has beguiled us throughout the novel, has become a harassed and untidy matron, her figure and her sparkle gone, a change that comes inevitably, Tolstoy suggests, to a woman with growing children and growing family responsibilities. Maria is depressed by her pregnancy, convinced that she looks dowdy and unattractive. The men are preoccupied with their own activities, Nicolai with the estate, Pierre with politics. But the overwhelming impression is of care for the children, energy, loyalty between the parents, and a loving instinct which soothes and outweighs the inevitable differences and problems, of men and women performing with some success their allotted roles, of family life as creative, satisfying, vital, ongoing. This is what the Rostov saga has been all about: love and loyalty that may not be able to cope with all eventualities, but can keep things going, can survive positively.

We have seen in *Family Happiness*, published ten years earlier, a somewhat different version of the story. Family living is a great deal more dubious, more negative. Duty, restriction, self-restraint, are more prominent than love. Vitality is deadened. In 1889 Tolstoy's story *The Kreutzer Sonata* was published. It expresses the full obsessional bitterness of Tolstoy's reaction against the family, and in the process it exposes with alarming clarity much of the damage inherent in Victorian attitudes towards marriage, towards women, towards sex and towards children. It extrapolates from Tolstoy's attitudes to his own family –

neither his wife nor his children demonstrated the moral nobility he demanded and this was an acute disappointment to him – a perverse logic which leads the story's central character to murder his wife, and to believe that the murder was inevitable.

Like Tolstoy himself Pozdnyshev, who is in a way the *only* character in *The Kreutzer Sonata*, has had a dissolute youth, frequenting brothels and making use of any available woman in the belief that this was not only normal behaviour for a young man of his class, which it was, but that sexual release was essential for his health. At the same time, when he thinks of marriage he has in mind a pure, irreproachable woman; it is out of the question that he should marry a woman of tainted reputation.

The story is riven with contradictions, some, but not all, of which Pozdny-shev and his creator recognize. It is just these contradictions which are so revealing, for they arise out of an inability to be rational about sex and women. When Pozdnyshev exploits women he can rationalize his use of them. As long as he pays them everything is all right. Money is a substitute for personal in-volvement: 'I remember how I once worried because I had not had an oppor-tunity to pay a woman who gave herself to me (having probably taken a fancy to me) and how I only became tranquil after having sent her some money – thereby intimating that I did not consider myself in any way morally bound to her...' (Chapter 3). But when he marries, because of his previous relations with women and his growing doubt about them, it is more difficult to rationalize his intimacy with his wife. Looking back on his life as he relates his story to a fellow-traveller on the train, crossing the vastness of Russia for several days and nights, Pozdnyshev condemns himself for profligacy. But he condemns his wife, and all women, too, for have they not deliberately put themselves up for sale and decked themselves out and exposed their bodies just like prostitutes? And because man is a victim of his sex drive, because man must have woman, the woman has a position of immense power at the same time as being degraded:

... on the one hand woman is reduced to the lowest stage of humiliation, while on the other she dominates. Just like the Jews: as they pay us back for their oppression by financial domination, so it is with women. 'Ah, you want us to be traders only, – all right, as traders we will dominate you!' say the Jews. 'Ah, you want us to be merely objects of sensuality – all right, as objects of sensuality we will enslave you,' say the women. Woman's lack of rights arise not from the fact that she must not vote or be a judge – to be occupied with such affairs is no privi-lege – but from the fact that she is not man's equal in sexual intercourse and has not the right to use a man or abstain from him as she likes – is not allowed to choose a man at her pleasure instead of being chosen by him. You say that is monstrous. Very well! Then a man must not have those rights either. As it is at present, a woman is deprived of that right while a man has it. And to make up for that right she acts on man's sensuality, subdues him so that he only chooses formally, while in reality it is she who chooses. And once she has obtained these means she abuses them and acquires a terrible power over people. (Chapter 9)

Women, Pozdnyshev argues, dominate society because of men's weakness. The mixture of resentment and zeal for reform is clear. The answer is not equality between men and women, the same opportunities for choice and action for women as for men, but the elimination of sex altogether, which he tries to prove is an artificial and unnatural need anyway. Tolstoy himself, in trying to come to terms with his own sexual urges, which led him to do things he despised himself for, decided in the end that total abstinence was the only solution, and Pozdnyshev echoes this. And like Tolstoy he cannot rid himself of the deep-seated belief that whatever injustices they suffer, women are the cause of the whole nasty business. Like so many Victorians he felt that upper-class women ought to be above sex, yet he couldn't help recognizing that it was men who prevented them. It was a vicious circle that tormented Tolstoy – he seemed never to be able to forgive his wife for being his wife. If it weren't for women, men could not indulge their sexuality, if it weren't for men women would not be corrupted, and he did distinctly see sexual pleasure in women as corrupt. 'The husband must cultivate that vice in his wife in order to derive pleasure from it' (Chapter 11). And later, 'All the women who might help the progress of mankind towards truth and goodness he converts, for the sake of his pleasure, into enemies instead of helpmates. See what it is that everywhere impedes the forward movement of mankind. Women!' (Chapter 13).

We can see the confusion in the argument, yet the logic is present too. Pozdnyshev penetrates the double standard, he understands that men cannot both place women on pedestals and exploit them; and yet he insists that they must stay on their pedestals. Like so many Victorians, Tolstoy (speaking through Pozdnyshev) wanted women to be not equal with men, but superior. His own wife fails him, and although he recognizes that it is not her fault, it is nevertheless she who must be punished.

The marriage is a failure from the start:

What were the first symptoms of my love? Why that I gave way to animal excesses, not only without shame but being somehow even proud of the possibility of these physical excesses, and without in the least considering either her spiritual or even her physical life. I wondered what embittered us against one another, yet it was perfectly simple: that animosity was nothing but the protest of our human nature against the animal nature that overpowered it. (Chapter 13)

Because of sex husband and wife become enemies and grow to hate one another. 'That hatred was nothing but the mutual hatred of accomplices in a crime,' Pozdnyshev says. They have several children, the only possible justification for sex, but when this justification ceases, when his wife is told by her doctor that she must have no more children and is shown how this can be prevented, the war intensifies:

She was not well and the doctors told her not to have children, and taught her how to avoid it. To me it was disgusting. I struggled against it, but she with frivolous obstinacy insisted on having her own way and I submitted. The last excuse for our swinish life – children – was then taken away, and life became viler than ever. (Chapter 18)

His outrage at the idea of contraception is increased for the effect of freedom from childbearing, in his eyes at least, gives his wife a new vitality, a new confidence, a greater sense of herself as an attractive woman, which he finds deeply offensive and leads him to interpret her relationship with a musician who visits the house as an adulterous one.

In Pozdnyshev's attitude to children we again see a fearful logic overriding the implicit contradictions. The only justification for sex is childbirth, and to redeem themselves from the animality of copulation women must not only bear children, they must suckle them themselves, however difficult or injurious to the health this may be. Yet children cause nothing but suffering and anxiety, continual worry over their welfare, neurosis on the part of the mother about whether she is handling them properly.

Not to have children is selfish indulgence, because it frees the parents from the burden of anxiety. But this is how Pozdnyshev describes the growth of their family:

Even now, when I do but remember my wife's life and the condition she was in during the first years when we had three or four children and she was absorbed in them, I am seized with horror! We led no life at all, but were in a state of constant danger, again followed by a desperate struggle and another escape – always as if we were on a sinking ship. Sometimes it seemed to me that this was done on purpose and that she pretended to be anxious about the children in order to subdue me. It solved all questions in her favour with such tempting simplicity. It sometimes seemed as if all she did and said on these occasions was pretence. But no! She herself suffered terribly, and continually tormented herself about the children and their health and illnesses. It was torture for her and for me too; and it was impossible for her not to suffer. (Chapter 16)

Marriage was poisoned by the children who might have been expected to be a consolation and a pleasure. Not only was family life completely unsettled, punctuated by crises of illness and accident, but the parents soon began to use the children as weapons in their own warfare. And all the time, we are to understand, their sexual life continued, aggravating Pozdnyshev's obsessions.

There is no suggestion that change or separation might be desirable, for Pozdnyshev sees it all as inevitable, that is what married life is like for most people, nothing can be done. In the end, convinced that his wife is having an affair with the violinist who plays the 'Kreutzer' Sonata accompanied by her, Pozdnyshev finds a solution in murder:

What was terrible you know, was that I considered myself to have a complete right over her body as if it were my own, and yet at the same time I felt I could not control that body, that it was not mine and she could dispose of it as she pleased, and that she wanted to dispose of it not as I wished her to. (Chapter 25)

Pozdnyshev is frustrated, obsessed, confused, he hates his wife because he hates himself, blames her because he blames himself, yet there is so much truth in the story, so much of Tolstoy's diagnosis is apt and revealing, that it cannot be dismissed as frenzied distortion. Injustice and inequality is sharply focused, the potential mutilations of family life ruthlessly exposed. Yet just as it exposes a core of truth about nineteenth-century life it reveals, through the character and attitudes of Pozdnyshev, a core of prejudice which is just as real.

The story is told entirely from the male point of view, egocentric, a total lack of curiosity about women other than sexually. Pozdnyshev's wife has no personality and no existence, except as his antagonist. She says and does nothing that is not directly apposite to their conflict. The story is extreme, yet it represents the way in which we have seen so many Victorian husbands regard their wives, and so many Victorian wives invite that kind of regard, and suggests a perfectly logical interpretation of a great deal of what I have been writing about. The attitude to women and to children has a grim typicality. We can read the story as the ultimate comment on Victorian marriage, a comment that arises not out of a new or more creative way of thinking of human relationships, but out of a tormented inability to make sense of the old. In so many ways, throughout his fiction, Tolstoy's diagnosis is right but, just as he despised and distrusted doctors, he had no faith in palliatives. If there was to be a cure it had to be drastic.

The bitter invective of *The Kreutzer Sonata* is a reflection of Tolstoy's own bitterness at human weakness and human failure. We have to admire him for the impossibly demanding standards he set himself, yet we have to condemn him for his lack of human sympathy and tolerance. There is something of Tolstoy in most of the great Victorian men, diluted very often by hypocrisy and compromise, and particularly detectable in attitudes to women, marriage and the home. The egocentric, authoritarian male point of view dominated Victorian life: what Victorian literature demonstrates is both its power and its destructiveness, and the fascinating process of reaction against it. It can be argued that this process of reaction, which we can see operating, with differing levels of awareness and varying motives and purpose, in all the authors I have been discussing, even those who seem to affirm a highly conventional ideal, is one of the most signal features of social and cultural life in the nineteenth century. The very centrality of marriage and the continual preoccupation of women made this inevitable. Relationships between husband and wife, parents and children, home and the family, were explored, idealized and worried over to an extent that had never occurred before, a reflection of the enlarged importance of the family; and the novel itself, the chief vehicle for this exploration, to a great extent owed its vast success to this preoccupation. Marriage and the family demanded to be written and read about.

In the closing years of the century Henry James wrote about individual relationships between men and women, isolating them and examining them closely yet with a diffusely objective point of view. He wasn't concerned with marriage as an institution, as a unit of society, but he was very much concerned with marriage and all kinds of human relations as a web of intimacy, of involvement, of loyalties recognized and flouted. If Meredith was the first novelist to remove marriage systematically from the iron grip of social expectations, James carried on the process of stripping it of all possible supports and disguises with an intensified, less amiable focus. He exposed the layers of vulnerability and betrayal with astringent curiosity.

Henry James' fiction does not really constitute a reaction against Victorian marriage, or against any of the relationships he examined, however cruel or unjust. His was a movement onwards and inwards, not a revolution. We have seen something of the backlash, which had features I have not mentioned, Ibsen's portrait of the doll's house wife, for instance, and Samuel Butler's damning attack on the corruption of the patriarchal system in *The Way of All Flesh* (1903). In the last twenty years or so of the nineteenth century the awareness of the failures and injustices of marriage and family life was both bitter and exciting. Attitudes changed of course, but on the whole nothing much came of this awareness, nothing to shake seriously the established institutions of society – apart, that is, from a number of remarkable novels.

A great deal of Victorian literature is about people accepting, or rejecting, or compromising over, the status of women and children as individuals. That many men, like Tolstoy and Dickens, remained baffled and tormented by this question, that many women, like Charlotte Brontë and George Eliot, were unable to follow unequivocally what instinct and reason suggested, is symptomatic of the social and psychological intensity of the issue. By the end of the century moral confusion over marriage, and its viability as a rational way of life, provoked a great deal of the kind of muddle and contradiction which *The Kreutzer Sonata* reveals, but nowhere else does it appear in so concentrated and agonized a fashion. In that story Tolstoy is defeated, for the only solution he can find to centuries of inequality and injustice and irrationality is wholly negative, a denial of human need. The fact that the greatest novelist of the century was defeated by the contradictions of marriage and family life suggests that we should not underestimate their depth and influence.

ACKNOWLEDGMENTS

THE SOURCES of the illustration material reproduced in this book are as follows: Mary Evans picture library, pp. 15, 81, 95, 204, 211; Thackeray's *Ballads* (1897 edition), pp. 26, 67; Thackeray's *The Newcomes* (1855), pp. 43, 55; Dickens' *Dombey and Son*, by Hablôt Browne (Phiz), p. 119; illustrations from contemporary sources, pp. 106, 129, 143, 170, 180, 194.

LIST OF DATES

This selective chronology includes publication dates of books relevant to the subject, and also dates of legislation affecting women's status.

1792 Mary Wollstonecraft *A Vindication of the Rights of Women*
1794 Ann Radcliffe *The Mysteries of Udolpho*
1796 Fanny Burney *Camilla*
1797 Thomas Gisbourne *An Enquiry into the Duties of the Female Sex*
1811 Jane Austen *Sense and Sensibility*
1813 *Pride and Prejudice*
1814 *Mansfield Park*
1816 *Emma*
1818 *Persuasion*
 Susan Ferrier *Marriage*
 Walter Scott *The Heart of Midlothian*
1825 Richard Carlile *Every Woman's Book*
1828 Bulwer Lytton *Pelham*
1831 Mrs John Sandford *Woman in her Social and Domestic Character*
1836 Bulwer Lytton *England and the English*
1839 INFANTS' CUSTODY ACT
1841 Charles Dickens *The Old Curiosity Shop* (serialized 1840–41)
1842 Mrs Sarah Stickney Ellis *The Daughters of England*
1844 Charles Dickens *Martin Chuzzlewit* (serialized 1843–44)
 William Thackeray *The Luck of Barry Lyndon*
 Benjamin Disraeli *Coningsby*
1845 *Sybil* or *The Two Nations*
1847 Anne Brontë *Agnes Grey*
 Charlotte Brontë *Jane Eyre*
 Emily Brontë *Wuthering Heights*
 William Thackeray *Vanity Fair* (serialized 1847–48)
1848 Anne Brontë *The Tenant of Wildfell Hall*
 Charles Dickens *Dombey and Son* (serialized 1846–47)
 Elizabeth Gaskell *Mary Barton*

Charles Kingsley *Yeast*

Geraldine Jewsbury *The Half-Sisters*

1849 William Thackeray *The History of Pendennis*

The Book of Snobs

Bulwer Lytton *The Caxtons*

Charlotte Brontë *Shirley*

'Hints for Husbands' and 'Hints for Wives' columns begin to appear in *The Family Friend*

1850 Charles Dickens *David Copperfield* (serialized 1849–50)

1851 Charles Kingsley *Alton Locke*

1852 William Thackeray *The History of Henry Esmond*

1853 Charles Dickens *Bleak House* (serialized 1852–53)

Dinah Craik *Agatha's Husband*

Elizabeth Gaskell *Ruth*

The Englishwoman's Domestic Magazine begins publication, and includes articles on topics such as 'The Comfort of the Family' and 'How to Manage a Husband'

1854 Charles Dickens *Hard Times*

1855 Elizabeth Gaskell *North and South*

Geraldine Jewsbury *Constance Herbert*

William Thackeray *The Newcomes* (serialized 1853–55)

George Drysdale *Physical, Sexual and Natural Religion*, later published as *Elements of Social Science*

1857 MATRIMONIAL CAUSES ACT

Anthony Trollope *Barchester Towers*

Charles Dickens *Little Dorrit* (serialized 1855–56)

Chambers' Journal publishes a series on 'A Woman's Thoughts about Women'

1858 George Eliot *Scenes from Clerical Life*

Anthony Trollope *Dr Thorne*

1859 Ivan Turgenev *On the Eve*

Leo Tolstoy *Family Happiness*

George Meredith *The Ordeal of Richard Feverel*

William Thackeray *The Virginians* (serialized 1857–59)

George Eliot *Adam Bede*

1860 *The Mill on the Floss*

Emily Eden *The Semi-Attached Couple*

George Meredith *Evan Harrington*

1861 Mrs Henry Wood *East Lynne*

1862 Anthony Trollope *The Small House at Allington*

Frances Power Cobbe 'What Shall We Do With our Old Maids?', in *Fraser's Magazine*

1863 Elizabeth Gaskell *Sylvia's Lovers*
George Eliot *Romola*
Frances Power Cobbe *Essays on the Pursuits of Women*
British Workwoman begins publication

1864 Anthony Trollope *Can You Forgive Her?*

1865 George Meredith *Rhoda Fleming*
Charles Dickens *Our Mutual Friend* (serialized 1864–65)
John Ruskin *Sesame and Lilies*

1866 George Eliot *Felix Holt the Radical*

1867 Elizabeth Gaskell *Wives and Daughters*
Elizabeth Lynn Linton *Sowing the Wind*
Ouida *Under Two Flags*

1869 John Stuart Mill *The Subjection of Women*
W. E. H. Lecky *A History of European Morals* (2 vols)
Leo Tolstoy *War and Peace*
Mrs Sarah Stickney Ellis *The Education of the Heart*

1870 MARRIED WOMEN'S PROPERTY ACT
Wilkie Collins *Man and Wife*
Elizabeth Lynn Linton *Ourselves: A Series of Essays on Women*

1871 George Meredith *Harry Richmond*

1872 George Eliot *Middlemarch* (serialized 1871–72)

1873 Wilkie Collins *The New Magdalene*

1874 MARRIED WOMEN'S PROPERTY ACT AMENDMENT ACT
Thomas Hardy *Far from the Madding Crowd*

1876 Charlotte Yonge *Womankind*
Leo Tolstoy *Anna Karenina*
George Meredith *Beauchamp's Career*
George Eliot *Daniel Deronda*

1877 Elizabeth Lynn Linton *The World Well Lost*
Ivan Turgenev *Virgin Soil*
Joseph Shillito *Womanhood: Its Duties, Temptations and Privileges*

1878 MATRIMONIAL CAUSES ACT

1879 George Meredith *The Egoist*

1880 Charles Kingsley *Sanitary and Social Lectures and Essays*
George Gissing *Workers in the Dawn*
Henry James *Portrait of a Lady*

1881 Frances Power Cobbe *The Duties of Women*

1882 MARRIED WOMEN'S PROPERTY ACT

FURTHER READING

THIS IS A very selective list of twentieth-century writing on the Victorian period that I have found particularly useful. Many of these books are essential texts in the study of the nineteenth century. I have included very few works of literary criticism, only those which are both relevant to my particular approach and are genuinely illuminating.

As general guides I found these helpful: J. F. C. Harrison's *The Early Victorians* (London and New York, 1971), and Geoffrey Best's *Mid-Victorian Britain* (London, 1971); E. Royston Pike's *Human Documents of the Industrial Revolution* (London and New York, 1966) and *Human Documents of the Victorian Golden Age* (London and New York, 1967). On women, Duncan Crow's *The Victorian Woman* (London, 1971), is a good survey, and Margaret Hewitt's *Wives and Mothers in Victorian Industry* (London, 1958) is a key text. Read Kate Millett's *Sexual Politics* (London and New York, 1971) for a healthily redressive study of women in literature. Read Claire Tomalin's *The Life and Death of Mary Wollstonecraft* (London and New York, 1974) for her description of early nineteenth-century childbirth. On the family and related subjects, J. A. Banks' *Prosperity and Parenthood* (London, 1954) and O. R. McGregor's *Divorce in England* (London, 1957) are essential reading, while on children the two volumes of Ivy Pinchbeck's and Margaret Hewitt's *Children in English Society* (London and Toronto, 1973) are comprehensive. On contraception in particular, J. A. and O. Banks' *Feminism and Family Planning in Victorian England* (Liverpool, 1964, and New York, 1972) and Peter Fryer's *The Birth Controllers* (London, 1965) contain the available information. On sexuality Steven Marcus's *The Other Victorians* (London, 1966, and New York, 1974) and Gordon Haight's article 'Male Chastity in the Nineteenth Century', *Contemporary Review*, November, 1971, are the most illuminating; Ronald Pearsall's *The Worm in the Bud* (London, 1969) is interesting but rather badly written and organized.

In general I found that Victorian women's magazines and family magazines never failed to increase my understanding of the period. Literary biographies I particularly relied on were Gordon Ray's excellent two volumes on Thackeray, *The Uses of Adversity* and *The Age of Wisdom* (Oxford, 1955, and 1958), Gordon Haight's *George Eliot: A Biography* (Oxford, 1968), Lionel Stevenson's *The Ordeal of George Meredith* (New York, 1953), and Edgar Johnson's *Charles Dickens, His*

Tragedy and Triumph (London, 1952) – although Angus Wilson's *The World of Charles Dickens* (London, 1970) is a marvellous read and vastly shorter.

A few titles of literary criticism, inevitably dominated by Barbara Hardy: *The Novels of George Eliot* (Oxford, 1967), *The Moral Art of Dickens* (London, 1970), her all too short study of Thackeray, *The Exposure of Luxury* (London and Pittsburgh, 1972), and her essay on Meredith's *Lord Ormont* and *The Amazing Marriage* in Ian Fletcher's *Meredith Now* (London, 1971). From the vast acreage of exposition of Dickens, Alexander Welsh's *The City of Dickens* (Oxford, 1972) is my selection, and similarly, from the lesser acreage on Jane Austen, Alistair Duckworth's *The Improvement of the Estate* (Baltimore, 1972). Inga Stina Ewbank's *Their Proper Sphere* (London, 1966) is a study of the Brontës as women writers. There is all too little on Thackeray, and most of the little there is on Meredith is heavy going. Arnold Kettle's essay on *Beauchamp's Career* in Ian Fletcher's collection (above) is a gratefully received exception. A more general book of literary and social interest is Guinevere L. Griest's *Mudie's Circulating Library and the Victorian Novel* (Indiana, 1970, and Newton Abbot, 1972).

INDEX